day trips® from
albuquerque

day trips® series

day trips® from albuquerque

second edition

getaway ideas for the local traveler

nicky leach

Globe
Pequot

Guilford, Connecticut

All the information in this guidebook is subject to change. We recommend that you call ahead to obtain current information before traveling.

Globe Pequot

An imprint of The Rowman & Littlefield Publishing Group, Inc.
4501 Forbes Blvd., Ste. 200
Lanham, MD 20706
www.rowman.com

Distributed by NATIONAL BOOK NETWORK

British Library Cataloguing in Publication Information available

Library of Congress Cataloging-in-Publication Data available

ISBN 978-1-4930-4424-5 (paper : alk. paper)
ISBN 978-1-4930-4425-2 (electronic)

∞™ The paper used in this publication meets the minimum requirements of American National Standard for Information Sciences—Permanence of Paper for Printed Library Materials, ANSI/NISO Z39.48-1992.

about the author

A former educator, Nicky Leach was born in the 7th-century cathedral city of Ely, near Cambridge, England. She moved to the western United States over 40 years ago, where she has worked as a publishing executive and freelance writer/editor ever since. She has authored or contributed to more than 60 guidebooks focusing on the natural and cultural history of the United States, from Florida to Hawaii to the West, and has received awards of excellence from the National Park Service for her visitor guides to US national parks. A meditator and healing practitioner, she believes that inner travel is as important as travel in the outside world, and that both are necessary for a balanced life. In addition to writing and editing books, she is a certified bodyworker and biodynamic craniosacral therapist. She may be reached through her website: nickyleachwriter-editor.com.

# dedication

To my dear friend and companion, longtime New Mexico writer Richard Mahler (1951–2017), who died on a wilderness trail in the Gila with his boots on in pursuit of what he loved. Your insatiable curiosity about the world and wish to keep learning and experiencing new things always inspired me, Richard. Thank you for the memories.

contents

southwest
day trip 01
landscape art, telescopes, and very good pie

west
day trip 01
mesa-top pueblos, volcanoes, and rock art

northwest
day trip 01
ranches and wineries in albuquerque's rural north valley

day trip 02
rock art and balloons

day trip 03
hot springs and hiking in the jemez mountains

day trip 04
cliff dwellings, canyons, and ancient springs in the española valley

day trip 05
georgia o'keeffe country

day trip 06
indian country

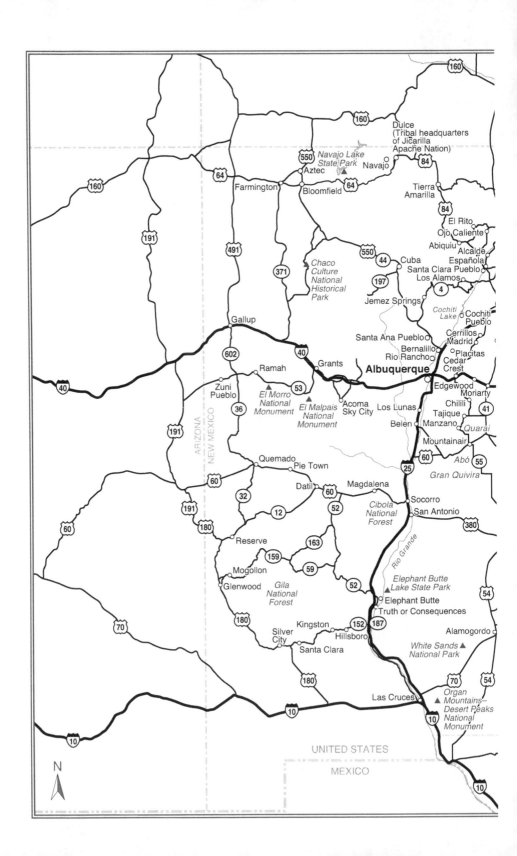

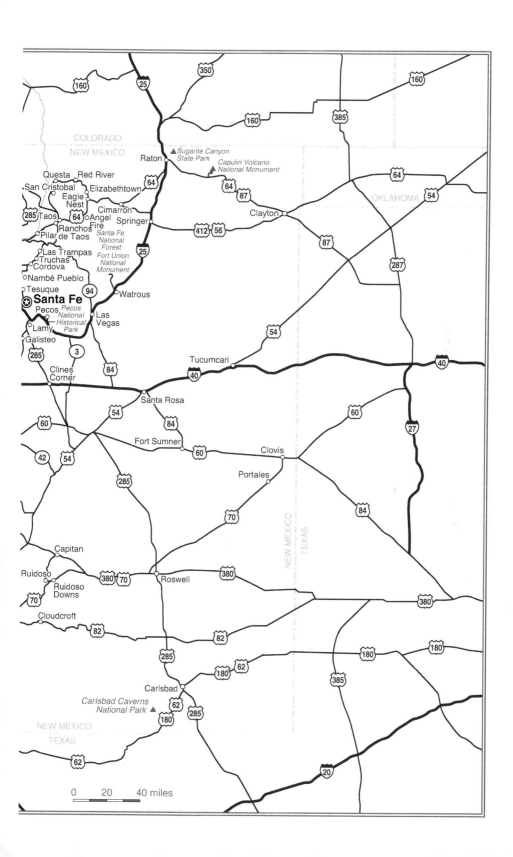

preface

I first visited New Mexico in 1980 on a youthfully romantic, madcap *On the Road*–style adventure across the US that involved long-haul Greyhound buses, one very old station wagon, and every national park campground I could find. By good fortune, I arrived in Santa Fe in early August, the weekend of Indian Market, and immediately immersed myself in the cultural commotion of that unique event on the Plaza. It was like stumbling upon a party at the end of the world that had been going on, pretty much unchanged, for centuries. Which, of course, is exactly what this remote outpost in the Southwest is all about.

A few years later, I traveled back for a fall trek to the top of Pecos Baldy with friends who had recently moved into a tiny converted adobe in the shadow of Rowe Mesa in the Pecos Valley. The weeklong trip took me from art openings and fireside meals of copious quantities of fresh-roasted green chiles to flamenco dancing, pueblo ruins, and a freezing night atop one of the state's highest mountains. I was a longtime Californian by then, but by the time I left New Mexico, I felt like I was only just beginning to understand new possibilities. I was in love.

I moved here in 1990 and have spent the last 30 years exploring New Mexico from top to bottom. I've been lucky enough to live in some remarkable historic homes in northern New Mexico: a Nature Conservancy ranch in remote backcountry near Hermit's Peak and Las Vegas, a solar-heated adobe adjoining Indian land in the shadow of Black Mesa in the Española Valley, a 6-acre canyon *hacienda* in Tesuque that once belonged to a Manhattan Project scientist, and a sprawling adobe home in the foothills southeast of Santa Fe, hand-built around an old log cabin by the German immigrant artist Helmut Naumer in the 1930s. This is not an uncommon experience in a state with adobe buildings that are 400 years old, but for a British person raised in an ancient cathedral town, or anyone who loves old things, there is something about fitting yourself into that unique history that soothes the soul. Soul is something that New Mexico has in abundance. In endless ways, the past informs the present here. *New* is always a relative term; it always gets jiggled with *tradition*, usually with extraordinarily creative results, as you'll find out.

This desert state is known for its expansive beauty, low population, and traditions. What is less clear initially, though, is that New Mexico is also a place of long cycles of immigration, as is the case with my home country of Great Britain. Indian origin stories tell of migration from other areas, even lower worlds, to arrive at the "Center of the World," whose boundaries are marked by geological landmarks that remind the people of how far they have come and how to live well in their homeland. Beginning in 1540 and continuing today—with new arrivals from Mexico and elsewhere in Latin America—Hispanics, too, came in waves, and they changed, and were changed by, the place they encountered. As recent arrivals, Anglos (meaning all of us who are not Hispanic or Indian) have had most of our preconceptions about what it means to live in a truly multicultural state scattered to the four winds. I've heard complaints from casual visitors to downtown Santa Fe that the area around the Plaza is just an "adobe Disneyland" with "museum Indians" and "fiesta Hispanics," and they felt it lacked authenticity. If that's the case, dig a little deeper. Get out of the tourist spots and spend time with real New Mexicans for a different view. You'll quickly discover that there's nothing fake about people's varied and interesting lives here. So explore off the beaten track. Real life trumps fantasy every time.

It's easy to imagine that because people have been here so long, and the landscape is so ancient, that nothing changes. On the surface that may seem true; spend some time here with an open mind, though, and you'll begin to find your life shifting in unexpected ways. The pace of life is completely different in New Mexico—deeper, slower, and more authentic. The changes that take place happen on such a deep level, it's only when you go elsewhere that you realize that you are seeing things completely differently. You'll find yourself more attuned to ancient natural rhythms: planetary movements, changing seasons, the agricultural calendar, and daily life as an art form expressed in a hundred ways, from painting and pottery to cooking, singing, dancing, and making music. This is part of the magic of New Mexico. Effort is counterproductive; just let it come to you.

Former New Mexico governor Lew Wallace (author of the classic *Ben-Hur*) captured the feisty spirit of the Land of Enchantment when he wrote, "Every calculation based on experience elsewhere fails in New Mexico." So leave your preconceptions at home and just enjoy the ride. A good time is all but guaranteed. *Bienvenidos y buen viaje!*

travel tips

Bicycling: Parts of these day trips can be done as enjoyable bike rides. Classic places to ride a bike are the SR 4 loop through the Jemez Mountains, beginning in Jemez Springs; SR 53 from Gallup to Zuni; the Enchanted Circle near Taos; and the Salt Missions Trail around Mountainair. You can rent bikes in Santa Fe at **Mellow Velo** (132 E. Marcy St.; 505-995-8356; mellowvelo.com) and in Taos at **Gearing Up Bike Shop** (616 Paseo del Pueblo Sur; 575-751-0365; gearingupbikes.com).

Buses and shuttles: Inexpensive ABQ Ride buses (505-243-7433; cabq.gov), Santa Fe Trails city buses (505-955-2001; santafenm.gov), the free Santa Fe Pick-Up shuttle for passengers riding the Rail Runner Express train (866-795-RAIL; riometro.org), and free hotel shuttles allow you to visit Santa Fe for day trips without a car, if you're so inclined. All the other day trips will require a car.

Camping: I've included a number of places to camp in the national forest and other federally managed public lands, as well as state parks and one or two private properties. Nearly all state parks and private campgrounds have developed facilities such as showers, flush toilets, and drinking water, as well as visitor amenities like visitor centers, boat launches, trails, and so on. National park campgrounds are usually developed but don't often have showers; state park campgrounds always have showers. National forest and Bureau of Land Management (BLM) campgrounds vary; some have developed facilities, while others maintain only primitive campsites with pit toilets and often no trash pickup or running water. Free, dispersed camping is allowed in national forests. Use wilderness ethics and "pack it in, pack it out."

Driving tips: It's best to tackle the labyrinthine streets of Santa Fe's compact historic downtown without a car. There is plenty of parking these days at two-hour street meters and in parking structures behind the Convention Center, in the Railyard, and next to the Roundhouse, as well as smaller structures on San Francisco Street and Cathedral Place. The PERA / South Capitol parking lot on Paseo de Peralta is free for visitors. My other piece of advice is to bear in mind, if you're doing these trips in winter, that snowstorms come in quickly and can create havoc on roads in northern New Mexico. I-25 at La Bajada—just after the exit to Cochiti Pueblo (SR 22) and a treacherous hill since Route 66 days—is notoriously slippery in snow and often closed by the State Highway Patrol. In Santa Fe, side streets are often icy and not plowed for days in winter, creating problems getting around. Backcountry roads are often dirt and become impassable during snowy and wet conditions. For information on road conditions, call 511 or (800) 432-4269 or visit nmroads.com.

Etiquette on Indian reservations: Indian reservations are sovereign lands. You are welcomed there as long as you observe the posted rules. Photographs, videotaping, sketching, and note taking are often not allowed, or allowed by permit for personal use only. Ceremonial dances are religious ceremonies, not staged performances. Observe them with the quiet respect you would maintain in a house of worship. Think of the dances as extended prayers for universal well-being; your role as spectator is to help those prayers succeed. Please don't talk or wave or otherwise disturb dancers or spectators. It's considered impolite to ask questions about dances or make comments about their meaning, and applause is inappropriate. Dress conservatively (no bare arms or shorts and flip-flops). Do not enter private homes without permission, but if you are invited into an Indian home to eat, accept with grace—it's a great honor—and do not refuse food, overstay your welcome, or offer to pay for food or tip your host; many other guests will also be invited on that day. In other words, be modest, be respectful, and show appreciation.

Fishing and hunting: Inexpensive fishing and hunting licenses are required and can be obtained from the **New Mexico Department of Game and Fish** (888-248-6866; wildlife .state.nm.us). Fishing licenses can be bought from over 200 vendors statewide, including outfitters, some grocery and hardware stores, and Walmart. The pueblos of Sandia, Picurís, and Taos and the Jicarilla Apache Nation offer limited draw hunting trips for elk, deer, and other big game on reservation lands in the mountains. **High Desert Angler** in Santa Fe offers guided fishing trips throughout northern New Mexico (505-988-7688; highdesert angler.com).

Golf: There are a number of challenging golf courses in New Mexico, and some of the most interesting are run by Indian pueblos, such as Cochiti, Santa Clara, Santa Ana, Pojoaque, and Isleta. Marty Sanchez Links de Santa Fe and Santa Fe Country Club have public 18-hole golf courses in Santa Fe; Quail Run offers a private 9-hole course in a luxury, gated community. For more information, contact **Sun Country Amateur Golf Association** in Rio Rancho at (505) 897-0864 or (800) 346-5319; suncountrygolf.org.

Hiking: An array of trails through every kind of landscape, from desert to volcanic to mountain forest, can be found in New Mexico. For more information, contact the **New Mexico Public Lands Information Center** in Santa Fe (301 Dinosaur Trail; 505-954-2002; public lands.org; open Mon through Fri 8 a.m. to 4:30 p.m.). The BLM and US Forest Service are in the same building.

Horseback riding: Horseback riding can be found on some northern New Mexico Indian reservations and resorts and through private companies, such as **Broken Saddle Riding Company** in Cerrillos on the Turquoise Trail on SR 14 (505-424-7774; brokensaddle.com).

National parks: New Mexico now has 18 units of the National Park System, not counting national historic trails. These include 2 national parks, 9 national monuments (4 of which are managed by the BLM), 3 national historical parks, 1 national preserve, and 3 national historic trails. Most have developed visitor facilities, and many have campgrounds; camping near the parks may be found on adjoining or nearby national forest or BLM lands and at private campgrounds. The four national monuments managed by the BLM are largely undeveloped, but Rio Grande del Norte and Organ Mountains–Desert Peaks have visitor centers and developed trails and campgrounds.

Pets: Where possible, I've indicated whether a lodging is pet-friendly. Many, however, have their own pets or ban them due to guests' allergies, so you're better off leaving Fido at home.

Reservations: Advance lodging and dining reservations are essential during the big tourist seasons in different parts of New Mexico: In Albuquerque, Balloon Fiesta (October); in Santa Fe, International Folk Art Market and Spanish Market (July), Indian Market (August), Fiesta (September), Thanksgiving, and Christmas; and in Taos, ski season (Thanksgiving to Easter).

River running and boating: Whitewater and flat-water river trips through the Upper and Lower Rio Grande Gorges and on the Chama River in northern New Mexico can be made using outfitters based in Taos and Santa Fe. **Los Rios River Runners** in Taos (575-776-8854; losriosriverrunners.com) and **New Mexico River Adventures** in Embudo (800-983-7756; newmexicoriveradventures.com) offer day trips on both rivers. For general information on Rio Grande river trips, contact the **Rio Grande Gorge Visitor Center** in Orilla Verde Recreation Area, part of Rio Grande del Norte National Monument, south of Taos (505-751-4899).

Sales tax: The sales tax average for New Mexico is 5.125 percent. In the destinations covered in this book, it varies between a low of 5.5 percent (parts of Lea and Lincoln counties) to 7.875 percent (Albuquerque), 8.4375 percent (Santa Fe), and 8.5 percent (Taos).

Seasonal travel: The trips in this guide span elevations of 5,000 to 10,000 feet and include a wide range of life zones, from low desert and mid-elevation grasslands to alpine and tundra on mountains, with their associated climates, vegetation, and wildlife. High-desert mountain travel is best in spring, summer, and fall, whereas low Chihuahuan Desert regions, such as the Truth or Consequences area, are mild in winter and popular with snowbirds. None of the destinations require you to dress up—business casual at most. Wear good sun protection; comfortable, breathable layers with roll-down sleeves and legs; a waterproof shell or down jacket in winter; a broad-brimmed hat; and sturdy boots, slip-ons, or walking sandals. Bring an easy-care item for dressier settings, if you want, such as a tailored jacket to throw on over jeans and cowboy boots. Santa Fe–style clothing—a showy getup of Western cowboy boots, Stetson, jeans or broomstick skirt, and brightly patterned woven wool jacket, dolled up with heavy Hispanic and Indian silver jewelry—is overrated; you won't see much of it among the general population in Santa Fe. Ethnic-influenced clothing and practical outdoor gear are more popular.

Skiing: Within a four-hour drive of Albuquerque are Ski Santa Fe, Taos Ski Valley, Angel Fire Ski Resort, Red River Ski Area, Sipapu Ski Area, and Sandia Peak Ski Area, which all have downhill runs, snowboarding, and ski lessons. You'll also find Nordic skiing, snowshoeing, and winter hiking at the Enchanted Forest Cross Country Ski Area near Red River, in and around Valle Grande National Preserve adjoining Bandelier National Monument in the Jemez Mountains, and many other places. For information on ski conditions, call **Ski New Mexico** (505-858-2422; skinewmexico.com).

Smoking: New Mexico now bans smoking in and around public buildings, institutions, and businesses, and 80 percent of lodgings are required to be nonsmoking.

State parks: New Mexico's excellent state park system encompasses a number of lakes that cool you down on a hot summer day. Most have sailing; boat launches; trails; campgrounds with developed facilities, including showers; and visitor centers. For more information, contact **New Mexico State Parks** at (888) 667-2757; emnrd.state.nm.us.

Staying healthy: The sun is strong in New Mexico and it shines 300 days of the year, so be sure to wear sun protection (sunscreen of SPF 30+, roll-down sleeves and trousers, broad-brimmed hat, neck protection, and polarized sunglasses). Don't underestimate the effects of higher elevations on your body: Even for the very fit, symptoms of altitude sickness include light-headedness, headaches, lack of energy, and nausea. If you're coming from out of state, it helps to acclimate in Albuquerque (5,000 feet) before heading up to Santa Fe and Taos (7,000 feet). The problem is exacerbated by dehydration, so drink plenty of water. To avoid electrolyte imbalances, a common problem when you're exerting yourself in summer, add a little unrefined sea salt to your water bottle and be sure to eat salty, high-energy snacks. In addition, cut back on caffeine, alcohol, and sugar, all of which can stress your adrenal glands. Daniel Gagnon, owner of **Herbs, Etc.** (1345 Cerrillos Rd., Santa Fe; 505-982-1265; herbsetc.com), has herbal tinctures and capsules that assist with altitude sickness and allergies (the worse culprits are piñon and juniper trees in March and grasses and weeds in summer).

Studio tours: Communities that have a lot of resident artists usually organize an open studio tour one weekend a year. Most are in the fall, but there are events in spring and summer, too. The best-known tours include Corrales, Abiquiu, Galisteo, Mountainair, Taos High Road, and El Valle. If you can time your trip to coincide with a studio tour, you'll gain access to many well-known artists' studios usually closed to visitors and meet a lot of people in quiet backcountry locations that are usually lightly populated.

Trains: In New Mexico, Amtrak's **Southwest Chief** train between Chicago and Los Angeles stops in Raton, Lamy (18 miles southeast of Santa Fe), Albuquerque, and Gallup. For information and reservations, call (800) 872-7245 or go to amtrak.com. The handsome **New Mexico Rail Runner Express** (866-797-RAIL; riometro.org) offers inexpensive regular daily train service on a 100-mile scenic corridor between Albuquerque and Santa Fe, starting at 4:32 a.m. and ending at 9 p.m. The Rail Runner stops at Belen, Isleta Pueblo, Los Lunas, Bernalillo County/Albuquerque International Sunport, Downtown Albuquerque, Los Ranchos/Journal Center, Downtown Bernalillo, Sandoval County/US 550, Kewa (Santo Domingo) Pueblo, Santa Fe County/NM 599, Zia Road, South Capitol, and Santa Fe Depot.

Wheelchair access: The Americans with Disabilities Act notwithstanding, you'll encounter many places in this rural state where it is not practicable to offer accessible lodgings, restaurants, businesses, and trails. Government buildings and facilities are required to be accessible.

Wineries: Vineyards were first planted in New Mexico by Franciscan monks in the 1600s, and in recent years a burgeoning number of family-run wineries have sprung up in areas that can support fruit growing, such as Los Ranchos in Albuquerque's North Valley, Alcalde and Dixon in the Lower Rio Grande Gorge, and the Mesilla Valley near Las Cruces. The Santa Fe Wine and Chile Fiesta, held at Los Golondrinas near Santa Fe in late summer, is a celebration of the state's viticulture and famed chile harvest. New Mexico wines now appear on wine lists at restaurants around the state that focus on locally raised foods. All have tasting rooms.

using this travel guide

The different sections of this guidebook use geographic directional headings (North, Northeast, East, Southeast, South, Southwest, West, Northwest). In most cases, compass directions relate to the New Mexico Tourism Department's geographic designations, and day trip chapters roughly follow designated scenic byways. This should make planning your trip using this book and local visitor information sources easier and more logical. I have also carefully designed the day trips to be either stand-alone outings you can do by gunning it up the highway—bypassing scenic byways—for a quick day trip or customized longer trips using several interconnecting outings.

Highway designations: Federal highways are designated I or US (note that most even-numbered roads are east–west and most odd-numbered roads are north–south). State routes are designated as SR or NM, county roads as CR, and forest roads as FR. Some reservation roads in Indian Country have their own designation: NR indicates Navajo Route.

Restaurants: This book uses dollar signs to indicate whether a hotel or restaurant is inexpensive, moderate, expensive, or very expensive. Before sales tax and tip, you'll pay $25 or less for typical meals for two people at a $ restaurant, $26–50 at $$, and $51–70 at $$$; anything above that, $$$$. Meal costs vary widely in New Mexico, depending on whether you are in a hot dining location (e.g., Santa Fe, Taos, or a luxury resort or country inn serving gourmet meals) or eating at one of New Mexico's many family-run places serving terrific regional cuisine. Many restaurants I've selected are run by chef-owners committed to regionally inspired dishes using local organic, sustainably grown produce and ethically raised meat and fish. Such places, though a bit more expensive, give you a true sense of what winemakers refer to as "tierra," a sensory experience of food that recognizes that "we become what we eat." My advice is that if you really want to try that hot restaurant, consider going there for lunch. Very often, some of their signature dishes are offered at lunchtime for a lower price. Don't worry, though: I'm on a tight budget, too. You'll find plenty of options for clean, delicious, unpretentious everyday food in the $ range in this book ("fun food," as a friend calls it) that won't break the bank.

Accommodations: For this guide, I've deliberately sought out diverse lodgings—from bed-and-breakfasts, artists' homes, and monasteries to nature reserves, spa retreats, Indian resorts, and historic railroad and Route 66 properties—that offer a full immersion in the experience of each place. This is how I myself travel (when I'm not camping in some beautiful spot), and it is my secret to quickly and easily tapping into the spirit of a location—its "sense of place." If I have one recommendation, it is this: Pay a bit more to stay in one of these unique lodgings in a historic location rather than a bland chain stranded at the far end of a noisy, commercial thoroughfare that could be Anywhere, America. This is particularly true in Santa Fe. Just like independent bookstores, what these lodgings offer is more than the sum of their parts. They deserve our support. You'll pay less than $100 at $ rates (although rarely below $85), $100–$175 at $$, and $176–$275 at $$$; anything above that, $$$$.

north

day trip 01

north

pueblo and peak:
sandia pueblo, sandia peak, placitas

This easy day trip is close by (a few miles north of downtown Albuquerque on I-25) but feels like a world away. Its focus is a visit to Sandia Pueblo and adjoining Sandia Crest, where a spectacular aerial tram ride to the summit offers incredible views of the city and Rio Grande valley as well as wildlife watching, hiking, biking, skiing, and scenic dining. The day trip ends with a side trip to the nearby village of Old Placitas.

sandia pueblo

The Tiwa-speaking pueblo of Tuf Shur Tia ("Green Reed Place") is located on 22,877 acres in Albuquerque's Northeast Heights. Built in AD 1300, it was one of several large pueblos consolidated along the Rio Grande that utilized the rich agricultural lands from the river to the mountains. The pueblo is built at the base of sacred Sandia Peak, where tribal members still conduct rituals and harvest plants and raise animals. During the 1680 Pueblo Revolt, the people of Sandia fled to Arizona, where they joined the Hopi Pueblos. In 1742 they returned and rebuilt their ruined pueblo.

With 3,000 residents, Sandia was once the largest pueblo in the area; that number has shrunk to just under 500 residents today. The tribe runs several successful commercial ventures. The most obvious is the attractive Chaco Canyon–style resort and casino, visible at the entrance to the pueblo, off Tramway Road, which has an 18-hole golf course; a well-regarded fine-dining restaurant, buffet, and casual dining; and an outdoor amphitheater that

north day trip 01

attracts national music acts. Nearby are a travel center, the largest American Indian–owned art market in the Southwest, and a buffalo preserve. The tribe also offers fishing at adjoining Sandia Lakes and elk and turkey hunting at a 15,500-acre mountain ranch near Eagle Nest near Taos.

where to go

Bien Mur Indian Market. 100 Bien Mur Dr. NE; (505) 771-7994; sandiapueblo.nsn.us/bien-mur-indian-market. From rattles and drums to fetishes, inlaid silver jewelry, and decorative pottery, you'll find an enormous selection of authentic Southwest Indian–made items at this large, attractive market next to the travel center. The tribe's 107-acre buffalo preserve is nearby, offering a rare chance to view an animal that is making a big comeback through Indian stewardship. Open Mon through Sat 9:30 a.m. to 5:30 p.m. and Sun 11 a.m. to 5:30 p.m.

Bobcat Ranch. Northern Ranches, PO Box 161, 2209 SR 38, Eagle Nest; (575) 377-2490; sandiapueblo.nsn.us/bobcat-ranch. Indian-guided seasonal elk and turkey hunts include all meals and lodging at this lovely, rustic 15,500-acre ranch in the northern Sangre de Cristo Mountains. Choose from 3-, 5-, and 7-day hunts. Call for more information and reservations.

Sandia Lakes Recreation Area. 100 SR 313; (505) 771-5190; sandiapueblo.nsn.us/sandia-lakes. Fish for rainbow trout in the winter and spring and catfish in the summer and fall at 3 stocked lakes just north of the casino-resort. Open daily 7 a.m. to 7 p.m. Apr through Sept; Wed through Sun 7 a.m. to 5 p.m. Oct through Mar. Tackle shop. Free. (Note: as of spring 2020, the Sandia Lakes Recreation Area is closed for restoration until further notice.)

where to eat

Bien Shur. Sandia Resort and Casino, 30 Rainbow Rd. NE; (505) 796-7500; sandiacasino.com/dining/bien-shur. This elegant rooftop-view restaurant is a popular place for a special night out. The emphasis is on continental-style dining featuring free-range poultry, seafood, and local meats such as bison, elk, lamb, and Black Angus beef accompanied by your selection of side dishes and 8 creative sauces. Business casual. Open Tues through Sat 5 to 10 p.m. $$$$.

Council Room Restaurant and Bar. Sandia Resort and Casino, 30 Rainbow Rd. NE; (505) 796-7500; sandiacasino.com/dining/council-room-restaurant. Breakfast, lunch, and dinner are served at this casual a la carte dining spot, which has a sports bar and booths. All the usual breakfast eggs and pastries; lunchtime soups, sandwiches, and burgers; and dinner steaks. Open daily 6 a.m. to 11 p.m. $–$$.

Thur Shan Buffet. Sandia Resort and Casino, 30 Rainbow Rd. NE; (505) 796-7500; sandiacasino.com/dining/thur-shan-buffet. Extensive all-you-can-eat buffet to stretch your dollar.

Depending on the time of day, items include breakfast eggs and pastries; salad and seafood bars; a meat-carving station; American dishes; Mexican, Italian, and Asian stations; home-made desserts; and a chocolate fountain. Open for breakfast Sun, Tues, and Sat 7 a.m. to 10:30 a.m. and Wed 7 a.m. to 9:30 a.m.; lunch Tues and Thurs 11 a.m. to 3:30 p.m., Wed 10 a.m. to 3:30 p.m., Fri 11 a.m. to 3 p.m., and Sat 11:30 a.m. to 3 p.m.; dinner Sun, Tues, and Thurs 4:30 to 9 p.m. and Fri and Sat 4 to 10 p.m.; Sunday brunch 11:30 a.m. to 3:30 p.m. Specials redeemed with Peak Rewards card points earned from casino include 2-for-1 on Tues, 50+ lunch discounted by $5 on Wed, military lunch for $6 on Fri, and sea-food buffet featuring snow crab on Fri and Sat nights. $–$$$.

where to stay

Sandia Resort and Casino. 30 Rainbow Rd. NE; (505) 796-7500; sandiacasino.com. There's no getting away from the fact that the focal point of this resort is the casino, but the 228 luxurious one- and two-bedroom and super suites, golf course, fine dining, and big-name musical acts playing the outdoor amphitheater are attractions in themselves. Once you're on the resort property, the views of the surrounding valley and mountains from this elevated foothills location, especially at sunset, are spectacular. $$–$$$$.

sandia peak ski area and tramway

The 10,000-foot Sandia Mountains (their name in Spanish is a reference to their watermelon hue at sunset) are a massive uplift of granitic rock topped with limestone. The facades facing the city are steep and rugged; the eastern side, reached by Sandia Crest Scenic Byway (see Northeast Day Trip 01), is gentler with forested slopes. Sandia Peak Ski Area is a winter sports haven (see Northeast Day Trip 01 for more information). The valley side of the mountains is the most popular hiking area in Albuquerque, as much for its challenges as its views of the Rio Grande valley and mountains 100 miles away. You don't have to get to the top using shank's mare (although some masochists enjoy the 9-mile straight-up La Luz Trail). Ride to the summit of 10,378-foot Sandia Peak and to the ski area in style aboard the Sandia Peak Aerial Tramway, the longest tramway in the world. The tram is top of the list of places that residents take visitors for a cracking view of the Duke City.

where to go

Cibola National Forest, Sandia Ranger Station. Exit 234 off I-25, follow Tramway Road east to the Sandia Peak Tramway; (505) 281-3304; fs.fed.us/recarea/cibola/recreation. The Four Seasons Nature Trail, otherwise known as Peak Nature Trail No. 97, in the Upper Tram area is a short interpretive loop introducing you to Cibola National Forest at Sandia Crest (elev. 10,300 ft.); Forest Service volunteers are available to help with information, and there are sometimes ranger hikes. Thirty miles of summit trails (accessed either from the west side or via 6-mile Sandia Crest Scenic Byway on the east side) offer easy to moderate hiking, mountain biking, and running in summer. Trail hounds will want to challenge themselves to do the breathtakingly steep La Luz Trail up Sandia Mountain. This rugged 9-mile trail is very exposed and has an elevation gain of 3,572 feet, so it's not for the faint of heart or the unfit. Bring plenty of water and high-energy food; wear good hiking shoes, layers, a hat, sunglasses, and sunscreen; and plan on taking the tram down.

Sandia Peak Aerial Tramway. Exit 234 off I-25, follow Tramway Road east to the Sandia Peak Tramway; (505) 856-7325; sandiapeak.com. The tram, built in 1966 by a Swiss company, spans 2.7 miles and climbs 3,819 feet up the sheer face of Sandia Peak. Allow about 15 minutes for the ride. A free ski museum is located at the base of the aerial tramway. A project of the New Mexico Ski Hall of Fame, it is a work-in-progress. The tram is open daily 9 a.m. to 9 p.m. in summer; Wed through Mon 9 a.m. to 8 p.m. in fall/winter. There is a fee.

Sandia Peak Chairlift. The ski lift is open for scenic rides in summer and fall on weekends, on the same schedule as Double Eagle II Day Lodge (see below). There is a fee.

where to shop

Double Eagle II Day Lodge. 10 Tramway Loop NE; (505) 242-9052; sandiapeak.com. This ski lodge at the base of Sandia Peak Ski Resort (see Northeast Day Trip 01 for more information on the ski area) has a mountain bike rental shop, a bike and accessory shop, a sandpit volleyball court, and a grill. Open weekends June to the first week in Sept and during Balloon Fiesta, the first 10 days in Oct.

where to eat

Double Eagle II Cafe. 10 Tramway Loop NE; (505) 242-9052; sandiapeak.com. Basic grill fare is offered here at the ski base area. Open weekends 10 a.m. to 4 p.m. $.

Ten 3. 30 Tramway Rd. NE; (505) 764-8363; ten3tram.com. A new view restaurant on Sandia Crest featuring locally sourced international cuisine. Bar is open Wed through Mon 11 a.m. to 5 p.m. and offers snacks, sandwiches, salads, and light meals in a casual atmosphere. Dinner restaurant is open 5 to 10:30 p.m. and features seafood, steaks, and other elegant fare. Note: Last tram down is at 9 p.m. in summer and 8 p.m. in winter, so plan accordingly. $–$$$$.

Two Mile High Café, Sandia Crest House. 701 Sandia Crest Rd.; (505) 243-0605; sandia cresthouse.com. Set atop Sandia Crest, this family-run gift shop and cafe offers well-priced snacks, beverages, sandwiches, salads, and burgers in a lovely setting. Open 10 a.m. to 5 p.m. weekdays and 10 a.m. to 7 p.m. weekends, weather permitting. $.

Sandiago's Grill at the Tram. 38 Tramway Rd. NE; (505) 856-6692; sandiagos.com. A view restaurant that offers a broad, updated, affordable menu of American and New Mexican favorites, including gluten-free items, at the base of the tramway. Open for lunch and dinner Sun, Mon, Wed, and Thurs 11 a.m. to 8 p.m. and Fri and Sat 11 a.m. to 9 p.m. $–$$.

placitas

Placitas is a quaint Spanish Colonial land-grant village in the Sandia Mountains due east of Bernalillo from I-25. To reach it, return to I-25 and drive north several miles, then drive east on SR 165 to where the road dead-ends at Placitas. It was originally settled in 1765 by 21 families from Bernalillo who farmed on lands formerly used by local Indians; they also grazed livestock, hunted, cut timber, gathered firewood, and foraged for food and herbs. Today only 4,763 acres of the San Antonio de las Huertas Land Grant remain intact; most of the original large grant is now owned by the federal government and managed by the US Forest Service and Bureau of Land Management. The road dead-ends just past the walled adobe village. Newer homes are springing up around the village, but it remains unspoiled. Note: There are no restaurants in Placitas anymore, so I recommend you eat in nearby Bernalillo (see Northwest Day Trip 01).

where to go

Jules' Poetry Playhouse. 11 Homestead Ln.; julesnyquist.com. Jules Nyquist is an award-winning poet and writing teacher who offers poetry readings, workshops, and retreats to creatives at her charming adobe studio in Placitas, which also doubles as a bookstore selling her poetry books, a daytime writing space for hire, and an overnight Airbnb rental. Contact her for directions and information. Open Tues through Sun noon to 6 p.m.

Placitas Studio Tour. 7 Placitas West Rd.; (505) 771-1006; placitasstudiotour.com. A combination of history, nature, and stunning views of the Jemez and other distant mountain ranges attracts numerous artists to live in Placitas. More than 60 artists working in a variety of media take part in the annual Placitas Studio Tour in May over Mother's Day weekend, an event run by the Placitas Mountaincraft and Soiree Society. Many artists' studios are open by appointment year-round. Visit the studio tour website for more information.

day trip 02

north

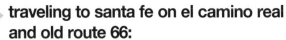

traveling to santa fe on el camino real and old route 66:
algodones, san felipe pueblo, kewa (santo domingo) pueblo, cochiti pueblo, la cienega

The one-hour drive north on I-25 to Santa Fe takes you from 5,000 feet in Albuquerque to 7,000 feet in the capital city and into a totally different landscape. It offers not only an interesting geography lesson but also a journey back through history. The freeway parallels the northern section of El Camino Real, "the Royal Road" between Mexico City and Santa Fe used by Spanish missionaries, explorers, soldiers, settlers, and traders for three centuries; it was particularly busy during the Mexican period (1821–48). It was displaced by the railroad in the 1880s, then the original Route 66 from 1926 to 1938, and finally the modern interstate. This day trip meanders along back roads close to the freeway; many locations were once important stops along the historic routes, including several Indian pueblos, natural landmarks, and rest and refuel stops. The route begins 5 miles north of Bernalillo in Algodones, reached by taking exit 248 to SR 313 (El Camino Real and Historic Route 66).

algodones

This sleepy Hispanic hamlet started out as a Spanish military garrison protecting travelers along El Camino Real. When Stephen Kearny and his huge Army of the West took New Mexico peacefully for the US in 1846, Algodones became a military supply depot and lodge for the US Army. The train passed through here in the late 1800s, and when Route 66 was

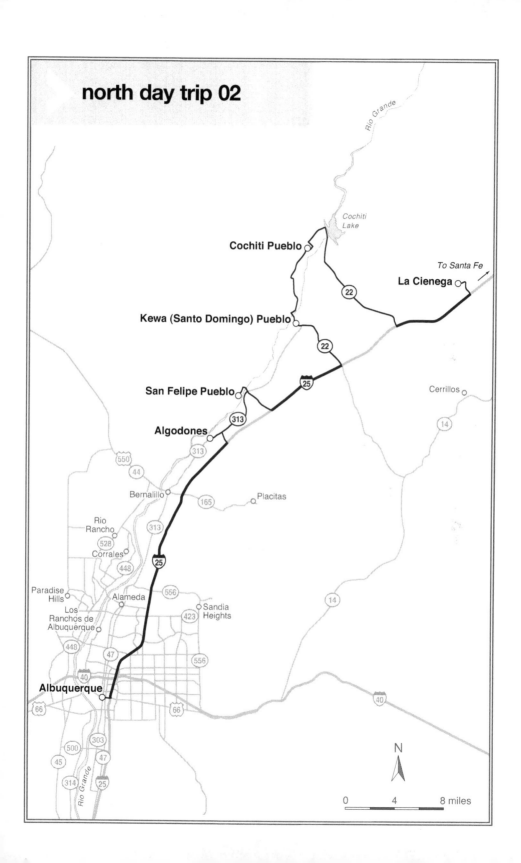

built in 1926, cars followed a road once taken by foot and horseback travelers. An attempt to bring visitors to this area by building a large arts/museum complex on the site of an old 1950s trading post at the Budaghers exit, just north of here, failed; the main interest now is the Mormon Battalion Monument near the end of W. Frontage Road. Until recently, Algodones's main attraction was Hacienda Vargas, the only lodging on the El Camino Real route in New Mexico, which occupied a historic adobe-brick building that once served as stage stop, train station, and post office; it has now closed but you can stop and enjoy the exterior of the historic building as you pass through on SR 313. There are no other services here, but it's worth a stop to enjoy a wine tasting at the family-run Casa Abril vineyard.

where to go

Casa Abril Winery and Vineyards. 1 Camino Abril; (505) 771-0208; casaabrilvineyards .com. This award-winning winery has been operated since 2001 by the Vigil/Romero family, whose deep roots in New Mexico go back to Spanish Colonial times. Not surprisingly, red and rosé wines here are made from Spanish and Argentinean grapes and celebrate Spanish heritage; moreover, it's worth a stop to meet the owner, taste an extensive number of wines, and learn about the history of the area. Tasting room open Thurs through Sun noon to 5 p.m. There is a fee.

Mormon Battalion Monument. W. Frontage Rd. Visible west of the interstate, just before you get to the Budaghers exit, heading north, this monument honors the members of the LDS Church who served in the Mormon Battalion during the 1846–48 Mexican-American War. The battalion, the only religious-based unit in the US Army, passed through Santa Fe in 1846 and followed the Rio Grande southward in rugged country. The monument consists of a 20-foot-high obelisk with a wheel on top and a plaque commemorating the challenging passage through the area. It was built by the LDS Church in 1940 at a location farther southwest, on US 85, and the dedication was attended by thousands of people, including the leaders of the LDS Church in Salt Lake City. It was removed in 1982, when I-25 was constructed, and was rebuilt on this dead-end road in 1996, after a newspaper drew attention to the forgotten memorial. A second monument on the east side of the road never materialized.

san felipe pueblo

Continue on I-25 to reach San Felipe, or Katishtya, one of the most traditional and least accessible of New Mexico's 19 pueblos. Tribal members speak Keres, lead a quiet, agricultural lifestyle, and make intricate beadwork. For visitors, the main contact with the pueblo is at the Black Mesa Travel Center and RV park adjoining Black Mesa Casino, and during the May 1 feast day of Saint Phillip, when hundreds of tribal dancers carry out the dramatic Green Corn Dance on the large sunken plaza. The pueblo holds an arts-and-crafts festival in October.

where to go

Black Mesa Casino. 25 Hagen Rd.; I-25, exit 252; (833) 867-6700; blackmesacasino .com. Sandia and San Felipe Pueblos have the only casinos on I-25 between Albuquerque and Santa Fe. They are popular places for a meal and a little gaming action as you travel between the cities. It's mostly slots, along with the usual poker, blackjack, and other card games. Second-tier musical acts play in the casino ballroom. Black Mesa Kitchen serves breakfast, soup, sandwiches, burgers, hot dogs, nachos, and New Mexican standards like Indian tacos and posole and green chile stew. Gas and snacks are sold at the travel center.

kewa (santo domingo) pueblo

Kewa (Santo Domingo) Pueblo is a few miles north of San Felipe Pueblo via I-25 and SR 22. It is the largest and most traditional of the pueblos; however, its proximity to the turquoise mines in Cerrillos and its inhabitants' great skill in creating gorgeous silver-and-turquoise jewelry and *heishi* (flat carved disks) made it a major prehistoric trading pueblo with the outside world, a tradition that continues today. Kewa, another Keresan pueblo, is also the best place in New Mexico to view the Corn Dance, which is performed several times a year, including New Year's Day and Easter, on the enormous plaza. The tribe's August 4 feast day of Saint Dominic is when you'll view the biggest and most majestic Corn Dance of the year, an all-day prayer for rain and a good crop. It's a spectacular explosion of pounding, hypnotic drums, and hundreds of brightly dressed dancers: The women wear buckskin leggings and towering *tabletas* (painted wooden headdresses), and the men are wreathed in evergreen boughs and clad in leather kilts with bushy coyote tails and jingle bells attached. It's an unforgettable experience. There is no casino here, but the tribe runs a small museum and a gas station/convenience store at the Cochiti exit from I-25. A Labor Day arts-and-crafts market at the pueblo features dancers and more than 350 vendors selling food and jewelry.

where to go

Santo Domingo Phillips 66 Gas Station. 1-25 and SR 22. Located at the turnoff for Kewa (Santo Domingo) and Cochiti Pueblos, this gas station and convenience store often has good fuel prices and is the last tribal gas station before you get to Santa Fe. There are two adjoining forecourts, so things move quite quickly. You'll usually find vendors set up in the dusty lot, selling jewelry and homemade bread baked in an *horno* oven. For information on visiting the pueblo, contact tribal headquarters at 134 Tesuque St. Mon through Fri 8 a.m. to 5 p.m.; (505) 465-2214.

cochiti pueblo

Cochiti Pueblo, the northernmost Keresan pueblo, is 13 miles northwest of I-25 via SR 22. The 528-member tribe has a diverse, modern economic base consisting of farming, ranching, commerce, and recreation. Cochiti artisans are known for their aspen drums and unusual ceramic figurines, the most famous of which are "storyteller dolls," revived and popularized by the potter Helen Cordero in 1964. The tribe invites visitors to attend its dances. Most are held in June, July, and August; the most important takes place on July 14, the feast day of San Buenaventura. Cochiti people trace their ancestry to the ancient pueblo now preserved at Bandelier National Monument on the other side of the Rio Grande. Modern tribal lands encompass a distinctive volcanic landscape, pierced by the Rio Grande, that came into being 1.1 million years ago when Jemez Volcano exploded, leaving behind the Jemez Mountains. The top visitor attractions at Cochiti Pueblo are all recreational. The tribe operates top-ranked Pueblo de Cochiti Golf Course and a small marina at Cochiti Lake and Dam. Spectacular 4,100-acre Kasha-Katuwe Tent Rocks National Monument, situated on tribal lands but managed by the BLM, preserves a dramatic array of tent-shaped hoodoo rocks that have eroded from the surrounding volcanic tuff, pumice, and ash. This is a favorite day hike for local residents and photographers and wonderful under a fresh snowfall (although it may be too slippery for hiking in winter, as the sun does not penetrate the corridors and melt the ice).

where to go

Cochiti Lake. 82 Dam Crest Rd., Pena Blanca; (505) 465-0307. Cochiti is one of four units for flood and sediment control on the Rio Grande operated by the US Army Corps of Engineers in conjunction with Galisteo, Jemez Canyon, and Abiquiu Dams. The construction of this dam and reservoir inundated Cochiti Pueblo lands in the 1960s, triggering lawsuits and a decline in traditional farming. The recreation area on the west side of the lake includes a visitor center, campgrounds with showers, trails, a marina, and a paved boat ramp. It's popular with boaters, windsurfers, and swimmers. Open year-round. There is a fee. During peak season, campsites may be reserved 6 months ahead through recreation.gov.

Kasha-Katuwe Tent Rocks National Monument. BLM, Rio Puerco Field Office, 100 Sun Ave. NE, Albuquerque; monument (505) 331-6259, field office (505) 761-8700; blm.gov/visit/kktr. This national monument was set aside in 2001 as part of the National Landscape Conservation System managed by the BLM. To get there, drive past the reservoir and then take graded FR 266/Tribal Road 92 for 3 miles. The 1.2-mile Cave Loop Trail is rated as easy. The more challenging 1.5-mile one-way Canyon Trail passes through the narrow canyons among the eerie, minaret-shaped hoodoos and makes a steep climb (630 feet) onto the surrounding mesa for wonderful panoramic views. The 1-mile Veterans Memorial Trail is an ADA-accessible loop that has great views into Peralta Canyon and the Jemez Mountains.

It is reached via a 3-mile dirt road. Be sure to scan the ground for tiny black pearls of volcanic obsidian, known locally as "Apache tears." (Note: These are federal property, still being studied by monument scientists, so please leave them where you find them.) Pit toilet, picnic tables, and parking lot; no visitor center or campground. Admission fee paid at booth. Open 8 a.m. to 4 p.m.; gate is locked at 5 p.m. Occasional ceremonial closures by the tribe are posted. No dogs allowed.

Pueblo de Cochiti Golf Course. 5200 Cochiti Hwy.; (505) 465-2230; cochitigolfclub.com. Designed by Robert Trent Jones Jr., this scenic 18-hole, par 72 course is ranked a four-star facility by *Golf Week* and has also received its architectural award; it is also featured on *Golf Digest*'s "America's Best Courses You Can Play" list. Its attractive three-level clubhouse houses the Kiva Bar and Grill for snacks and light fare and a full-service pro shop. Open year-round, sunup to sundown. $-$$.

la cienega

Named for its extensive wetlands, La Cienega (reached by taking exit 271 off I-25, just south of Santa Fe) is the final stop on this day trip, just as it once was on El Camino Real for travelers from Mexico City. Its principal attractions include the huge living-history museum El Rancho de las Golondrinas, adjoining Leonora Curtin Wetland Preserve, and a large petroglyph panel above the Santa Fe River in neighboring La Cieneguilla that contains hundreds of prehistoric Indian and Spanish Colonial carvings. La Cienega is a great choice for visitors who want to visit Santa Fe attractions but stay in the countryside. There are two excellent lodgings here, and restaurants are about 10 minutes away, off NM 14 in south Santa Fe. La Cienega is also close to Santa Fe Airport in southwest Santa Fe, which now offers daily flights to Denver on United Airlines and to Phoenix and Dallas/Fort Worth on American Airlines.

where to go

El Rancho de las Golondrinas. 334 Los Pinos Rd.; (505) 471-2261; golondrinas.org. "The Ranch of the Swallows," a 200-acre oasis at the end of El Camino Real, offers a vivid re-creation of the area's 18th- and 19th-century history and is an essential stop for families. Visit an 18th-century *placita* (small plaza), a water-powered mill, a blacksmith shop, a schoolhouse, a mountain village, and a *morada* (chapel) used by the Penitentes, and watch costumed volunteers baking bread, weaving, grinding corn, and tending goats, burros, sheep, and other animals. Golondrinas is best known for its popular themed weekends, including the Civil War (May), Spring and Fiber Fest (June), Wine Festival (July), New Mexico Beer and Food Festival: Panza Llena (Aug), and Harvest Festival (Oct). This place is huge and exposed; wear walking shoes and a broad-brimmed hat, and bring food and water. Kids may get tired, so plan accordingly. Open seasonally June 1 to Oct 6 for self-guided tours Wed through Sun 10 a.m. to 4 p.m.; a free guided tour (limit 25 people) is available at 10:30 a.m. Docent-led tours are available by reservation with 2 weeks' advance notice Wed through Sun in summer and in Apr, May, and Oct when the museum is closed; allow 2 hours. Food on themed weekends; otherwise bring a picnic. No dogs allowed. Admission fee; free for children 12 and under.

La Cieneguilla Petroglyphs. BLM, Taos Field Office; (575) 758-8851; blm.gov/visit/la-cieneguilla-petroglyphs. Part of the BLM's La Cienega Areas of Critical Environmental Concern, this petroglyph site is right along the main road above the Santa Fe River. Park at the gravel area on the west side of the road, and walk the loop trail around the escarpment, which has been carved with hundreds of rock art symbols from the prehistoric and Spanish Colonial era. Open daily. Free.

Leonora Curtin Wetland Preserve. (505) 471-9103; santafebotanicalgarden.org. This 35-acre working wetland preserve and outdoor laboratory, adjacent to Rancho de las Golondrinas, is overseen by the Santa Fe Botanical Garden. It is a sanctuary for native plants and animal species and is a great place to go birding. To reach the preserve, take the La Cienega exit (exit 271) off I-25. Turn right on W. Frontage Road, driving north for approximately 1.5 miles. Open May through Oct, Sat and Sun 9 a.m. to 3 p.m. Guided tours when docents are available; Fourth Saturday 8 a.m. bird walk with Rocky Tucker. Free.

where to eat

Blue Heron Restaurant. Sunrise Springs Spa Resort, 242 Los Pinos Rd.; (877) 977-8212; sunrisesprings.ojospa.com/dining/blue-heron-restaurant. The newly restored Blue Heron Restaurant, under the watchful eye of well-known executive chef Rocky Durham, has once again become a destination dining spot known for its gorgeous setting and creative use of seasonal ingredients, including veggie bowls with a variety of add-ons featuring organic produce from its own Ojo Farm and eggs from on-site chickens. It is open to the public as well as resort guests Mon through Sun for breakfast 7 to 11 a.m. (Sun to 10:30 a.m.), lunch noon to 4 p.m., and dinner 5 to 9 p.m.; brunch on Sun 11 a.m. to 2 p.m. $–$$$.

where to stay

Sunrise Springs Spa Resort. 242 Los Pinos Rd.; (877) 977-8212; sunrisesprings.ojospa.com. Now owned by the folks who operate Ojo Caliente Hot Springs, northwest of Santa Fe, Sunrise Springs has roared back to life after a hiatus and offers personal wellness retreats and experiences in a beautiful, peaceful environment. There's a playful ambiance at this shady 70-acre, sustainably built eco-resort with its weeping willows, ponds, view restaurant, sacred medicine wheel, hot springs, saltwater pool, sweat lodge, spa, and 32 garden rooms and 20 artisan casitas set amid trails landscaped with native plants. Guests can book a variety of packages; the basic Soak and Stay includes unlimited soaks in the hot springs and saltwater pool and overnight lodging, with a la carte dining, spa treatment, and activity options. Luxurious New Mexico–style rooms have Wi-Fi, phones, a full bath, locally made herbal toiletries, a minifridge, and microwaves on request; casitas have kitchen and sitting areas. Yoga and fitness classes are offered in a studio, while bodywork treatments, including craniosacral therapy, polarity, and spiritual healing, are available at an integrative spa. Play is big on the agenda here, and guests are encouraged to interact with recently fostered puppies in the Puppy Patch and take part in the Catnips and Catnaps program at the Cat Corral, a joint project with the Española Humane Society shelter, where guests play with and can (and frequently do) adopt puppies, kittens, and cats awaiting their "furr-ever home" (Note: the Puppy Patch and Cat Corral are open to nonguests every afternoon 1 to 4 p.m. by appointment). $$$$.

day trip 03

north

>>> riding the rails to historic santa fe:
guadalupe historic district and railyard
park, santa fe plaza, barrio de analco

A new spin on the classic Santa Fe outing, this trip advocates ditching your car in the parking lot at one of the Albuquerque Rail Runner train stops—Downtown Albuquerque, Los Ranchos, Downtown Bernalillo, Sandoval County (US 550/I-25), or Kewa (Santo Domingo) Pueblo—and riding the train for a long weekend. (If you prefer to drive, simply follow I-25 into downtown Santa Fe to reach each destination.) The Rail Runner terminates at Railyard Park in the Guadalupe Historic District, one of two new burgeoning warehouse arts districts in Santa Fe. Walk or take the free Santa Fe Pick-Up shuttle a couple of blocks north of the Santa Fe River to the Plaza, the heart of the downtown historic district, where attractions include the Santa Fe style convention center, the nearby New Mexico History Museum and Governor's Palace, the New Mexico Museum of Art, and La Fonda, the "Inn at the End of the Santa Fe Trail." Following Old Santa Fe Trail a couple of blocks south, over the river, you'll find Barrio de Analco, Santa Fe's oldest quarter, with its lovely old San Miguel Chapel and distinctive New Mexico capitol, dubbed the Roundhouse. From the Plaza, the Georgia O'Keeffe Museum and Lensic Performing Arts Center on the west and the Cathedral Basilica of St. Francis, Loretto Chapel, and Institute of American Indian Arts Museum on the east anchor San Francisco Street, a haven for gifts, fine art, historic trading posts, bars, music venues, and bookstores. In the evening, take in a show at the Lensic, which has a variety of nightly offerings. Santa Fe is a foodie's haven: Selecting just a couple of places to recommend out of 250 possibilities in this town of 83,000 people is a headache in itself. Next day, enjoy a leisurely breakfast and then catch the shuttle to explore the delightful Canyon Road Arts District and Museum Hill on the East Side, allowing time later to take in the hugely

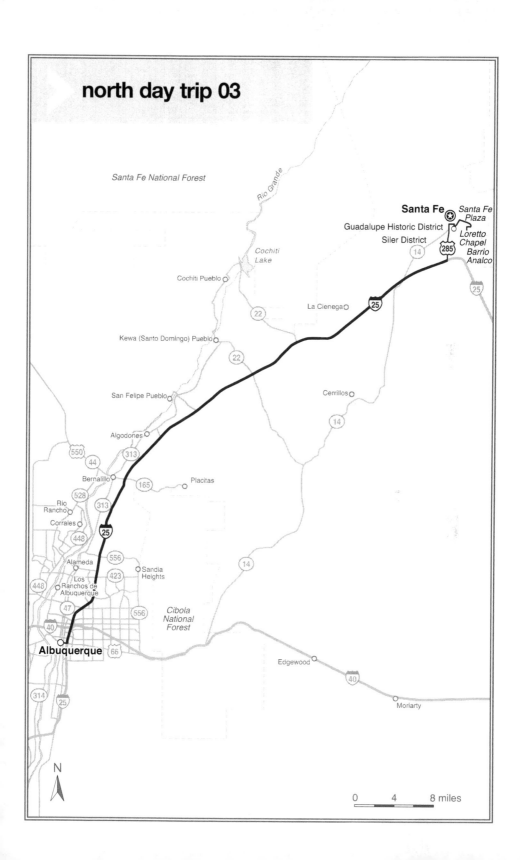

north day trip 03

Santa Fe National Forest

Rio Grande

Santa Fe *Santa Fe Plaza*
Guadalupe Historic District
Siler District
Loretto Chapel
Barrio Analco

Cochiti Lake

Cochiti Pueblo

14

285

25

La Cienega

25

22

Kewa (Santo Domingo) Pueblo

22

Cerrillos

San Felipe Pueblo

14

Algodones

550 44

313

Bernalillo 165 Placitas

528

313

Rio Rancho

Corrales 448

25 556

Alameda 423 Sandia Heights

448 Los Ranchos de Albuquerque

47 556

40

Albuquerque 66

14

Cibola National Forest

Edgewood

40

Moriarty

314

25

N

0   4   8 miles

popular Meow Wolf art installation, south of downtown, in the vibrant new SIDI arts district south of Siler and Cerrillos Roads (North Day Trip 04). Note: Most Santa Fe museums are closed on Monday.

guadalupe historic district and railyard park

In the 1970s, South Guadalupe Street, between the river and Cerrillos Road, was the place where counterculture types sold their arts and crafts, squeezed among the garages and upholstery shops beside the branch railway line that historically connected the Chile Line to the north with the mainline train station to the southeast in Lamy. Under the aegis of the Trust for Public Land, which purchased 50 acres in the railyard and to the south on Baca Street, the railyard was earmarked for development into a 13-acre park and mixed-use area. After a long and spirited community debate, Railyard Park opened in September 2008. It now includes landscaped trails and open space, live-work lofts, an adobe hotel majority owned by Picurís Pueblo, a youth arts center, the historic train station (now also housing the Santa Fe Tourism Center), the popular farmers' market, a brewpub, museums, performing arts spaces, galleries, restaurants, quirky boutiques and a branch of REI, and two movie theaters: one a restored arthouse cinema run by the author of *Game of Thrones*, and the other a first-run movie theater with armchair seating and food service.

where to go

Santa Fe Farmers' Market. 1607 Paseo de Peralta, Ste. A; (505) 983-4098; santafe farmersmarket.com. This award-winning trackside green building houses one of the top-10 organic farmers' markets in the country, which is open year-round. Local vendors, in booths both inside and trackside, sell homemade salsa, mustard, and chutney; baked goods, including sourdough breads from locally grown and milled flour and flatbread pizzas; herbal remedies; garlic oil; goat cheese and soap; grass-fed meats and free-range eggs; organic produce; cut flowers and native plants; and lavender items. The summer market includes a popular Cook with the Chef program featuring talented Santa Fe chefs like Deborah Madison. Saturday market open year-round. Hours are 8 a.m. to 1 p.m. Oct through May and 7 a.m. to 1 p.m. June through Sept; Tuesday market open 7 a.m. to 1 p.m. May through Nov only; Wednesday market open 3 to 6 p.m. July through Sept only. Also open in the same building during market hours are the Farmers' Market Gift Shop selling local and global gifts, Vivac Winery tasting room, and Café Fresh, serving organic espresso and farm-fresh foods. A branch of Second Street Brewery is located on the north end of the building.

Santuario de Guadalupe. 100 S. Guadalupe St.; (505) 983-8868; santuariodeguadalupe santafe.com. Built in 1776–96, this is the country's oldest shrine to Our Lady of Guadalupe, the apparition of the Virgin who appeared to the Indian Juan Diego in Mexico City on December 12, 1531. A beautiful statue of Our Lady of Guadalupe by Mexican sculptor Georgiana Farias can be viewed outside the church. Mass takes place in the new adjoining church Wed through Fri at 6:30 a.m., Sat at 8 a.m. and 5 p.m., and Sun at 8 a.m., 10 a.m., and 5 p.m. The former adobe church building is now a museum displaying historic photographs and artwork, including carved santos and the largest oil painting of Our Lady of Guadalupe in the US. It was painted in 1783 by one of Mexico's most renowned painters, José de Alcíbar, and brought up El Camino Real by cart from Mexico City; there is also a performance space. Open Mon through Fri 9 a.m. to 4 p.m.; Sat 10 a.m. to 4 p.m. in summer. Closed weekends Nov through Apr. Free.

SITE Santa Fe. 1606 Paseo de Peralta; (505) 989-1199; sitesantafe.org. This modern gallery in an old beer warehouse is known for its large-scale, cutting-edge art installations by international artists, such as Andy Goldsworthy. In 2019 its facade was remodeled with aluminum cladding and exhibit galleries were expanded for a bold new look. Skywatching in the Sky Terrace and lectures in the state-of-the-art auditorium. Open Wed through Sat 10 a.m. to 5 p.m. and Sun noon to 5 p.m. Admission fee.

where to shop

Ark Books. 133 Romero St.; (505) 988-3709; arkbooks.com. A mainstay for esoteric and New Age books, music, meditation gear, jewelry, and other items, this place is a pleasant hangout behind REI in Railyard Park. Author readings and signings. Open Mon through Sat 10 a.m. to 6 p.m. and Sun 11 a.m. to 5 p.m.

Double Take. 320 Aztec St.; (505) 989-8886; santafedoubletake.com. Double Take is one of the largest consignment stores in New Mexico and a favorite spot for gently used designer and everyday clothing for men, women, kids, and babies; vintage Western wear; Southwest furniture; handmade pottery; art objects; and Indian and antique jewelry. Open Mon through Sat 10 a.m. to 5 p.m.

LewAllen Contemporary. 1613 Paseo de Peralta; (505) 988-3250; lewallengalleries.com. One of the largest contemporary galleries in the Southwest, with more than 11,000 square feet of exhibit space, LewAllen was founded more than 30 years ago by famed art collector Elaine Horwitch and has been expanded under subsequent owners. Look for art by Forrest Moses, Fritz Scholder, Emmi Whitehorse, and Judy Chicago, among others. Open Mon through Sat 10 a.m. to 6 p.m.

where to eat

Amaya. Hotel Santa Fe, 1501 Paseo de Peralta; (505) 982-1200, (855) 825-9876; hotel-santafe.com. For breakfast, lunch, or dinner, this lovely restaurant off the main lobby and overlooking the grounds of Hotel Santa Fe, complete with a dining tipi, offers delicious food inspired by northern New Mexico's Hispanic and Native American cultural traditions. At breakfast, there's a whole roster of classic local dishes, from huevos rancheros and burritos to eggs Benedict and other egg dishes. At lunch, try the red chile tortilla soup, followed by organic greens topped with grilled achiote chicken, Scottish salmon, or shrimp, or perhaps sample the bison burger. At dinner, Red Mesa dinner items include wonderful Native-inspired renditions of quail, ruby trout, and elk tenderloin, alongside mainstream entrees like filet mignon, salmon, and duck. Artisan sourdough bread is from Sage Bakehouse across the street (a fun spot for coffee and pastries in the morning). $–$$$$.

Cowgirl Santa Fe. 319 S. Guadalupe St.; (505) 982-2565; cowgirlsantafe.com. Effortlessly hip Cowgirl is Grand Central for serious late-night boozing and bopping on Guadalupe. The restaurant specializes in "deep Southwestern barbecue with a twist" served by spunky guys and gals in cowboy gear. The menu runs the gamut from mesquite-spiced barbecue and juicy steaks to jerked chicken, Louisiana specialties, and New Mexican fare like huevos rancheros and the "Mother of All Green Chile Cheeseburgers," a burger made from ground, locally raised beef and bison and applewood-smoked bacon, topped with brie and green chile served with truffle fries. The tiny bar features live music nightly by local fixtures and the occasional late-night jam with a big-name musician following a local gig (one night it was Blues Traveler, in town to record a new album). Open Sun through Thurs 11 a.m. to 11 p.m. and Fri and Sat 11 a.m. to 11:30 p.m. (summer); happy hour Mon through Fri 3 to 6 p.m. $$–$$$.

Paper Dosa. 551 W. Cordova St.; (505) 930-5521; paper-dosa.com. Chef-owners Paulraj Karuppasamy and wife Nellie Tischler, who met working at a restaurant in San Francisco, bring the unique tastes of South Indian cooking to Santa Fe at this popular restaurant just south of Railyard Park, which has a pretty patio for outdoor dining. Starting life as a catering firm hosting the occasional pop-ups, Paper Dosa has been a hit from the start, with its delicate dosas (thin crepes made from fermented rice and lentil batter), uttapams (a thicker pancake version of a dosa with the ingredients baked in), idlis (pillow-shaped rice cakes), vadas (lentil fritters), sambars (stews), fragrant curries, and farmers' market salads bursting with the smells, colors, and tastes of Paulraj's homeland. The three-course Tasting Menu features soup, salad, or pakora, followed by your choice of uttapam or dosa and meat, seafood, or vegetarian curry. The a la carte menu is extensive. Open for dinner Tues through Sun 5:30 to 9 p.m. $$–$$$.

where to stay

Hotel Santa Fe, the Hacienda, and Spa. 1501 Paseo De Peralta; (855) 825-9876; hotel santafe.com. This handsome hotel, built in the Pueblo Revival style, echoes an ancient Indian pueblo and is the only tribally owned lodging and restaurant in Santa Fe. It is my top pick for accommodation with a unique perspective. It's hard to beat for price, atmosphere, and proximity to Railyard Park and downtown. The hotel is majority owned by Picurís Pueblo;

its interior showcases beautiful Indian pottery as well as fine curated art in the annex, and sculptures by famed Apache sculptor Allan Houser grace the grounds. The 162 newly remodeled Southwest-style standard rooms and suites have specially made king-size beds with Western headboards, Navajo rugs and other art, and marble bathrooms, and are quiet and comfortable. The 35 spacious suites in the Hacienda annex all have fireplaces and for only a slightly higher cost than the main hotel (particularly off-season) offer some nice perks: butler service and an inclusive breakfast buffet and afternoon wine and cheese in a dedicated sitting room. There's nightly Indian flute music and storytelling in the cozy lobby/bar, and every Monday night at 6 p.m. there are cultural talks by Southwest Seminars, a nonprofit organization specializing in Southwest studies (southwestseminars.org; 505-466-2775). A small spa located in the quiet Hacienda annex offers a variety of body treatments. The on-site restaurant, Amaya, which started out as Corn Dance Café, one of the first restaurants in the country to offer creative Native American cuisine and retains that heritage, is excellent; you may be tempted never to leave the hotel. To reach the Plaza, 6 blocks away, walk or take the purple London taxi brought over by the hotel's longtime British managing partner. $$$–$$$$.

santa fe plaza

Built as administrative headquarters of New Spain by Pedro de Peralta in 1608–10 and reclaimed from Pueblo Indian revolutionaries by Don Diego de Vargas in 1693–96, Santa Fe is the oldest capital city in the country. Santa Feans still congregate on the Plaza for art festivals and fairs, the Spanish Market, the Indian Market, Fiestas de Santa Fe, and the Christmas Nativity play *Las Posadas*. You'll see people strolling and sitting on benches, eating street food from food carts, dancing to free live music under the gazebo, and browsing arts and crafts made by Pueblo vendors under the portal of the Palace of the Governors on the Plaza's north side. The surrounding architectural styles reflect New Mexico's history: adobe Spanish Pueblo Revival and Territorial Revival, also known as Santa Fe style, a term

la conquistadora

A small side chapel at the cathedral—all that remains of the original church—displays a small wooden statue of the Virgin Mary known as La Conquistadora, Our Lady of Peace, *the oldest representation of the Madonna in the US.* La Conquistadora *returned to Santa Fe with de Vargas during the Reconquest. She is carried in a procession as part of religious commemorations during October's Santa Fe Fiesta celebration commemorating de Vargas's reconquest of New Mexico in 1692.*

that embraces both the historic and modern versions of the style. Stores on the Plaza, once the main shopping area, now sell pricey American Indian art and Western memorabilia and clothing. The southeast corner is anchored by historic La Fonda, the most elaborate of a series of inns serving travelers on the Santa Fe and Chihuahua Trails since the 1600s. San Francisco Street runs along the south side of the Plaza. St. Francis Cathedral Basilica is at the east end, and the Lensic Performing Arts Center is at the west end, with shops, restaurants, and bars in between.

where to go

Cathedral Basilica of St. Francis of Assisi. 131 Cathedral Place; (505) 982-5619; cbsfa .org. Archbishop Jean Baptiste Lamy's cathedral was built between 1869 and 1886 from local sandstone directly over an earlier church. With its French Romanesque Revival stained glass and pale statuary, Corinthian columns, and unfinished bell towers, it was deliberately designed to outshine traditional adobe churches filled with folk art *santos* made by local artisans. The cathedral's massive bronze double doors chronicle 400 years of Roman Catholic history in New Mexico. A beautiful statue of an American Indian saint now stands near that of Lamy himself. Open daily 6 a.m. to 5:45 p.m. Free. Mass daily.

Georgia O'Keeffe Museum. 217 Johnson St.; (505) 946-1000; okeeffemuseum.org. The world's largest permanent collection of art by Georgia O'Keeffe is displayed in 10 unpretentious galleries at this private museum and includes some of the artist's most famous paintings, such as large-scale flowers and bleached desert bones, as well as abstracts, nudes, landscapes, cityscapes, and still lifes. Revolving exhibits interpret O'Keeffe's influences and impact on other artists. There's a good short film on O'Keeffe and unique O'Keeffe art items and souvenirs in the gift shop. The museum runs tours of the artist's home in Abiquiu, workshops, and youth art programs. Seasonal tours of the artist's home leave from The O'Keeffe: Welcome Center next to Abiquiu Inn. Main museum is open daily 10 a.m. to 5 p.m. (until 7 p.m. on Fri evenings, when most art openings take place at galleries and museums around town). Admission fee; under 18 free.

IAIA Museum of Contemporary Native Arts. 108 Cathedral Place; (505) 983-8900; iaia .edu/mocna. The old post office, designed by Santa Fe style architect extraordinaire Isaac Rapp, is now occupied by the prestigious Institute of American Indian Arts, which displays the largest contemporary American Indian art collection in the US, some 7,500 pieces, including work by former students and teachers such as Allan Houser, Dan Namingha, Estella Loretto, Linda Lomahaftewa, Darren Vigil Gray, and T. C. Cannon. Open Mon and Wed through Sat 10 a.m. to 5 p.m., Sun noon to 5 p.m. Admission fee; under 16 free.

Lensic Performing Arts Center. 211 W. San Francisco St.; (505) 988-1234; lensic.com. An $8.2 million upgrade in 2001 made this 1931 movie palace—a rare example of churrigueresque (Spanish baroque) architecture—into Santa Fe's premier performing arts venue and is now home to seven different arts organization that put on more than 200 performances a year. The theater sponsors community shows, works-in-progress readings, school performances, old movie showings, and fund-raisers. There's something scheduled most evenings. The box office also sells tickets to other Santa Fe shows.

Loretto Chapel. 207 Old Santa Fe Trail; (505) 982-0092; lorettochapel.com. This charming chapel was built by Archbishop Lamy for the Sisters of Loretto, who came to Santa Fe to establish a school for young women—the Loretto Academy—on the site of what is now the Inn at Loretto. Famous for its "miraculous" spiral staircase built by a mysterious carpenter, which winds to the choir loft without benefit of center support or nails, it's frequently used for weddings and concerts. Open Mon through Sat 9 a.m. to 5 p.m. and Sun 10:30 a.m. to 5 p.m. Admission fee.

New Mexico History Museum/Palace of the Governors. 113 Lincoln Ave.; (505) 476-5200; nmhistorymuseum.org. This diverse, modern 96,000-square-foot history museum is the main unit of the Museum of New Mexico and a must-visit in Santa Fe. It features well-conceived interactive exhibits, including several that interpret important Spanish Colonial treasures housed in the Palace of the Governors, the oldest state capitol in the country. The famed Palace of the Governors, which fronts onto the Plaza, is now folded into this museum, along with the Palace Press and the Fray Angelico History Library and Archives opposite the city library. The History Museum's core exhibit presents state history through six periods.

New Mexico Museum of Art. 107 W. Palace Ave.; (505) 476-5072; nmartmuseum.org. Completed in 1917, this photogenic Pueblo Revival museum—the oldest example of Santa Fe style—celebrates New Mexican art through the centuries in its extensive permanent collection and revolving exhibitions, now numbering 20,000 artworks and growing. The museum's attractive St. Francis Auditorium is home to the annual summertime Santa Fe Chamber Music Festival (505-982-1890; santafechambermusic.com), which also holds concerts at the Lensic; lunchtime rehearsals are free.

Note: Museum of New Mexico (MNM; museumofnewmexico.org) includes four state-run museums in Santa Fe: the New Mexico History Museum/Palace of the Governors and the New Mexico Museum of Art off the Plaza, and the Museum of International Folk Art and the Museum of Indian Arts and Culture/Laboratory of Anthropology on Museum Hill (see North Day Trip 04). In all, MNM runs seven state museums and seven state historic sites. If you plan to visit several, purchase the **New Mexico Culture Pass,** which for just $30 offers admission to each of the sites and is valid for 12 months. Hours for MNM units in Santa Fe are Tues through Sat 10 a.m. to 5 p.m. (daily in summer). Admission fee; under 16 free. Free admission every Fri 5 to 7 p.m. May through Oct and the first Fri of the month Nov through Apr, on Wed for New Mexico seniors 60+, and on Sun for New Mexico residents.

Santa Fe Community Convention Center. 201 W. Marcy St.; (800) 777-2489; community conventioncenter.com. The 72,000-square-foot convention center that replaced the old

Sweeney Center in 2008 is a beautiful Santa Fe style LEED Gold-certified green building located atop a 13th-century pueblo that predates the founding of Santa Fe. It has 40,000 square feet of meeting and convention rooms, a ballroom, a landscaped courtyard, art galleries, and an underground car park. Open Mon through Fri 8 a.m. to 5 p.m. The convention center is also home to TOURISM Santa Fe (505-955-6200, 800-777-2489; santafe .org), the Santa Fe Convention & Visitors Bureau. Visitor information is also available at the Plaza Visitor Information in the Plaza Galeria (10 a.m. to 6 p.m. daily; 505-955-6215) and the Railyard Visitor Information Center in the Santa Fe Depot (9 a.m. to 5 p.m. Mon through Sat; 505-955-6230).

where to shop

Andrea Fisher Fine Pottery. 100 W. San Francisco St.; (505) 986-1234; andreafisher pottery.com. A classy shop specializing in historic and contemporary Southwestern Indian pottery. Pieces are arranged by pueblo, family, and artist and include examples of historic work by famed San Ildefonso potter Maria Martinez and several generations of the celebrated Santa Clara Naranjo family. Open Mon through Sat 9:30 a.m. to 5:30 p.m. and Sun 11:30 a.m. to 5:30 p.m.

Collected Works Bookstore. 202 Galisteo St.; (505) 988-4226;collectedworksbookstore .com. This popular independent bookstore, owned by Dorothy Massey, has been in business for over 40 years and occupies a 4,000-square-foot building on the corner of Galisteo and Water Streets, near Coyote Cafe. It's very strong in regional titles and hosts regular author readings and signings. On-site cafe. Open daily 8 a.m. to 6 p.m. or to 8 p.m. during special events.

Todos Santos Chocolates. 125 E. Palace Ave., #31; (505) 982-3855. One of the top chocolate makers in the country, New Orleans native Hayward Simoneaux is an artist in confectionery. In this miniscule corner shop in historic Sena Plaza, he conjures unusual chocolate combinations featuring chile and lavender, fruit, nuts, and sugar, and themed items such as Day of the Dead skeletons and handmade edible heart *milagros* (Mexican religious charms) covered in gold leaf. Creative gift wrapping enhances a unique souvenir from Santa Fe. Open Mon through Sat 10 a.m. to 5 p.m. and Sun noon to 4 p.m.

where to eat

Cafe Pasqual's. 121 Don Gaspar Ave.; (505) 983-9340; pasquals.com. Former Alice Waters cohort Katherine Kagel's globally inspired Mexican eatery, snugged into a tiny former corner drugstore near the Plaza, turns out heavenly meals that channel Asia by way of the Americas. Try huevos Motuleños, a Yucatecan breakfast specialty; smoked trout hash; or the huevos rancheros, taken to new heights by superb red chile. All the food here is organic and sustainably sourced. Fresh Mexican salsas made from fire-roasted tomatoes and chiles spark everything. The dining room alone—with its bright Mexican tiles, banners, and homages to San Pasqual, patron saint of the kitchen—is an instant "happy pill." No breakfast reservations; come early to avoid the line. Open daily 8 a.m. to 3 p.m. for breakfast and lunch, and then dinner starting at 5:30 p.m. $$–$$$.

Tia Sophia's. 210 W. San Francisco St.; (505) 983-9880; tiasophias.com. Squeeze into a booth next to the politicos at this traditional New Mexican hot spot, which is run by the Maryol family, who also own the equally popular **Tomasita's** in the Railyard (505-983-5721; tomasitas.com). This is the best red and green chile in Santa Fe, according to many, and offers an unpretentious, lively atmosphere. Open 7 a.m. to 2 p.m. daily. $–$$.

where to stay

La Fonda Hotel. 100 E. San Francisco St.; (505) 982-5511, (800) 523-5002; lafondasanta fe.com. A 1923 National Historic Landmark taking up the whole southeastern corner of the Plaza, La Fonda is the one building that everyone should walk through (among other things, it has an old-fashioned newsstand in its indoor shopping arcade). Santa Fe style reaches its apotheosis here. The 167 modern Southwestern rooms have been luxuriously renovated and upgraded in 29 different room types, from queens to suites, some with balconies and fireplaces, all with hand-painted furnishings, Nespresso coffeemakers, and flat-screen TVs. A kaleidoscope of light filtering through hand-painted windows fills the sunken dining room, La Plazuela, a good place for Southwestern dining at moderate prices. The Fiesta Lounge has reliably good local live music and dancing. A sunset drink at the rooftop Bell Tower bar is memorable. $$–$$$$.

barrio de analco

Spanish colonists clustered north of the Santa Fe River around the Palace of the Governors. But the earliest residents of Barrio de Analco ("Neighborhood on the Other Side of the River") in the early 1600s were Mexican Indians, who helped build San Miguel Mission Church; as elsewhere on the frontier, they were used as a buffer between Spaniards and local Indians. Over the years the Barrio de Analco neighborhood was rebuilt and became more inclusive. Today state buildings dominate, but some of the old charm remains. A stroll along Old Santa Fe Trail and East De Vargas Street gives you a sense of Santa Fe during its oldest days. Barrio de Analco is located 3 blocks south of the Plaza, immediately across the river.

where to go

New Mexico State Capitol (Roundhouse). Paseo de Peralta at Old Santa Fe Trail; (505) 986-4600; nmlegis.gov. Built in 1966 and remodeled in 1992, the four-story Roundhouse architecturally echoes the Zia Pueblo sun sign or circle of life, the same symbol on the New Mexico state flag. The Governor's Gallery has rotating exhibits of artwork by New Mexicans, and walls throughout the building display paintings, photographs, weaving, and mixed-media work by some of the state's best-known artists. The grounds have sculptures by Allan Houser, Glenna Goodacre, and others. Ask for a walking tour brochure. The legislative session takes place every January, convening for 60 days in odd-numbered years and 30 days in even-numbered years. Open for self-guided tours Mon through Fri 7 a.m. to 6 p.m. and Sat 9 a.m. to 5 p.m. Memorial Day to last Sat in Aug. Free.

San Miguel Chapel. 401 Old Santa Fe Trail; (505) 983-3974; sanmiguelchapel.org. Built between 1610 and 1625 atop a 12th-century pueblo and rebuilt in the 1700s following the Pueblo Revolt, this iconic adobe church, administered by the Christian Brothers and dedicated to Saint Michael the Archangel, protector of the Catholic Church, symbolizes the faith of the masses at the heart of the Holy City of Faith and is one church you should definitely visit. Inside are a 1798 painted *reredos*, or altar screen; buffalo- and deer-hide religious paintings from 1630; and the 780-pound San José Bell, cast in 1356 in Spain, shipped to Mexico, and then brought here by oxcart in the 1800s. It is the oldest bell in America. Audio tour. Gift shop. Open Mon through Sat 10 a.m. to 4 p.m. The 5 p.m. Sunday mass is a moving experience. Admission fee.

where to eat

The Pink Adobe. 406 Old Santa Fe Trail; (505) 983-7712; thepinkadobe.com. Opened in 1944 by artist Rosalea Murphy, this family-owned historic adobe restaurant and famous Dragon Room bar is one of Santa Fe's most popular local hangouts, especially when the state legislature is in session. The menu has barely changed since the 1940s, when Murphy developed her French-influenced New Mexican cuisine. The classics are a starter of Gypsy Stew, a soothing take on green chile chicken stew made with sherry-infused broth; Steak Dunnigan, a huge charbroiled grass-fed New York strip steak topped with mushrooms and hot green chile served with spinach almandine and potatoes; and a dessert of homemade deep-dish apple pie made with pecans, raisins, nutmeg, and cinnamon served with rum hard sauce. "The Pink" adjoins the ultraluxe **Inn of the Five Graces** (150 E. De Vargas St.; 505-992-0957; fivegraces.com), whose 13 brilliantly colored bed-and-breakfast rooms and suites are furnished with exotic items from Seret's, a large import store selling trade items that its owners have brought back from Morocco, Asia, and elsewhere. On-site spa. The Pink Adobe is open for dinner Tues through Sun 5:30 to 9 p.m. Dragon Room open 4 p.m. to close. $$–$$$$.

Restaurant Martín. 526 Galisteo St., corner of Paseo de Peralta; (505) 820-0919; restaurant martinsantafe.com. Award-winning Santa Fe chef Martín Rios's eatery just west of the capitol is the kind of deceptively simple *chef-patron* place you might find in France, where eating well *en famille* is an everyday art, not a special occasion. Using classical techniques to bring out the character of fresh, local, seasonal ingredients, Rios's artful food personifies what he calls "Progressive American" cuisine. Dinner here is quite simply "an experience." A creamy chilled spring pea soup is topped with citrus-marinated Gulf prawns and jicama. A brûléed

Maytag blue cheese adds cream and crunch to a fresh beet, jicama, and citrus-sparked salad. A country mustard-coated organic chicken breast sensuously oozes *jus* onto a pillow of creamy risotto below. A luxurious milk chocolate–Grand Marnier crème brûlée snaps to attention with a bite-size muffin and pool of intense berry coulis. The restaurant is spacious and comfortable and offers several rooms for dining and an extensive patio for outdoor dining. Dinner Tues through Sat 5:30 to 10 p.m. $$$–$$$$.

where to stay

Drury Plaza Hotel. 828 Paseo de Peralta; (505) 424-2175; druryhotels.com. One of several unique flagship historic properties in the popular family-run Drury Hotels chain, the Drury Plaza Hotel occupies the completely restored green building that once housed an imposing hospital close to Canyon Road and the Plaza. The boutique hotel is quiet, spacious, airy, filled with art, and has off-street parking. It offers popular all-in Drury amenities, such as a rooftop pool, fitness center, and free nightly Kickback happy hour drinks and food, hot breakfast, soda and popcorn, and in-room Wi-Fi. $$–$$$$.

day trip 04

north

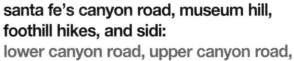

santa fe's canyon road, museum hill, foothill hikes, and sidi:
lower canyon road, upper canyon road, museum hill, siler district (sidi)

The highlights of this day two exploration of Santa Fe include art galleries along historic Lower Canyon Road, the Randall Davey Audubon Center and Santa Fe Open Space foothill trails at the top of rustic Upper Canyon Road, the four enjoyable cultural museums on Museum Hill off Old Santa Fe Trail, and last but by no means least, the wildly popular art fun house installation of Meow Wolf: House of Eternal Return, linchpin of the gentrifying SIDI (Siler District) arts district, south of Siler and Cerrillos Roads. Away from the compact downtown, you'll need transportation to get around. For those riding the Rail Runner or without a car, the free daily Santa Fe Pick-Up shuttle operates between 10 a.m. and 5:30 p.m. and transports visitors around Downtown, Railyard Park, Canyon Road, and Museum Hill. To reach Meow Wolf, take Santa Fe Trails Bus Route 2 from the Downtown Transit Center next to the Museum of Art. The bus travels along Cerrillos Road (NM 14); the closest stop is Calle de Cielo, and from there, it's a four-minute walk to Meow Wolf close by on Rufina Circle. There is no taxi service in Santa Fe now, but if you have a smartphone, you can call for an Uber or Lyft ride to your destination.

Note: Most museums in Santa Fe offer free entrance between 5 and 8 p.m. on Friday evenings, when most art openings take place, especially along Canyon Road, where you'll meet as many locals as out-of-towners enjoying the diverse art and free food and drink. The traditional Canyon Road Christmas Eve Farolito Walk is a unique event that attracts thousands of visitors for an atmospheric stroll among *farolitos* (small sand-filled bags with

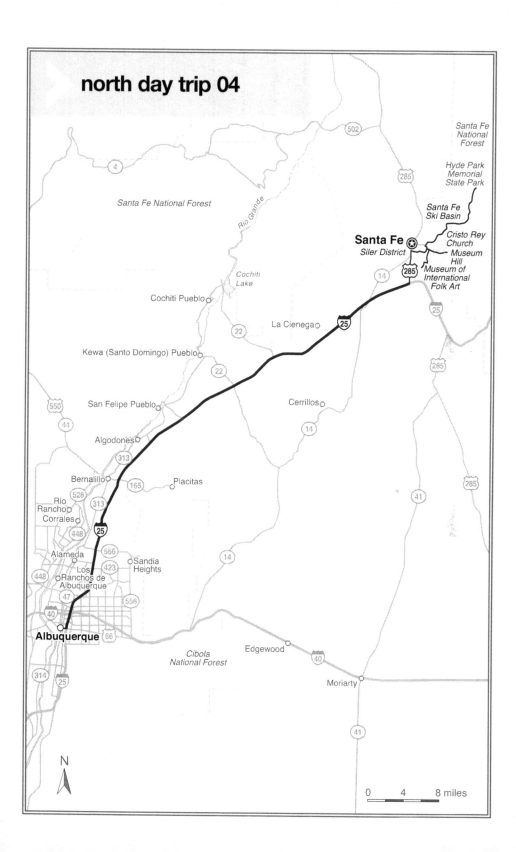

north day trip 04

votive candles that are often generically known by the incorrect name of *luminarias*), bonfires (properly known in northern New Mexico as *luminarias*), carol singers, and hot cider vendors.

lower canyon road

More than 100 unique galleries, restaurants, businesses, and museums occupy historic adobe homes in one of Santa Fe's most storied old neighborhoods: Lower Canyon Road. In prehistoric times, it was a footpath used by Pueblo Indians to travel between the Santa Fe River valley and Pecos Pueblo. Hispanic settlers used it for hauling cut firewood by burro from the mountains to sell in town. Sheep and goats grazed hillsides, and farmers grew chiles, beans, and peaches, drawing the water for irrigation from *acequias*, or communal ditches. Acequia Madre, the "Mother Ditch," runs parallel to Canyon Road on the south side. In the 1920s, a group of Anglo artists settled along Camino del Monte Sol, between Canyon Road and Old Santa Fe Trail, fixing up adobe homes and mingling with Hispanic neighbors. As Santa Fe grew in popularity, families sold their land, and real estate boomed on the East Side. Protected by ordinances, this historic district remains authentic and enjoyable to visit, even though home prices are now out of reach of struggling artists.

where to go

El Zaguán: James L. Johnson House and Garden. 545 Canyon Rd.; (505) 983-2567; historicsantafe.org. A rambling Territorial *hacienda*, El Zaguán began as a 24-room family compound in the early 1800s, was bought as a temporary home by anthropologist Adolph Bandelier in 1890, and was converted to apartments by two sisters in the 1920s. Six low-cost small apartments are still rented to artists and writers annually; apply through Historic Santa Fe Foundation (number above). The public areas and beautiful shady garden are open Mon through Fri 9 a.m. to 5 p.m. Free.

Santa Fe Religious Society of Friends Meeting House (Olive Rush Home). 630 Canyon Rd.; (505) 983-7241; santafefriends.org. The first female Anglo artist on Canyon Road was Olive Rush, an illustrator and student of Howard Pyle who became interested in plein air painting and moved here in 1920. She left her adobe home to the Quakers, and it is still in use as a meeting house. Hour-long silent worship meetings take place at 9 and 11 a.m. with a potluck lunch at 12:30 p.m. on the first Sunday of the month. Workshops are sometimes held here.

where to shop

Gerald Peters Gallery. 1005 Paseo de Peralta; (505) 954-5700; gpgallery.com. Art maven Gerald Peters built this 8,500-square-foot Santa Fe style gallery, close to Canyon Road, in 1998 to showcase his collection of Taos Society and Santa Fe Colony artists. Galleries also display American impressionists, American modernists (including Georgia O'Keeffe), abstract expressionists, contemporary realists, modern sculpture, and vintage and contemporary photography. Sculpture garden. Open Mon through Sat 10 a.m. to 5 p.m.

Morning Star Gallery. 513 Canyon Rd.; (505) 982-8187; morningstargallery.com. Billed as the largest gallery in the country devoted to antique American Indian art, Morning Star focuses on Plains Indian beadwork, quillwork, ledger drawings, and parfleche, but it also has Southwestern pottery, baskets, textiles, and jewelry. Open Mon through Sat 9 a.m. to 5 p.m.

Turner Carroll Gallery. 725 Canyon Rd.; (505) 986-9800; turnercarrollgallery.com. North Carolina natives and art history buffs, the Carrolls sell work by established international contemporary artists. This is an intelligent and very vibrant gallery, with revolving exhibitions to date by artists from Romania, Ireland, France, Russia, and Mexico. Open daily 10 a.m. to 6 p.m.

Ventana Fine Art Gallery. 400 Canyon Rd.; (800) 746-8815; ventanafineart.com. Located in a historic brick schoolhouse, Ventana is a popular destination for contemporary art lovers, with two airy rooms displaying local artists such as plein air painter Barry McCuan as well as a landscaped sculpture garden. Open Mon through Sat 9:30 a.m. to 5 p.m. and Sun 10 a.m. to 4 p.m.

where to eat

Geronimo. 724 Canyon Rd.; (505) 982-1500; geronimorestaurant.com. In 2009 chef-owner Eric DiStefano and his partners bought not only Mark Miller's Coyote Cafe—the restaurant that put Santa Fe fine dining on the map in the 1980s—but Geronimo, where DiStefano had a stellar reputation as executive chef. Sadly, Chef DiStefano passed away suddenly in 2016, but his crack team continues his legacy today, which is great news for the restaurant's many fans. The lovely old *hacienda* offers an elegant menu of seasonal global eclectic dishes, including signature dishes such as Telicherry Rubbed Elk Tenderloin and Cast Iron Seared Diver Scallops and new Asian fusion dishes like Green Miso Sea Bass. One of the best choices in Santa Fe for a memorable evening out. Dinner only. Reservations required. $$$$.

The Teahouse. 821 Canyon Rd.; (505) 992-0972; teahousesantafe.com. This European-style teahouse with a bohemian vibe is located in a rambling old adobe and a great spot to rest and refresh yourself. It imports and custom blends more than 100 teas, including several rooibos and matcha varieties, in addition to coffee drinks. The Teahouse menu has been substantially expanded under new owners and now offers breakfast, lunch, and dinner. Breakfast specials include several popular versions of eggs Benedict and, on the lighter side, feathery Eggs Confetti, scrambled using steam from the espresso machine. Between 11 a.m. and 5 p.m., the extensive lunch menu includes lighter fare such as salads, wraps, soups, and sandwiches and entrees such as slow-cooked stews, chicken potpie, meat loaf, and lasagna, perfect for a warm-up on a chilly day; between 5 and closing at 9 p.m., you'll find dinner menu additions such as wild salmon. But of course, you can't beat teatime treats here. I think the homemade crumbly scones and clotted cream and lemon curd are the best I've had outside England. Open daily 9 a.m. to 9 p.m. $–$$$.

where to stay

Inn on the Alameda. 303 E. Alameda St.; (888) 984-2121; innonthealameda.com. This enchanting bed-and-breakfast's location, a block from Canyon Road, is unbeatable. The 59 traditional and deluxe rooms and 12 gorgeous casita-style suites are attractively furnished in Santa Fe style and are very comfy; many have patios, balconies, and fireplaces. Extensive breakfast buffet and wine and cheese reception are included in the reasonable rates. $$–$$$.

upper canyon road

Camino Cabra, the main bus route to Museum Hill, crosses the top of Lower Canyon Road about a mile from Paseo de Peralta. Canyon Road doglegs past Cristo Rey Church to head east on Upper Canyon Road. You'll need a car for this section. The long country lane climbs past shambling adobes and the Upaya Zen Center to dead-end—2.5 miles from the Plaza— at the delightful Randall Davey Audubon Center and intersecting trail system adjoining the old Santa Fe reservoir, high above Santa Fe.

where to go

Cristo Rey Church. 1120 Canyon Rd.; (505) 983-8528; cristoreyparish.org. Santa Fe style architect John Gaw Meem designed this lovely church, the nation's largest adobe building, in 1940 to commemorate the 400th anniversary of Coronado's exploration of the Southwest. It houses the huge 1760 painted stone altar screen that was originally installed in the old military chapel near the Plaza. The church is at the turnoff for Upper Canyon Road. Open Mon through Fri 8 a.m. to 4 p.m.; closed noon to 1 p.m. for lunch. Free.

Randall Davey Audubon Center & Sanctuary. 1800 Upper Canyon Rd.; (505) 983-4609; randalldavey.audubon.org. Great bird-watching, short trails, an education center, and a historic artist's home are the draws at this 135-acre former sawmill and farm, which has been the New Mexico headquarters of the Audubon Society since the 1980s. Artist Randall Davey, who owned the property from 1920 to 1964, made his home in the converted Martinez mill and used the family *hacienda* for his studio. The center is open Mon through Sat 8 a.m. to 4 p.m. Bird-watching tours every Sat at 8 a.m.; tours of Randall Davey House every Fri at 2 p.m. Admission fee.

Santa Fe Canyon Preserve. (505) 988-3867; nature.org/wherewework/northamerica/ states/newmexico/preserves. This 335-acre nature preserve adjoining Randall Davey Audubon Center at the top of Upper Canyon Road is owned by the Nature Conservancy. Trails explore a thriving bosque, ponds, the ruins of a Victorian-era dam, and more than 140 species of birds along the original route of the Santa Fe River. Note: This trail creates an important foothills link with the popular Atalaya Trail, behind St. John's College to the south, and the 25-mile Dale Ball Trail system to the north, which ends at Hyde Park Road. Those trails are administered by the Santa Fe Open Space and Trails Division (505-992-9868; santafecountynm.gov/open_space_and-trails_program). Open daily. Free.

museum hill

The four cultural museums clustered on Museum Hill, off Old Santa Fe Trail, offer excellent coverage of the human story, here and around the world, and their proximity to one another on this quiet, wooded campus far from the busy downtown are their greatest attractions. There are 360-degree views, a labyrinth, massive sculptures by Indian artists, and popular community events on Milner Plaza, such as the Santa Fe International Folk Art Festival, the world's largest folk art fair, in July. Museum Hill Cafe, the only cafe here, is between owners and currently closed. The closest restaurants are Harry's Roadhouse and Cafe Fina on Old Las Vegas Highway (See Where to Eat below) and restaurants on Old Santa Fe Trail and Canyon Road. For information, visit museumhill.net. Adjoining is the lovely Santa Fe Botanical Garden, a pleasant place to stroll and sit.

where to go

Museum of Indian Arts and Culture/Laboratory of Anthropology. 710 Camino Lejo; (505) 476-1269; indianartsandculture.org. The core exhibit at this lively Indian arts museum, part of Museum of New Mexico, is "Here, Now, and Always," which uses images, voices, music, architecture, and 1,300 cultural objects to tell the story of Indians in the Southwest. Galleries display pottery and other artifacts from the adjoining Laboratory of Anthropology, which has been an important repository for artifacts excavated by the archeologist Edgar Lee Hewett and others since the early 1900s. Revolving contemporary Indian art exhibits, lectures, day trips, resource center, and other programs. Open Tues through Sat 10 a.m. to 5 p.m., daily in summer (MNM hours; see North Day Trip 03). Admission fee; under 16 free.

Museum of International Folk Art. 706 Camino Lejo; (505) 476-1200; internationalfolkart .org. The repository of the world's largest collection of international folk art, the museum began with 2,500 objects collected and donated by Florence Bartlett and expanded exponentially with donations of 106,000 objects from designer Alexander Girard and 2,600 objects from Lloyd Cotsen of Neutrogena. Today the extensive collection numbers 130,000 objects. The museum's most popular exhibit is the 10,000 miniature figurines from 100 countries, which are displayed in charming dioramas that appeal to the entire family. The Neutrogena Wing has revolving exhibits of textiles, costumes, and masks. The Bartlett Wing and Hispanic Heritage and Contemporary Hispanic Wings feature traditional New Mexican folk art by famed *santeros* (artists who create carvings and other artwork depicting saints and other religious figures) like Charlie Carrillo. Concerts, lectures, and other special events are held in the auditorium. Open Tues through Sat 10 a.m. to 5 p.m., daily in summer (MNM hours). Admission fee; under 16 free.

Museum of Spanish Colonial Arts. 750 Camino Lejo; (505) 982-2226; spanishcolonial .org. This newer private museum is the only one in the country dedicated to exhibiting and interpreting Spanish Colonial art. It is run by the Spanish Colonial Arts Society, which was founded by writer Mary Austin and artist/writer Frank Applegate in 1928, and is best known for organizing the popular Spanish Market on the Plaza every July. It occupies the former home of the director of the Laboratory of Anthropology, a low-slung adobe building designed, like the other museums on Museum Hill, by Santa Fe style genius John Gaw Meem. On display are about 3,000 artifacts from the society's collection. Open Tues through Sun 10 a.m. to 5 p.m., daily in summer. Admission fee; under 16 free. Free for New Mexico residents on the first Sunday of the month.

Santa Fe Botanical Garden at Museum Hill. 725 Camino Lejo, Ste. E; (505) 471-9103; santafebotanicalgarden.org. Founded by and run by community members over 20 years ago, Santa Fe Botanical Garden, adjoining Museum Hill, proves that high-desert gardens can be just as lush and enchanting, with its colorful mix of native and nonnative plants. Trails wander through arroyos and pathways on the property and connect Museum Hill with Old Pecos Trail, making for a very pleasant place to take a breather and enjoy the views. Free.

Wheelwright Museum of the American Indian. 704 Camino Lejo; (505) 982-4636; wheelwright.org. The only Santa Fe museum open on Mondays year-round, the tiny Wheelwright is, for my money, one of Santa Fe's most interesting museums. It was built in 1937 by New Englander Mary Cabot Wheelwright and Navajo medicine man Hastiin Klah, who, certain that Navajo culture was disappearing, founded this museum to record ritual knowledge from Navajo elders. Their fears about the Navajo culture proved unfounded, so in the 1970s the Wheelwright changed its name and mission to reflect an expanded focus on contemporary Southwest Indian art. The main gallery has revolving exhibits of historic and contemporary art; a second gallery has one-person exhibits. Downstairs an authentic trading post sells artwork, jewelry, pottery, books, and folk art. By the way, the building—in the shape of an eight-sided Navajo hogan—was designed by artist/master builder William Penhallow Henderson, a major exponent of Santa Fe style. He and his wife, poet Alice Corbin Henderson, came to Santa Fe to treat Alice's tuberculosis and built a home in the Canyon Road area. Henderson was part of the group known as the Cinco Pintores ("Five Painters"). Open daily 10 a.m. to 5 p.m. Admission fee; under 12 free. Free on the first Sun of the month to all visitors.

where to eat

Cafe Fina. 24 Old Las Vegas Hwy.; (505) 466-3886; cafefinasantafe.com. Located in an attractive converted Fina gas station at the junction of Old Las Vegas Highway, I-25, and US 285, Cafe Fina is light and bright and a great spot to meet for healthy, reliably good modern Southwest comfort food. Owner Murphy O'Brien, a veteran of well-known restaurants like Coyote Cafe and Mu Du Noodles, has stacked the menu with crowd-pleasers. Try huevos Motuleños, the regional breakfast classic of Mexico's Yucatan; savory corn cakes with chipotle-marinated shrimp (with an egg on top, New Mexico style), a classic of Coyote Cafe's Cantina; or the green chile cheeseburger made with poblano (not Big Jim) chiles, grass-fed beef raised down the road in Pecos, and local Tucumcari cheese served with a lovely fresh salad or fries (or both). They turn out a delectable daily array of baked goods: fresh pies, including a fresh organic pumpkin pie with a flaky crust in fall that is an annual delight; a rustic individual fruit galette; a yummy bacon-date scone; iced gingerbread cookies; macaroons; and homemade granola. There's even a drive-thru. Note: O'Brien has recently opened the restaurant in the refurbished historic Legal Tender Saloon in nearby Lamy for dinners on weekends (see Northeast Day Trip 01). Open for breakfast and lunch Mon through Fri 7 a.m. to 3 p.m. and Sat and Sun 8 a.m. to 3 p.m.; dinner Thurs through Sat 5:30 to 8:30 p.m. $–$$.

Harry's Roadhouse. 96 Old Las Vegas Hwy.; (505) 989-4629. Locals flock to this arty roadhouse eatery for its eclectic menu, neighborhood vibe, and decent prices. Waits are common, but things move quickly and efficiently. Breakfast eggs with homemade turkey sausage and salsa jump-start mornings; at lunch or dinner try juicy burgers, a chopped salad, Moroccan couscous, trout, or catfish. The stars of the menu are the flaky pies and airy baked goods made by Harry's wife, Peyton. Patio and bar. Open daily. $–$$.

where to stay

Inn of the Turquoise Bear. 342 E. Buena Vista St.; (505) 983-0798, (800) 396-4104; turquoisebear.com. There are 8 beautiful Southwestern guest rooms with fireplaces, vigas, and other details in this timeless historic B&B built in the early 1920s by poet Witter Bynner, Santa Fe's answer to famed Taos salon-hostess Mabel Dodge Luhan. Willa Cather, D. H. Lawrence, Robert Oppenheimer, and other major artists and thinkers stayed here and enjoyed Bynner and longtime companion Robert Hunt's outrageous "Bynner's bashes." Full gourmet breakfast. Afternoon tea includes house-made baked goods and pie on Fri. Gay-friendly. $$.

siler district (sidi)

In the past, the long commercial route into town along Cerrillos Road (NM 14) may have been the place to find less-expensive lodging away from the downtown core. With its bland strip malls and chains, the route offered little for tourists. Even so, with sky-high rents in Santa Fe and a low supply of affordable housing crippling the city, the newer subdivisions, loft developments, live-work studios, and regenerating neighborhoods off Cerrillos around Second Street and increasingly farther south have become a mecca for those on tighter budgets, including many working-class Santa Feans, young people, and artists working on large-scale projects who need more space. That's particularly true of the grittier, slowly gentrifying, mixed-use industrial zone on the south side of the Santa Fe River between Siler Road and Cerrillos—dubbed the Siler District, or SIDI—where live-work warehouses and old commercial buildings are now populated by artists, entrepreneurs, breweries, coffee shops, chocolatiers, and local businesses. The shift has been gradual yet inexorable, and then in March 2016 it seemed to suddenly explode with the opening of art collective Meow Wolf's entrancing and decidedly psychedelic House of Eternal Return. Since it opened, the project has been a massive hit with locals and tourists alike—it made $6 million in its first year alone—and is now Santa Fe's top visitor attraction. Not surprisingly, the prototype is now expanding; it will open in Las Vegas in 2020 and Denver in 2021.

where to go

Meow Wolf: House of Eternal Return.1352 Rufina Circle (look for the huge iron sculpture of a robot); (505) 395-6369; meowwolf.com. Meow Wolf is the brainchild of a 400-strong group of artists who over a number of years have been slowly incubating this very un–Santa Fe style permanent art installation for kids of all ages, as part of an effort to improve youth culture and contemporary art in Santa Fe. The project took off when *Game of Thrones* author and local resident George R. R. Martin, a major supporter of the arts in Santa Fe and owner of the Jean Cocteau Arts Cinema in the Railyard, purchased an old 20,000-square-foot bowling alley complex on Rufina Circle as a home for the Meow Wolf Arts Complex, which was established in 2008. The House of Eternal Return features room after room of colorful, clever, artful, and interactive experiences that engage the senses and offer fresh perspectives: Think futuristic Victorian haunted fun house meets immersive art experience meets children's museum. There is something here for everyone. It's open late, so this is a good option for a fun evening out and allows you to fit it into a busy day of sightseeing in Santa Fe. Purchase tickets online or through the box office ahead of time, and reserve an entrance time. Allow yourself plenty of time to experience the large exhibit; there is no time limit once inside, but there may be a line in the parking lot to get in, so plan accordingly. The complex also includes a children's learning center, a cafe and bar, and an events venue. Open Mon, Wed, Thurs, and Sun 10 a.m. to 8 p.m. and Fri and Sat 10 a.m. to 10 p.m.

where to eat

Dr. Field Goods. 2860 Cerrillos Rd.; (505) 471-0043; drfieldgoods.com. Located in a strip mall just south of Siler Road, Dr. Field Goods is a lively spot for warm, comforting, well-prepared, local farm-to-table food, from burgers and wood-fired pizzas to tacos, sandwiches, and salads. Try the classic Cubano sandwich, shrimp tacos, or red chile buffalo enchiladas. Portions are huge, but smaller meals are available. There is a full-service butcher shop next door if you can't resist taking home some sausages, bacon, or other meat. $—$$.

Second Street Brewery Rufina Taproom. 2920 Rufina St.; (505) 954-1068; second streetbrewery/rufina-taproom. Popular Second Street Brewery opened this 20,000-square-foot space, which includes a brewery, canning line, restaurant, and taproom, in 2017, and it's a great spot to grab a microbrew and some good fish-and-chips or other pub food and watch some live music after a trip to nearby Meow Wolf. Open daily noon to midnight; original brewery location is beside the train tracks on Second Street, with a third location in the Railyard in the Farmers' Market building. $–$$.

where to stay

Silver Saddle Motel. 2810 Cerrillos Rd.; (505) 471-7663; santafesilversaddle.com. Located across the lot from Dr. Field Goods, the Silver Saddle is a friendly, family-run vintage adobe motel that retains its classic 1950s Route 66 atmosphere and character and feels homey and welcoming. Lovingly upgraded and furnished, this is Santa Fe's most popular budget motel, with small but spotless themed single-story rooms that include homages to Route 66, cowgirls, and other icons of the West. All have flat-screen TVs, microwaves, one or two queen beds, and showers; those in back have kitchenettes and are quieter, so I usually recommend trying to snag one of those, especially if you plan on staying a few days. Free continental breakfast on an attractive patio adjoining the reception. $.

worth more time

If you have a car and want to get outdoors and move, head up Hyde Park Road, just northeast of downtown, for a scenic 29-mile drive to the 10,000-foot-elevation **Santa Fe Ski Basin** (505-982-4429; skisantafe.com). Some long and challenging trails into the Big Tesuque Creek watershed and other areas of **Santa Fe National Forest** (505-438-5300; fs .usda.gov/santafe) leave from either side of the road, but you can also just pull off and start walking. The most popular day hike is Aspen Vista, just below the ski basin, which attracts thousands of leaf-peepers at the end of September. The scenic chairlift at the ski basin is another way to appreciate fall color—during ski season, it's kept busy by skiers enjoying groomed trails. Developed camping is available in several national forest campgrounds and in Hyde Memorial State Park, which has showers.

The quintessential Santa Fe day outing is to do a long hike in the forest, then stop at **Ten Thousand Waves,** known locally as "The Waves" (3451 Hyde Park Rd.; 505-992-5003;

tenthousandwaves.com), for a soak in a private hot tub or the communal tub and one of the best massages in Santa Fe. Fourteen rooms are available, if you want to spend the night, and include Zen rooms, Townsman rooms, and Emperor's rooms, all decorated in stripped-down Japanese style and featuring proprietary yuzu- and evergreen-infused toiletries and unlimited soaking in the communal pool. **Izanami** (505-982-9304; open Tues 5 to 10 p.m. and Wed through Sun 11:30 a.m. to 10 p.m.; Fri and Sat happy hour 4 to 5 p.m.), the on-site upscale, woodsy Japanese pub, offers a unique dining experience with *izakaya*, or small plates designed for sharing. The seasonal Japanese menu, developed by executive chef Kim Muller, uses organic meat and local produce and stars Wagyu beef done several ways, chicken, lamb, sushi, vegetarian dishes, fresh pickles, and yuzu desserts; there's also an extensive sake list assembled by master sake sommelier Deborah Fleig, one of only 40 such sommeliers in the US. $$–$$$$.

day trip 05

north

>>> **badlands to bombs—past meets present between santa fe and los alamos:** tesuque village, tesuque pueblo, pojoaque, las barrancas, san ildefonso pueblo, los alamos

Picking up US 285/84 off I-25 at Santa Fe, a drive north of town takes you into the colorful *barrancas* (badlands) of the Santa Fe watershed between the Sangre de Cristo and Jemez mountain ranges to visit traditional Hispanic villages and the Indian pueblos of Tesuque, Pojoaque, and San Ildefonso. At Pojoaque, US 502 veers west into the Española Valley toward the Jemez Mountains, passing the villages of Jacona, Jaconita, and El Rancho and Black Mesa, a prominent geological landmark sacred to local Indians. The highlights of this day trip are San Ildefonso Pueblo, home to famed potter Maria Martinez during the early 20th century, and Los Alamos, where the Bradbury Science Museum interprets the historic Manhattan Project that brought international scientists here in the 1940s to create the world's first atomic bomb. This day trip connects with Northwest Day Trips 03 and 04.

tesuque village

Five miles north of the Fort Marcy neighborhood in Santa Fe is the village of Tesuque, a mixture of family compounds, artist retreats, and walled second homes. You can reach Tesuque quickly by driving north on US 285/84 and turning off near the Santa Fe Opera, but it's much more pleasant to get there by dawdling through the dense bosque, horse paddocks, and adobes along Bishop's Lodge Road (CR 73A). Just north of downtown, the road opens

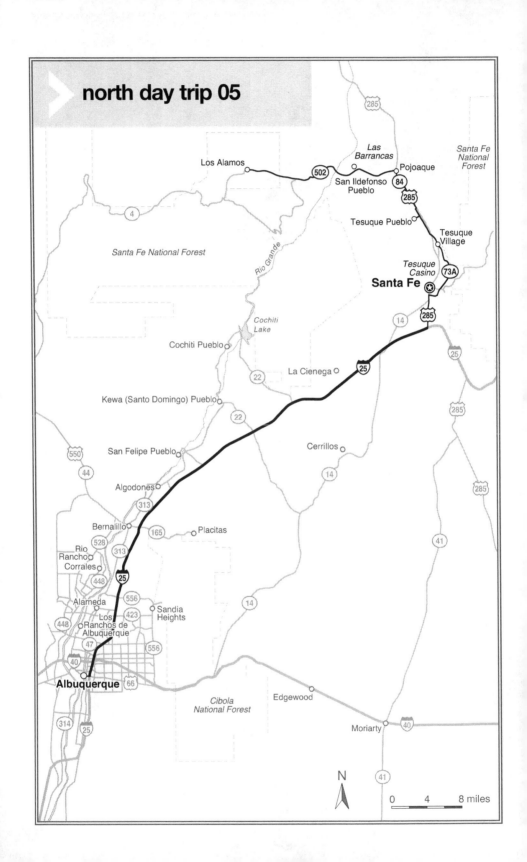

north day trip 05

out as it passes the Governor's Mansion, offering panoramic views, especially at sunset. As the road approaches the south end of Tesuque, it starts to narrow considerably and hugs Big Tesuque Creek, which comes out of Big Tesuque Canyon, the lower end of the Winsor Trail into the mountains. The road winds past Shidoni, a good place to enjoy the sculpture garden and gallery, and emerges in the main village by Tesuque Village Market. The market is a community hub for coffee, tasty meals on the patio, and freshly made deli items.

where to go

Santa Fe Opera. 7 miles north of Santa Fe on US 285/84; (505) 986-5900, (800) 280-4654 (box office); santafeopera.org. With its mast-and-sail architecture floating up out of the piñon-juniper hills north of town, Santa Fe Opera's landmark building is reminiscent of the Sydney Opera House. This also is a world-class opera. It was completely rebuilt in 1997, with many green elements but primarily a roof that now protects summer-season operagoers from the elements without losing the spectacular "sensurround" feeling of the landscape. Since it was founded in 1957, Santa Fe Opera has presented more than 170 different operas, by 85 composers, including 15 world premieres, performed by the world's greatest opera stars. One-hour Backstage Tours take place late May through late Aug, Mon through Fri at 9 a.m. Tours of the grounds, known as the Opera Ranch, and a Meet the Artists presentation by one of the opera apprentices, take place on Fri at 10 a.m.; fee charged for both. Opera Insider Tours are free every Sat at 8:30 a.m. and include coffee and pastries, a talk about the opera, and a backstage tour.

Winsor Trail, New Mexico Public Lands Info Center. 301 Dinosaur Trail; (505) 954-2002, (877) 276-9404; center open Mon through Fri 8:30 a.m. to 4:30 p.m. To reach the trailhead, take a sharp right onto CR 72, a mile past Bishop's Lodge Resort (currently closed for renovations), and cross Big Tesuque Creek into residential Big Tesuque Canyon. There's limited parking for a shady creekside hike on the popular Winsor Trail, quite a workout as you head up from the national forest boundary into the ski basin alongside Little Tesuque Creek

tesuque wildlife

Between 1999 and 2006, I lived on a historic 6-acre property in Big Tesuque Canyon that was once owned by a Manhattan Project scientist and his family. The canyon has been used since Pueblo times as a thoroughfare into the mountains, and first rights on the acequia (irrigation ditch) in the canyon still go to Tesuque Pueblo down in the valley. Rabbits, coyotes, raptors, mountain birds, and other wildlife are abundant. Black bears have been known to frequent the orchards in the canyon and the trail when food is scarce, so keep your wits about you.

(if you go all the way, you'll need a car on Hyde Park Road to get back). The mile-long hike to the trailhead from the parking lot through private property, or just beyond the forest boundary to the second stream crossing, offers a nice way to stretch your legs or walk the dog.

where to shop

Shidoni Gallery and Sculpture Garden. 1508 Bishop's Lodge Rd.; (505) 988-8001; shidoni.com. Opened in 1973, Shidoni was one of the world's leading fine-art casting facilities and showplaces, continuously owned by the same family since it opened. Although the foundry has been shuttered, you can still roam a 5-acre sculpture garden with 500 works, the largest in New Mexico, and an art gallery displaying indoor and outdoor works by local artists nestled among the apple orchards. Open Mon through Sat 10 a.m. to 5 p.m. Free.

where to eat

Tesuque Village Market. 138 Tesuque Village Rd.; (505) 988-8848; tesuquevillagemarket .com. Under new ownership, this country market has gone slightly more upscale (and even has a branch on Venice Beach, California), with wood-fired pizza ovens and natural and organic offerings supplementing authentic Mexican and New Mexican dishes, fresh-roasted meats, and decadent baked goods that will break any diet. Tesuque is home to many laid-back celebrities. You may end up standing in line to pay for your tortilla soup, fresh tamales, and éclairs behind someone you recognize, but it's good manners here to respect privacy and keep your fandom to yourself. Open daily 7 a.m. to 9 p.m. $–$$.

where to stay

Four Seasons Resort Rancho Encantado. 198 SR 592; (505) 946-5700, reservations (800) 819-5053; fourseasons.com/santafe. Set far from the madding crowd, in the foothills of Tesuque along SR 592, this relaxing resort on a former dude ranch offers 65 luxurious casitas and suites and 57 acres in which to get away from it all, whether hiking, horseback riding, bicycling, lazing by the pool, getting a spa treatment, or eating in the excellent on-site restaurant Terra, a great place to experience the property. $$$$.

tesuque pueblo

Return to US 285/84 to visit the conservative 450-member pueblo of Tesuque on 17,000 acres of irrigated farmland and badlands adjoining the Rio Grande. It was founded in the 1100s, then abandoned during the Pueblo Revolt, during which time Tesuque people were the first to suffer losses against the Spanish before acting as messengers and spreading word of the revolt to other tribes. The best time to visit is on Christmas Day, when there are dances honoring sacred animals on the large plaza (built in 1694). Tesuque artists are reviving the brightly painted ceramic rain-god figurines made as curios in the golden age of railroad tourism. The tribe's main commercial enterprises are an attractive new casino along US 84/285, a campground and picnic area across from the distinctive sandstone landmark called Camel Rock, and Santa Fe Suites off South St. Francis Drive in Santa Fe. Permits for camping and fishing on tribal lands are available from the tribal office. For more information, call the tribal office at (505) 983-2667.

where to go

Tesuque Casino. 7 Tesuque Rd.; (800) 462-2635; tesuquecasino.com. This elegant, soaring, 72,000-square-foot casino is New Mexico's newest and has been a big hit since it opened in 2018 on the site of the former flea market adjoining Santa Fe Opera. It has slots, bingo, table games, and plenty to keep gamblers busy while also offering an attractive destination for a night out. Nightly entertainment by local musicians is offered in the bar, while concerts by big-name acts take place in the 4,000-square-foot event center. The Cottonwood Kitchen, the attractive on-site restaurant, is professionally run and has an exhibition kitchen, an open-plan bar-restaurant, and patio dining that takes advantage of sweeping views. The menu focuses on seasonal fare and offers a variety of dishes from a half-pound burger, prime rib, and crab legs to Skuna Bay salmon and free-range chicken, all at reasonable rates; bar snacks include a delectable spinach and artichoke dip.

pojoaque

After being abandoned several times, Tewa-speaking Pojoaque, which has had a presence in the area since AD 500, has made a big comeback. Its numerous attractive, modern visitor services straddle the junction of US 285/84 and US 502, long an important crossroads with travelers in the area. The recent governor of the pueblo, George Rivera, is the great-grandson of former governor Antonio Tapia (who left the pueblo in 1915 after a smallpox outbreak and helped reestablish it after 1932). He is a talented sculptor—his *Buffalo Dancer II* is installed in front of the Smithsonian's National Museum of the American Indian in Washington, DC. Its sibling, *Buffalo Dancer I*, sits at the entrance to the tribe's Buffalo Thunder Resort, the first Indian-owned luxury resort in northern New Mexico. The elegant property includes the Hilton Buffalo Thunder and Homewood Suites by Hilton hotels, a casino, three golf courses, a luxury spa, and four restaurants. Dances at the pueblo are open to the public on the tribe's feast day (December 12) and Reyes Day (January 12).

where to go

Poeh Cultural Center and Museum. 78 Cities of Gold Rd.; (505) 455-5041; poehcenter .org. Although it appears modern, Pojoaque Pueblo is firmly rooted in the past. It is reintroducing bison on its lands and encouraging young people to learn traditional arts under the tutelage of established potters, painters, sculptors, and weavers at this cultural center.

Exhibits in the museum interpret all the Pueblo people, with particular emphasis on the six Tewa-speaking pueblos of northern New Mexico. The featured artist here is Santa Clara potter Roxanne Swentzell, from a long line of Pueblo potters, whose distinctive female sculptures are a powerful homage to the lives of Native women. In October 2019, 100 sacred ancient Pueblo pots were returned to the tribal museum from the National Museum of the American Indian, and the pottery will be the core exhibit in a new educational resource center. In addition to being a museum, Poeh Cultural Center will become an immersive learning center used by all Tewa tribes in the area. Artist demonstrations take place every Fri and Sat between Memorial Day and Labor Day. The eye-catching cultural center is constructed in the form of a traditional pueblo. Open Mon through Fri 9 a.m. to 5 p.m. and Sat 10 a.m. to 4 p.m.

where to eat

Red Sage Grill at Buffalo Thunder Resort. 20 Buffalo Thunder Trail; (505) 819-2056; redsage-sf.com. Back in the 1980s, Mark Miller's Coyote Cafe put Santa Fe on the national culinary map. Miller pioneered and then wrote the book—literally—on the chiles, spices, and traditional foods of the Southwest. Red Sage, with its huge dry-aged steaks, savvy wine list, strong cocktails, and *Urban Cowboy* meets *Nick and Nora* elements, was begun by Miller in Washington, DC; opened as a fine-dining restaurant at Buffalo Thunder; and now continues on, without Miller, refining earthy New American cuisine in a diverse menu. Steaks are still the star attraction, and you can choose from an 8-ounce filet mignon, a 16-ounce Cowboy Steak, and 12-ounce buffalo and New York strip steaks, as well as other cuts of meat. Entrees include free-range chicken, Chilean sea bass, lobster tail, seared diver scallops, and a vegetarian pasta dish. Select ingredients are sourced from local farmers through Tewa Farms. The lounge menu offers flatbreads, tacos, sliders, and queso fundido. A good time to sample Red Sage is at happy hour daily from 3 to 6 p.m., when prices on drinks and bar food are reduced. Dinner 5 to 9 p.m., until 10 p.m. Sat and Sun. Bar open until 11 p.m. $$–$$$$.

where to stay

Hilton Buffalo Thunder. 20 Buffalo Thunder Trail; (505) 455-5555; buffalothunderresort .com. The main resort has 395 modern Pueblo-style rooms and suites, an enormous casino, a full-service spa, high-end shopping, a large theater with world-class entertainment, 4 dining options, and 3 golf courses. Nearby Homewood Suites by Hilton has 79 "contemporary-calm" suites with fireplaces. A destination unto itself, this beautiful resort is filled with contemporary Indian art by prizewinners from Indian Market. $$–$$$$.

las barrancas

Drive west on US 502 toward the Jemez Mountains and Los Alamos following the braided Pojoaque River wash. The road skims the southern margin of the Española Valley. To the north are Las Barrancas ("the Badlands"), a series of eroded pinkish sandstone rocks made up of sediments that have been washed down from the mountain ranges, which have yielded skeletons of long-extinct southwestern camels. At their feet sit the little Hispanic settlements of Jacona and Jaconita (pronounced Hac-ONA and HAC-onita) and El Rancho amid fertile irrigated farmlands in the bosque. Having lived out here at one time, I can recommend turning off and exploring the back roads. The area has no formal trails or attractions but is a lovely place to walk in arroyos and through bosque, relax, and enjoy killer views.

where to stay

Rancho Jacona. 277 CR 84; (505) 455-7948; ranchojacona.com. This lovely family-run historic adobe retreat is set on 35 acres in Jacona, perfectly positioned between Pojoaque and San Ilefonso Pueblo. There are 12 fully furnished and stocked casitas of various sizes for rent, a pool, walking trails to the riverbed, and landscaped grounds. A great place to use as a base while you explore the area. Rates are nightly and sliding scale, depending on number of nights you stay; monthly rates are available for extended stays. $$–$$$$.

san ildefonso pueblo

Black Mesa is sacred to the 1,524-member San Ildefonso Pueblo, whose residents retreated to the mesa to protest de Vargas's 1692 Reconquest. The pueblo was founded around AD 1300 by refugees from the Mesa Verde area of southwestern Colorado and from nearby Bandelier National Monument. The pueblo is famous around the world for the polished black ceramics of Maria and Julian Martinez and their son Popovi Da. San Ildefonso has a visitor center, museum, and many art studios selling work. Buffalo and Deer Dances are held on the large plaza on the tribe's feast day, at Easter, and at Christmas; dances are also performed during the summer. San Ildefonso's fame as an art pueblo has ensured that it is one of the most visited pueblos in New Mexico.

where to go

San Ildefonso Pueblo Museum. (505) 455-3549; sanipueblo.org. San Ildefonso people reconnected with their ancestral roots in 1908, when archeologist Edgar Lee Hewett showed elder Julian Martinez and his potter wife Maria samples of the pottery he was uncovering on the nearby Pajarito Plateau. The Martinezes were skilled in making polychrome pottery, but these ceramics were subtle black-on-black pieces with an *avanyu* (water serpent) motif. Maria worked closely with Hewett, reviving the firing technique to create the black-on-black pottery. Maria, Julian, and their son Popovi Da ushered in a renaissance in ceramics at San Ildefonso, creating pottery that is collected around the world. This small museum has examples of Maria Martinez's pottery as well as examples of other arts and crafts. Open daily; call for hours. Free.

los alamos

US 502 crosses the Rio Grande via historic Otowi Bridge and winds up onto the Pajarito Plateau to Los Alamos. Several spots along here are used as practice routes by weekend climbers; watch for them as you drive by. The city "on the Hill" is, and has been since 1942, a company town, albeit a rarified, intellectual one. The Manhattan Project, which raced to beat the Germans in creating the world's first atomic bomb, ended up here by an interesting fluke: Robert Oppenheimer had attended the Los Alamos Ranch School, an outdoors-oriented school for wealthy boys, and thought the location—isolated but within 45 minutes of Santa Fe—perfect. The government commandeered the school campus and installed world-renowned scientists in a think-tank atmosphere designed to promote maximum creative thinking in a short time. The town is quiet and retains its bunker mentality and look: A series of mysterious numbered buildings are interspersed with historic Ranch School buildings that house an arts center and the history museum. Manhattan Project National Historical Park was set aside by President Obama in 2015 to tell the story of the Manhattan Project and includes sites in Los Alamos; Hanford, Washington; and Oak Ridge, Tennessee. It is run jointly by the National Park Service and the Department of Energy. You cannot visit the lab itself, but you can take a walking tour of downtown starting from the park's Los Alamos Unit visitor center, which is staffed by rangers, and also visit the Bradbury Science Museum.

where to go

Art Center at Fuller Lodge. 2132 Central Ave.; (505) 662-4493; fullerlodgeartcenter.com. Fuller Lodge is the town's main art center, with workshops, classes, revolving exhibits, and a gift shop selling work by local artists in a historic building. The Los Alamos Historical Society runs a small local-history museum nearby on Juniper Street. Open Mon through Sat 10 a.m. to 4 p.m. Free.

Ashley Pond Park. 109 Central Park Sq.; (505) 661-4891; secretcityconcertseries.com. Every Friday night in the summer, the Los Alamos Concert Series offers some big-name musical acts at this small community park located at 20th Street between Trinity Drive and Central Avenue. A building on the bank of this pond houses the Los Alamos County Council and the Municipal Court. Free.

Bradbury Science Museum. 1350 Central Ave.; (505) 667-4444; lanl.gov/museum. Run by Los Alamos National Laboratory, this museum in an old icehouse on Ashley Pond fills you in on the Manhattan Project and is your main source of information for what LANL has been doing since then. Kid-friendly, with 60 interactive exhibits and a historical film. Open Tues through Sat 10 a.m. to 5 p.m. and Sun and Mon 1 to 5 p.m. Free.

Manhattan Project National Historical Park Los Alamos. 475 20th St., Ste. C; (505) 661-6277; nps.gov/mapr. Set aside in 2015 to protect and interpret 17 sites at Los Alamos National Laboratory and 11 sites in downtown Los Alamos, which together form Project Y, the visitor center of the Los Alamos Unit of the new national historical park should be your first stop for information on visiting the individual historic sites in Los Alamos. You can watch a film about the Manhattan Project, talk to park rangers, and pick up a walking tour booklet of the different sites; these include the Ice House Memorial, Ashley Pond, the Oppenheimer and Groves sculptures, Fuller Lodge, Los Alamos History Museum, Stone Power House, Bathtub Row, the Hans Bethe House, the Women's Corps Dormitory, the WWII Cafeteria, and the Bradbury Science Museum (see separate entries for Ashley Pond, Fuller Lodge, and Bradbury Science Museum above).

Pajarito Mountain Ski Area. 397 Camp May Rd., off SR 501; (505) 662-5725; pajarito .ski. After the Manhattan Project, volunteers built ski runs and a lodge here in the 1950s for winter recreation; the 4,000 members of the Los Alamos Ski Club continue to manage the facility today. This is a 750-acre ski hill, not a resort, but there's good skiing on 44 trails and lessons in telemark skiing, cross-country skiing, snowboarding, and alpine skiing. No snowmaking. Usually open mid-Nov to mid-Mar, depending on snow conditions. The 5 lifts operate Sat and Sun, 9 a.m. to 3 p.m. Seniors and youngsters under the age of 6 ski free. Cafe open Wed through Sun.

where to eat

Blue Window Bistro. 1789 Central Ave., #3088; (505) 662-6305; labluewindowbistro.com. This charming, airy restaurant has been a popular spot for a meal for 30 years. It's open from lunchtime through dinnertime, so is convenient for when you just need to eat. At lunch, there are homemade soups, salads, crepes, wraps, and sandwiches, and a midafternoon menu that includes appetizers, Pacific Rim surf-and-turf, fish-and-chips, and a variety of light meals. Dinner kicks it up a notch with entrees such as Eggplant Napoleon, free-range Southwest chicken, and different takes on fresh Atlantic salmon. Open Mon through Fri for lunch 11 a.m. to 2:30 p.m. and dinner 5 to 8:30 p.m. Midafternoon and dinner menu served in the lounge 2:30 to 8:30 p.m. $$–$$$.

Ruby K's Bagel Cafe. 1789 Central Ave., Ste. 2; (505) 662-9866; rubykbagel.com. This hip, modern cafe is locally owned and serves tea, coffee drinks, fresh bagels and cream cheese, soups, sandwiches, panini, and salads. Since its opening a couple of years ago, it has gone a long way toward filling the need for a community meeting place that also serves good food and coffee. There are occasional poetry readings and local events held here, and the cafe gives away its leftover food to local food banks and homeless shelters. Free Wi-Fi. Open Mon through Fri 7 a.m. to 4 p.m. and Sat and Sun 7 a.m. to 3 p.m. $.

where to stay

The Canyon Inn. 80 Canyon Rd.; (505) 510-2253; canyon-inn-los-alamos-us.book.direct. The Canyon Inn is an English-style B&B in a mountain home that really operates as a home-style boardinghouse. The simple accommodations include 4 bedrooms with private baths and shared kitchen facilities. Food is provided; guests prepare their own meals at their leisure in the kitchen. Barbecue available outside. There is a terrace, shared television lounge, and free Wi-Fi is available throughout the building. $.

northeast

day trip 01

northeast

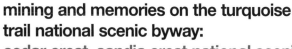

mining and memories on the turquoise trail national scenic byway:
cedar crest, sandia crest national scenic byway, madrid, cerrillos, galisteo basin, lamy

New Mexico is the oldest mining district in the US. Around AD 1000, Pueblo-run mines at Cerrillos supplied turquoise that was used for trade and ritual in Mexico's Aztec empire and New Mexico's Chaco Canyon; it was as important in the prehistoric world as gold is to us today. The first Spanish colonists, who self-funded expeditions to New Mexico in hopes of finding gold, quickly set up lead and silver mining operations at Cerrillos, likely making that settlement older than Santa Fe. Under American rule, Golden became the site of the first gold rush west of the Mississippi in 1825; Golden and Cerrillos are ghost towns now. The most popular destination on this drive is the former coal-mining town of Madrid (pronounced MAD-rid), which has become a back-road artists' haven. Famous for its Christmas illuminations and parade, the oldest tavern in New Mexico, an old-time melodrama theater, and a summer blues festival, Madrid is a popular year-round tourist destination. Like Cerrillos, it has been used as a backdrop for movie shoots, most famously 2006's *Wild Hogs*, which was shot entirely on location here. To start the tour, take I-40 east to exit 125 at Tijeras, then head north on NM 14. The scenic highway winds between the Sandia and Ortiz Mountains.

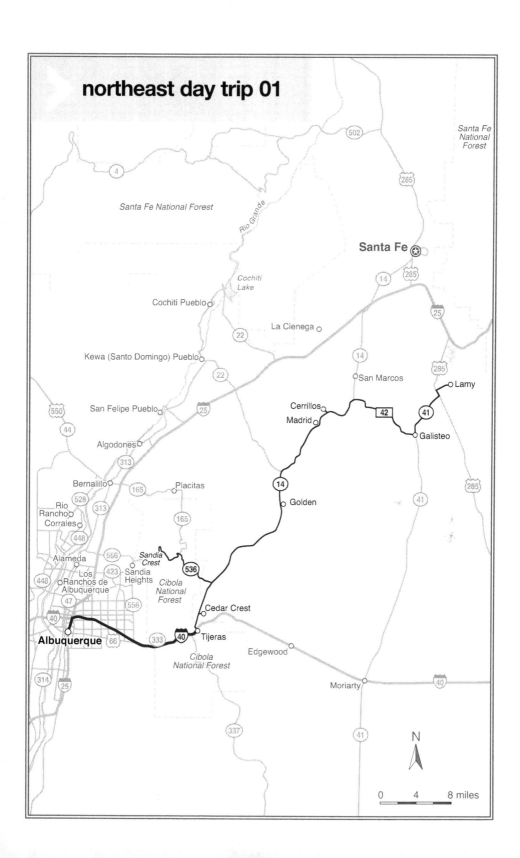

cedar crest

This mountain town just north of I-40 has alpine charm and is a good place to gas up and have a meal at the start of the scenic byway.

where to eat

Greenside Cafe. 12165 N. NM 14, Ste. B1; (505) 286-2684; greenside.cafe. There aren't a lot of interesting places to eat in Cedar Crest, but the Greenside Cafe, an attractive cafe in the Village of Bella Vista, a strip mall, is an exception. It serves tasty New Mexican food, such as chilaquiles for breakfast, and American favorites such as chicken-fried steak, burgers, soups, sandwiches, and homemade ice cream for lunch and dinner all week. Open Tues through Sat 11 a.m. to 8 p.m. and Sun 10 a.m. to 8 p.m. $–$$.

sandia crest national scenic byway

The scenic byway (SR 536) heads west off NM 14 and winds through the 1.9-million-acre Cibola National Forest to the top of the 10,000-foot Sandia Mountains, where you'll find skiing and hiking in cool pine forests. Their name means "watermelon," a reference to the pinkish hue of the mountains at sunset. They drop off steeply into the Rio Grande valley and taper more gently on the east.

golden: the oldest gold-mining town in the west

The gold-mining town of Golden, off NM 14 in the foothills of the Ortiz Mountains, boomed in 1825, long before the gold rushes in California and Colorado. It busted not long after, then boomed again in 1879, when a second gold strike occurred. Lack of water made mining difficult in this remote location, and by 1889 the settlement was mostly abandoned. Ranching is the main occupation in the area now, and Golden is a ghost town that has seen better days. Of interest are the remains of two 14th-century Indian pueblos, the general store, and the pretty 1830 whitewashed Catholic church, one of the most-photographed attractions on the Turquoise Trail. The church was restored by historian, author, and local priest Fray Angelico Chavez in the 1960s.

where to go

Sandia Peak Ski Area. SR 536, off NM 14, 6 miles via Sandia Crest National Scenic Byway; (505) 242-9052 (general info), (505) 857-8977 (snow report); sandiapeak.com. About 45 minutes from Albuquerque, this 200-acre suburban ski resort with on-site restaurants has 39 runs and a terrain park with skateboarding funboxes, rails, and jumps. It operates 4 lifts with a capacity of 4,500 skiers per hour. Vertical drop is 1,700 feet. It can also be reached from the west side via Sandia Peak Tramway (see North Day Trip 01). Open Dec through Mar, depending on snow.

Tinkertown Museum. SR 536, off NM 14; (505) 281-5233; tinkertown.com. This family museum, 2 miles from NM 14, celebrates Americana. Its main focus is a three-ring circus and miniature Wild West town that were carved by the late painter Ross Ward, a lover of circuses and traveling shows who worked on his "hobby" for 40 years. The entrance wall is made of 50,000 glass bottles. Guided tour. Gift shop. Open daily Apr through Oct, 9 a.m. to 6 p.m. Admission fee.

madrid

Madrid's mines date to the mid-1850s. Coal Gulch, as it was then known, was connected by a railroad spur to the main line of the Santa Fe Railroad, for which it supplied coal, and the town grew to a population of 2,500 by 1892. By the early 20th century, the mines had been bought by the Albuquerque and Cerrillos Coal Company, which built schools, hospitals, a company store, a tavern, and an employees' club. The company emphasized civic pride, and employees were required to support and turn out for town events. The most famous were Madrid's Christmas illuminations, which were powered by 500,000 kilowatts of electricity from coal-fed generators. Summer bluegrass and jazz concerts took place in a ballpark that was the first in the nation to be floodlit. After World War II, the mines closed and the town dwindled. In the 1970s the town's then-owner, the late Joe Huber, son of the former mine superintendent, successfully revived the town by virtually giving away old miners' homes to artists. They loved the setting and stayed, converting miners' cottages and shacks into a funky assortment of art studios, galleries, bed-and-breakfasts, cafes, and eclectic boutiques selling ethnic clothes and imported and locally made goods.

The main attractions for visitors, aside from strolling Main Street, are clustered around the old mine shaft. You can see the mine shaft and exhibits on town history at the museum; get tickets to see a seasonal melodrama at the Engine House Theatre next door, and enjoy the authentic atmosphere in the historic Mine Shaft Tavern. The Christmas illuminations and parade have been revived, making Madrid a festive place for Christmas shopping. More information is available at visitmadridnm.com.

where to go

Engine House Theatre Melodrama. 2846 NM 14; (505) 438-3780; themineshaftavern
.com/engine-house-theatre. Kids as well as adults will enjoy rooting for the heroes and boo-
ing the dastardly villains in the melodramas put on at this 135-seat theater, which is located
in the old Engine Repair House. It is part of a complex that also contains the Mine Shaft
Tavern and the Old Coal Town Museum. The theater is open seasonally between Memorial
Day and mid-Oct. Admission fee.

Old Coal Town Museum. 2846 NM 14; (505) 438-3780; themineshafttavern.com/madrid
-old-coal-town-museum. You can see the coal-mine shaft (located next to the tavern of the
same name) and learn about the town's history at this little museum. The kids will enjoy the
old mining gear and restored 1901 steam locomotive. Open Fri through Mon 10 a.m. to
4:30 p.m. Admission fee.

where to shop

Gifted Hands Gallery. 2851 NM 14; (505) 471-5943; ghgmadrid.com. This gallery, located
in a cottage just north of the Mine Shaft Tavern, sells all kinds of attractive art made by local
and American Indian artists. Items include everything from carved fetishes and handmade
jewelry to fabric art, photography, and paintings. Open daily 10 a.m. to 5:30 p.m.

Johnsons of Madrid Fine and Fiber Art Gallery. 2843 NM 14; (505) 471-1054; collectors
guide.com/sf/g279.html. The oldest gallery in Madrid, directly across from the Mine Shaft
Tavern, Johnsons sells fine and wearable art by 100 artists and is the working studio of the
Johnsons. It has receptions one Saturday a month from 4 to 7 p.m. Open daily 10 a.m. to
5 p.m.

where to eat

The Mine Shaft Tavern. 2846 NM 14; (505) 473-0743; themineshafttavern.com. The
original Mine Shaft Tavern burned down on Christmas Day 1945, but the current tavern,
built in 1947, is still the oldest drinking establishment in New Mexico. Even if you aren't into
the hearty burgers, strong drinks, and live music for which the tavern is famous, wander in
and take a look. Among other attractions, its 40-foot bar is the longest in New Mexico, and
there's a wonderful painting over the bar depicting Madrid history by Tinkertown creator
Ross Ward. Open Mon through Fri 11:30 a.m. to 8 p.m. and Sat and Sun 11:30 a.m. to
9 p.m. $.

where to stay

Java Junction B&B. 2855 NM 14; (505) 438-2772; java-junction.com/bnb. This artsy
one-bedroom studio is above Madrid's main coffee spot. It has a queen-size bed, 6-foot-
long claw-foot tub, full kitchen, Wi-Fi, TV, A/C, private patio, and complimentary continental

breakfast. The coffee shop downstairs is colorfully decked out with novelty mugs, hot sauce bottles, and a variety of New Mexico food gifts, carved wood kitchen items, and cookbooks by local authors; it serves its own "joe," pastries, pies, and breakfast burritos. Pet-friendly. $.

cerrillos

Named for the "Little Hills" around it—the source of staggering amounts of turquoise, silver, zinc, and lead—by the 1880s Cerrillos had grown big enough to support 21 saloons and 4 hotels and was in the running for territorial capital. Both Sarah Bernhardt and Lillie Langtry sang at its Clearlight Opera House on Main Street. It's a ghost town now; the few residents are the usual charming dreamers and artists drawn to mining towns all over the West. Cerrillos has been used as a backdrop for many movies, including *The Hi-Lo Country* and *Young Guns.* Its main attraction, Cerrillos Hills State Park, protects a number of Cerrillos's 221 historic mines. The park is a source of local pride, since it was community activism that succeeded in getting the land set aside in 2003.

North of Cerrillos, NM 14 winds through a breathtaking area of hills, arroyos, and dramatic rocks known as Garden of the Gods, the northwestern margin of the Galisteo Basin, and then continues past the old state penitentiary and burgeoning Turquoise Trail businesses, schools, and residential areas into south Santa Fe. Note: the final destinations on this day trip are reached by driving east cross-country through the villages of Galisteo and Lamy, then north on US 285 to its junction with I-25, to pick up the next day trip, which takes you through the Pecos River valley, following the Santa Fe Trail.

where to go

Broken Saddle Riding Company. 26 CR 59A (Vicksville Road); (505) 424-7774; broken saddle.com. This well-regarded stables is the only one in the state offering smooth-riding, gaited horses like Tennessee walkers and Missouri fox-trotters that use all four legs for power. Rides explore some of the stables' scenic 5,500 acres, including mining areas, overlooks, and canyons. Open year-round 6 a.m. to 8:45 p.m.

Casa Grande Trading Post, Cerrillos Turquoise Mining Museum, and Cerrillos Petting Zoo. 17 Waldo St.; (505) 438-3008; casagrandetradingpost.com. This classic roadside attraction is in a family-built 28-room adobe stuffed with historic glass bottles, railroad paraphernalia, and items made from local turquoise and other rocks. There are goats, llamas, chickens, and other small animals in the petting zoo, and the family offers tours of their own personal turquoise mine for a fee. Open daily 9 a.m. to 5 p.m.

Cerrillos Hills State Park. 37 Main St.; (505) 474-0196, emnrd.state.nm.us/SPD/cerrillos hillstatepark.html. This 1,116-acre park has 5 miles of trails for use by hikers, mountain bikers, and horseback riders that allow visitors to explore some of the pre-1900 mines in the Cerrillos area deemed safe for entry. A visitor center with information, exhibits, a gift shop, and snacks is open Fri through Tues 2 to 4 p.m. only. Your best bet is to visit the Amigos de Cerrillos Hills State Park website for complete visitor information (cerrilloshills.org). Open sunrise to sunset daily. Admission fee.

Ortiz Mountains Open Space. 582 CR 55; (505) 471-9103; santafecountynm.gov/open_space_and_trails_program. The 1,350-acre wilderness preserve in the beautiful piñon-juniper foothills of the Ortiz Mountains is a great place for wildlife watching on 6 miles of trails for hikers. It's now run by Santa Fe County Open Space and is only open for guided tours by reservation; call for more information. Admission fee.

where to eat

San Marcos Cafe and Feed Store. 3877 NM 14; (505) 471-9298. Located in San Marcos/Lone Butte, halfway between Cerrillos and the state penitentiary, this quaint country cafe in a colorful old adobe with wooden floors is a welcome oasis along the increasingly busy Turquoise Trail. It has creative breakfast dishes such as Eggs San Marcos and lunchtime standards such as burgers, quiche, and enchiladas. The cafe is known for its enormous homemade cinnamon rolls, which are perfect for sharing with a cup of coffee. Open daily 8 a.m. to 2 p.m. $.

Santa Fe Brewing Co. Taproom. 35 Fire Place, NM 14; taproom (505) 424-3333, event space (505) 557-6182; santafebrewing.com. Santa Fe Brewing Co., the state's oldest microbrewery, is located just past the state penitentiary and offers some refreshing brews made from hops grown along the Rio Grande. You'll find Saturday brewery tours, daily beer tastings, and the Bridget at Santa Fe Brewing, a popular open-air event center next door, which often hosts big-name touring musical acts, brews, and food trucks such as Jambo's Cafe. Open Mon, Tues, and Sat 11 a.m. to 10 p.m.; Wed, Thurs, and Fri 11 a.m. to 10:30 p.m.; and Sun noon to 8 p.m. Tours are offered Sat at noon. Other taprooms are in Santa Fe, Eldorado, and Albuquerque.

where to stay

Casita del Abuelo Airbnb at Crystal Mesa Farm. 27 Crystal Mesa Rd., Santa Fe; (505) 474-5224; crystalmesafarm.com. Located on a farm 25 minutes southeast of Santa Fe near the ancient site of San Marcos Pueblo, one of the major pueblos in the Galisteo Basin, this loft casita is an open-plan guesthouse with two sleeping areas—a queen downstairs and a futon double in the loft—a kitchen, and a sitting area. The farm was a full bed-and-breakfast's paradise for many years, and the hosts are welcoming and knowledgeable. Kids will enjoy visiting with potbellied pigs, goats, and more. Wi-Fi but no TV. Budget-friendly and charming. $.

galisteo basin

The Galisteo Basin is a haunting area of grasslands, ranches, old Pueblo ruins, and rock art that is increasingly popular with artists seeking peace and quiet yet proximity to Santa Fe. To reach the Galisteo Basin, turn right onto a well-signposted dirt road at the Garden of the Gods, near Lone Butte, and head east. Following the great drought of 1276–99, the Galisteo Basin had one of the biggest concentrations of Indian pueblos in the state, which were occupied by Rio Grande farmers who had left the overcrowded riverine areas. **Arroyo Hondo,** one of the largest, was in ruins by the 1400s, its residents dead from starvation. **San Marcos Pueblo** focused on making a new kind of pottery that used a galena glaze derived from lead mined in the Cerrillos Hills. These pueblos are not open to visitors. During Spanish Colonial times, the quiet Hispanic village of **Galisteo** was known for its sheep ranches, which supplied wool to Hispanic weavers. Although there are no visitor services here, Galisteo is now a retreat for artists. Northeast of Galisteo, you'll pick up US 285, the main highway linking I-40, at the Clines Corners exit east of Albuquerque, and I-25, just past Eldorado, a large rural community about 20 minutes southeast of Santa Fe.

lamy

A short detour off US 285 leads to historic Lamy, the main railroad station for Amtrak passengers traveling between Chicago and Los Angeles on the Southwest Chief. Though sleepy now, Lamy was once the site of El Ortiz Hotel, a historic Fred Harvey railroad hotel, now demolished. What does remain, though, is the Legal Tender, a 19th-century saloon in a former mercantile opposite the depot. In 2006 the railroad donated the saloon to a Lamy nonprofit for use as a volunteer-run railroad and history museum. They, in turn, in 2018 donated it to Winslow Arts Trust, headed up by Allan Affeldt, owner of the restored La Posada in Winslow, Arizona, and the Plaza Hotel and newly rebuilt and reopened Castañeda Hotel in Las Vegas, New Mexico (see Northeast Day Trip 02). Affeldt worked his magic on the Legal Tender, keeping its charming bordello meets honky-tonk atmosphere, decorating walls with old Southwest Chief menus and other memorabilia from the museum collection, and getting the old flashing neon sign going again (it is very dark out here at night).

where to eat

Legal Tender Saloon. 151 Old Lamy Trail; (505) 466-1650; legaltenderlamy.com. Murphy O'Brien, owner of nearby Cafe Fina, and nephew Rory O'Brien worked with Allan Affeldt to reopen the Legal Tender as a weekend dinner restaurant in 2019, taking inspiration from classic Fred Harvey dishes for their select menu of appetizers and small plates. These include corn chowder, spinach salad with pomegranate seeds and warm bacon dressing, classic wedge salad with blue cheese or green goddess dressing, pecan-smoked ribs, liver and onions, poached shrimp roll, New Mexico beef fillet, local trout with succotash, and a decadent sundae, salt caramel boudin, and fruit galette. Open Fri, Sat, and Sun 5 to 8:30 p.m. Irish musician Gerry Carthy plays folk music on Fri eves and piano music and vocals by Charles Tichenor on Sun eves. Reservations essential. Full menu available in dining rooms and bar. $–$$.

day trip 02

northeast

>>> **traders, ruins, and refuges on the santa fe trail:**
pecos, el valle, las vegas, watrous, cimarron, clayton, raton

When Mexico declared its independence from Spain in 1821, the Santa Fe Trail between Franklin, Missouri, and Santa Fe became the main route west for explorers, mountain men, settlers, miners, soldiers, government surveyors, tourists, and outlaws. Scores of merchants made the arduous 900-mile journey by wagon train, attracted by huge profits to be made from trade with Santa Fe and the connecting Chihuahua Trail to Mexico City. When the trail reached the Great Plains, it split. The hot, dusty Cimarron Cutoff southern route exposed travelers to Indian attacks, while the Mountain Branch went through rough terrain. In 1851, soon after the territory became American, the US Army built Fort Union near where the branches converged; travelers arriving safely at Fort Union were assured of a military escort all the way to Santa Fe.

The arrival of the railroad in 1888 rendered the trail obsolete, but trail buffs will find wagon ruts, landmarks, and historic locations along this route, best undertaken as a long weekend trip. Pick up the trail east of Santa Fe (officially "north" on I-25). The drive passes through the scenic Pecos River valley, the natural break between the Sangre de Cristo Mountains and Glorieta Mesa, and continues onto the plains, east of Las Vegas. Highlights include the cultural remains of Paleo-Indians and Indian pueblos, Hispanic villages, backcountry art studios, early American trading posts and ranches, wildlife refuges, the Wild West village of Cimarron, a young volcanic field, and the railroad town of Las Vegas.

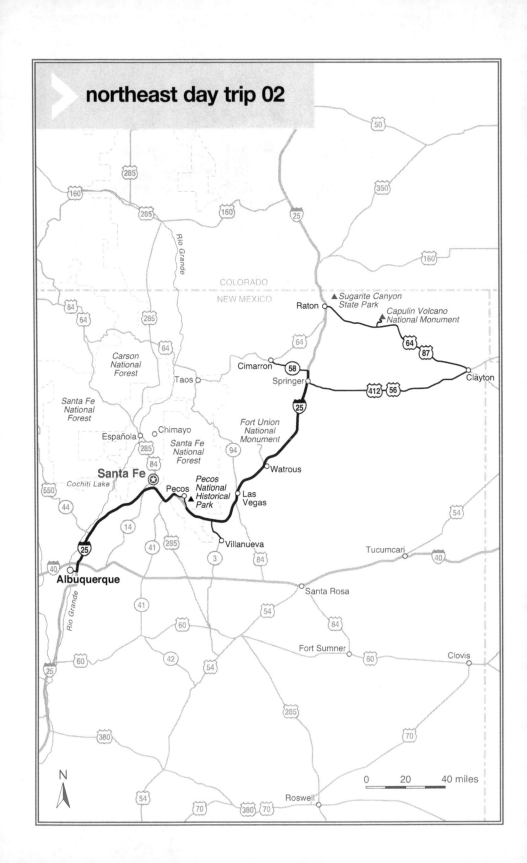

pecos

Of the several pueblos visited by Spanish conquistador Coronado in 1540, among the most important was Cicuye, a 650-room gateway pueblo that controlled trade between Pueblos and Plains tribes like the Apache and Comanche. Spanish priests built a mission and oversaw the construction of a huge adobe church at Cicuye, while noblemen settling nearby lands required Pueblo people to tithe part of their harvest and products in return for "protection." The demands of these newcomers during a time of cyclical drought, dwindling food supplies, and susceptibility to European diseases devastated even powerful pueblos like Cicuye, which had emptied out by the early 1830s, its remaining residents having joined Towa-speaking relatives at Jemez Pueblo. The ruined pueblo became a popular attraction along the Santa Fe Trail for travelers staying at nearby Kozlowski's Stage Stop the night before reaching Santa Fe.

To reach Pecos National Historical Park, take the Rowe exit and follow signs on SR 63 to Pecos, the village between the park and the Sangre de Cristo Mountains. Pecos offers visitor facilities and access to hiking, hunting, camping, fishing, horseback riding and packing, and other outdoor activities in Pecos Canyon and the 223,000-acre Pecos Wilderness portion of Santa Fe National Forest. For information, stop at the Pecos ranger station on Main Street (505-757-6121; fs.usda.gov/detail/santafe). Open Mon through Fri 8:30 a.m. to 4:30 p.m.; closed noon to 12:30 p.m. for lunch. Permits and maps sold Mon, Tues, Thurs, and Fri 8:30 a.m. to noon only.

where to go

Pecos National Historical Park. 1 Peach Dr.; (505) 757-7241; nps.gov/peco. Pecos's story is well told in its attractive log-and-glass E. E. Fogelson Visitor Center, named for the husband of the late actress Greer Garson, who donated the land for the national park. The museum has exhibits on 12,000 years of Indian history, the Civil War in New Mexico, Spanish settlement, and the Santa Fe Trail. It displays some of the 80,000 artifacts excavated in the early 1900s by A. V. Kidder, father of Southwest archeology. Kidder and fellow archeologists convened at Pecos annually and developed the important Pecos Classification, which uses comparative differences in regional ceramic making over a long period of time to date different periods of Southwest Pueblo culture. The remains of Cicuye Pueblo, a great kiva, and the Spanish mission church and adjoining *convento* can be viewed by walking a 1.25-mile trail behind the visitor center. Also protected in the park are numerous Santa Fe Trail wagon ruts; Greer Garson's Forked Lightning Ranch, originally designed for rodeo entrepreneur Tex Austin in 1926 by John Gaw Meem; Kozlowski's Stage Stop; Arrowhead Ruin, an early pueblo; and the site of the Battle of Glorieta Pass, the important 1862 Civil War battlefield where a unit of Union volunteers saved the West from the Confederate advance by cutting off their supplies. Free guided tours include Ancestral Sites (Fri through Mon), Civil War Walking Tour (Fri and Sun), Forked Lightning Ranch Tour (Sat and Mon), and Battlefield

Hike (Sat). Open daily 8 a.m. to 6 p.m. in summer, 8 a.m. to 4:30 p.m. in winter; visitor center closes at 5 p.m. in summer and 4 p.m. in winter. Free.

where to eat

Frankie's at the Casanova. 12 S. Main St.; (505) 757-3322; frankiesnm.com. Just north of the park, Frankie's serves authentic New Mexican food at breakfast and lunch daily and dinner on Fri and Sat featuring steak and seafood in addition to the regular menu. It is a great spot to meet locals. Open daily 8 a.m. to 2 p.m.; dinner Fri and Sat 5:30 to 8:15 p.m. $–$$.

where to stay

Our Lady of Guadalupe Abbey. PO Box 1080, Pecos; (505) 757-6415; pecosmonastery .org. The welcoming double Benedictine monastery of Our Lady of Guadalupe and Olivetan Benedictine Sisters of Our Lady of Guadalupe lies in tranquil Pecos Canyon, just north of the village and adjoining the Pecos River, and is a popular retreat center for locals and out-of-town visitors alike. Father Aidan, the British-born abbot, was a former bed-and-breakfast owner in another life, so you can be sure of a lovely stay here. The 5 newly upgraded double rooms in the main guesthouse have simple but comfortable and attractive furnishings, bathrooms with showers/baths, ceiling fans, shared kitchen facilities, and a lounge with Wi-Fi but no TVs or phones. Four Hermitage single rooms are available in a separate building on the hill for people wishing to make silent personal retreats; each has a kitchenette and bathroom for complete privacy, as well as a desk and view. Note: Hermitage rooms on the hill may not be available in winter due to access problems. Rates include simple meals in the refectory. Discounts for AARP and AAA members and Mon through Thurs stays. $.

Pecos River Cabins. 8 River Cabin Rd.; (505) 757-8752; pecosrivercabins.com. This cabin resort has a variety of options. Four modern cabins are available year-round and are attractive, comfortable, and with full amenities. The lodge can accommodate up to 8 guests in 3 bedrooms, and the River Studio sleeps 2 to 5 people in 2 bedrooms; both cabins can be configured as needed. The Pinon and Aspen cabins are studio casitas that sleep 2 people. Three charming seasonal cabins—2 sleeping 4 people and 1 sleeping 2—have electricity but no baths and kitchens; a bathhouse is nearby. Microwaves, minifridges, Wi-Fi, and small TVs are in each cabin. The cabins are popular with fly-fishers, bird-watchers, hikers, horseback riders, and those who enjoy outdoor life. Smoke-free; pets not allowed. $–$$$.

el valle

I-25 continues through the Pecos River valley to Villanueva; the area is dubbed El Valle. A 15-mile side trip south on SR 3 through Spanish Colonial villages and pretty mesa-and-badlands country offers a complete change of pace and the chance to visit art studios in Ribera, a family-run winery in El Barranco, and a small state park in Villanueva.

where to go

El Ancon Sculpture Park. I-25 N, exit 323, Ribera; (505) 421-7057; sculpture.org. Mixed-media artist Janet Stein Romero and her nationally known architect/sculptor husband Nicasio Romero work out of this delightful two-story adobe home and gallery, which they created 30 years ago. They also represent other area artists. Open by appointment.

Villanueva State Park. 135 Dodge Rd.; (505) 421-2957; emnrd.state.nm.us, newmexico-stateparks.reserveamerica.com (campground reservations). This 1,679-acre riverside park is set in a pretty canyon, 15 miles south of the turnoff on SR 3. It's a nice spot for a picnic, stretching your legs on two short trails, or fishing in the Pecos River. It has a visitor center and a developed campground with 33 sites, 12 of which have hookups. Open 7 a.m. to 9 p.m. Oct through Mar; 7 a.m. to 7 p.m. Apr through Sept. Admission fee.

where to eat

La Risa Bakery. 200 SR 3, Ribera; (505) 421-0040. A former cafe with a lot of fans, La Risa now operates as a bakery only, but it is still worth stopping by to see what baker Laura Boyd is rustling up, from pies to brownies to coffee cakes. Open Wed through Sun 10 a.m. to 6 p.m. $.

las vegas

Las Vegas was founded in 1835 at the edge of the Great Plains. It was the first major town in 600 miles for travelers on the Santa Fe Trail, and it had an important water source, Haye Springs Well, the oldest surviving well on the trail. The town boomed when the railroad arrived, outpacing Santa Fe in population growth by 1900. Wealthy easterners traveled by rail to Las Vegas to summer at Montezuma Castle, a luxury resort built by the entrepreneur Fred Harvey around natural hot springs. The historic hotel is now one of 13 United World College campuses offering the International Baccalaureate diploma and encouraging international relations. Another important educational institution, New Mexico Highlands University, is also located in Las Vegas.

During the 1898 Spanish-American War, Teddy Roosevelt recruited his Rough Riders from the Spanish-speaking population in Las Vegas; a small museum displays a special exhibit of artifacts from the period. The entire downtown is a designated historic district, with an astounding 900-plus listed structures. Las Vegas is named for its well-watered "meadows," a haven for wildlife in winter, and there are several wildlife refuges nearby. North of Las Vegas, SR 518 takes you into cool, forested mountains via Mora. The high-country route connects with Peñasco near Taos (see Northeast Day Trip 04).

where to go

Dwan Light Sanctuary (United World College). PO Box 249, Montezuma; (505) 454-4221; uwc-usa.org. Set on the United World College campus in Montezuma (see entry below), the unusual and striking Dwan Light Sanctuary is the result of a collaboration among conceptualizer Virginia Dawn, artist Charles Ross, and architect Laban Wingert. The project grew out of Dawn's dream of creating a quiet space for contemplation for people of all faiths. The sanctuary incorporates 12 angles of light within its circular space, and 12 large prisms in the apses and ceiling create a progression throughout the year of unique spectrum events. In addition, the sanctuary was designed to align with the sun, moon, and stars and to capture sunrise and sunset. Open daily for quiet contemplation from sunrise to sunset. Note: UWC is a closed campus. Visitors must first stop at the Moore Welcome Center to register and receive directions on accessing the sanctuary. Free.

Las Vegas Museum and Rough Riders Memorial Collection. 727 Grand Ave.; (505) 426-3205. This small hometown museum started out caretaking the Rough Rider collection and has since expanded to include 7,000 items covering all of Las Vegas's history. The main reason to visit, though, is to learn more about Teddy Roosevelt's Rough Riders, the heroes of the Spanish-American War, who were largely recruited in New Mexico because of their Spanish-speaking ability and fortitude. Open Tues through Sat 10 a.m. to 4 p.m. Donation.

Las Vegas National Wildlife Refuge. Route 1, Box 399, Las Vegas; (505) 425-3581; fws .gov/refuge/Las_Vegas. This 8,762-acre national wildlife refuge is one of several between Las Vegas and Raton, a unique ecosystem where the Rockies, the Chihuahuan Desert, and the Great Plains come together. The grasslands attract some 270 species of birds, including neotropical migrants, and herds of pronghorn antelope—like bison, a familiar sight in this area. It's located 7 miles southeast of town. Open 24 hours; headquarters office is open Mon through Fri 8 a.m. to 4 p.m. Free.

Montezuma Castle (United World College). PO Box 248, Montezuma; (505) 454-4221, (505) 454-4245 (tour information); uwc-usa.org. United World College, the two-year coed boarding school now housed in this distinctive 1884 Queen Anne–style former Fred Harvey hotel at the mouth of scenic Gallinas Canyon, restored and maintains the historic structure, which was once the showpiece of the Santa Fe Railroad and a major destination for families vacationing from the East. Note: UWC is a closed campus. All visitors must first stop at the Moore Welcome Center to register and be accompanied on campus by a UWC guide. During the school year, one-hour tours of the historic campus are conducted on Sat at 1 p.m.; alternatively, contact Kathy Hendrickson, owner of Southwest Detours (505-459-6987; southwestdetours.com), a local company offering tours of the UWC campus and the historic Plaza and Castañeda hotels in Las Vegas. Visitors may use the hot springs that dot the banks of the Gallinas River along Hot Springs Boulevard (SR 65). They are first come, first served and subject to UWC regulations, as they are on college property; swimsuits are required. Free.

Santa Fe Trail Interpretive Center. 116 Bridge St.; (505) 425-8803; lvcchp.org/santa-fe-trail.html. Located in the Bridge Street Historic District, this little center offers historic photos and artifacts, brochures, books, and other information for those wishing to follow the Santa Fe Trail, which passed near here. It is run by the Las Vegas Citizens Committee for Historic Preservation, which has been very active in local preservation. Las Vegas has one of the largest numbers of preserved historic structures in the state and is an active member of the Main Street Program. The center can provide you with good walking tour maps, and the website also offers virtual tours. Open Mon through Sat 10 a.m. to 3 p.m.

where to shop

Mayeur Projects. 200-202 Plaza Park; (505) 434-0016; mayeurprojects.com. Founded by French collector and entrepreneur Christian Mayeur, this contemporary art gallery and creative arts space is located in a historic building on the plaza. It focuses on socially engaged art of all types, including land art, and reflects the growing arts community springing up in a revitalizing Las Vegas. Open Fri, Sat, and Sun 11 a.m. to 5 p.m. and during special art shows; otherwise by appointment.

Tito's Gallery and Gifts. 157 Bridge St. (Old Town); (505) 425-3745. Located in the old police station, this family-run place sells Tito's handmade jewelry and regularly exhibits other artists' work. It has the largest selection of *santos* in town. Open Mon through Sat 10 a.m. to 5:30 p.m. Part of the Second Saturday Art Walk, an evening stroll around Las Vegas art galleries.

Tome on the Range. 247 Plaza St.; (505) 454-9944; tomeontherange.com. This wonderful independent bookstore will keep you captivated for hours and is particularly strong in regional titles. They offer a full roster of author readings and signings. Open 10 a.m. to 6 p.m. daily.

where to eat

Bar Castañeda. Castañeda Hotel, 524 Railroad Ave.; (505) 425-3591; kinlvnm.com. Independently owned and operated by chef Sean Sinclair, this atmospheric hotel bar and grill has become a hot new destination for drinks and dinner since it opened in the renovated Castañeda Hotel in 2019. The deft mixologist here serves killer cocktails, such as the Harvey Girl, and the popular menu highlights New Mexico seasonal foods and updated takes on classic Fred Harvey menu items, including oysters Rockefeller and a green chile cheeseburger and onion rings that gets a big thumbs-up from picky locals. The adjoining fine-dining restaurant, Kin, is set to open soon and will be a gourmet experience serving a chef's tasting menu of local, seasonal food. Open for happy hour and dinner Wed through Mon 3 to 10 p.m. $–$$.

Charlie's Spic and Span Bakery & Cafe. 715 Douglas Ave.; (505) 426-1921. A longtime favorite for delicious, reasonably priced New Mexican food. Breakfasts are particularly seductive—house-made corn tortillas and chile make everything shine, from enchiladas to burritos. Their fresh doughnuts are a local institution. Open daily for breakfast and lunch only. Free Wi-Fi. $.

Range Café Las Vegas. Plaza Hotel, 230 Plaza; (505) 425-3591; rangecafe.com. A sixth branch of the famed Range Café in Bernalillo opened insidethe Plaza Hotel in 2018 and has been a good match for traditional Las Vegas. Food here is fresh, local, and focused on big portions of modern American and New Mexican comfort food favorites. They do a mean huevos rancheros at breakfast; unusual burgers, sandwiches, salads, green chile stew, and soup, as well as enchiladas, burritos, and the like at lunch; and some additional entrees at dinner, from country-fried steak and meat loaf to rib eye and salmon. Desserts and pastries are big and indulgent, including cinnamon rolls as big as your head and homemade pies. Open for breakfast, lunch, and dinner. $–$$$.

World Treasures Travelers Cafe. 1814 Plaza; (505) 426-8638. This little cafe is a lovely surprise in the back of the Tapetas de Llana weaving cooperative shop in a historic building a few doors down from the Plaza Hotel. They serve delicious specialty coffee drinks, scones, croissants, and other baked goods at breakfast, and soups, sandwiches, salads, and quiche at lunchtime. $.

where to stay

Castañeda Hotel. 524 Railroad Ave.; (505) 425-3591; castanedahotel.org. The renaissance of the shuttered 1898 Castañeda Hotel next to the railroad station was a pipe dream for many Las Vegas residents. That was until 2014, when historic property entrepreneur Allan Affeldt and his artist wife Tina Mion bought Las Vegas's historic Plaza Hotel (see entry below) and took on the reconstruction of the derelict Mission Revival Castañeda through their nonprofit Winslow Arts Trust. It was all part of their vision to restore historic Fred Harvey railroad hotels, which had begun in the 1990s with the long and ultimately hugely successful restoration of La Posada in Winslow, Arizona. The couple oversaw every detail of the long, hard work of restoring the Castañeda, using original architectural plans and local workers and artisans to handcraft every detail, from installing new wood floors to rebuilding the grand staircase to hand-painting a new hotel sign and bed headboards; the transom windows in each room feature animals painted by Tina Mion. The rooms and public spaces are now light, airy, and welcoming; furnished with hand-selected period antiques; and have large windows from which you can watch the Southwest Chief train arriving and departing. The Castañeda is a work-in progress. It began reopening to guests in April 2019 as the 16 king and queen rooms and suites were completed. Room reservations are taken through a central booking system for the Plaza and Castañeda in Las Vegas and La Posada in Winslow, Arizona. $$.

Plaza Hotel. 230 Plaza; (505) 425-3591; plazahotellvnm.com. Presiding over the tree-filled Old Town Las Vegas Plaza Park, the 1882 brick-built Plaza Hotel was once considered the fanciest hotel in New Mexico Territory and has seen a lot of history come and go. It underwent a major restoration in 1982, when new owner Wid Slick and his Plaza Partnership took charge and put this grande dame back on the map. In 2014 Slick passed the baton to historic hotel aficionado Allan Affeldt, owner of the renovated La Posada in Winslow, Arizona, who bought the Plaza and tweaked the formula slightly to make it an attractive and affordable destination hotel. There are now 70 elegant and comfortable rooms featuring classic Southwest furnishings and art; 19 overlook the plaza and offer sitting areas and refrigerators. Downstairs is a gift shop filled with local books and arts and crafts by native artisans, a Harvey specialty; the perennially popular Byron T's Bar (named for the hotel's resident ghost); and a branch of the Range Café in Bernalillo, known for fresh New Mexican food, which also operates the lobby coffee and pastry bar. $–$$.

watrous

Watrous is about 19 miles north of Las Vegas. The settlement was named for Sam Watrous, a trader on the Santa Fe Trail who operated a general store in 1849. Ghost town buffs, take note: Six miles north of Watrous is Loma Parda, all that remains of a quiet Hispanic farming settlement used as a brothel and drinking haven by soldiers from nearby Fort Union. Keep on SR 161 to reach Fort Union.

where to go

Fort Union National Monument. SR 161, Watrous; (505) 425-8025; nps.gov/foun. Fort Union was one of the most important forts in the West, with a large parade ground, officers' quarters, and quartermaster's store, among other structures. The mostly adobe fort is in ruins now, worn down by the passage of time, and even its importance as a stop on the Santa Fe Trail feels tenuous, marked only by the deep ruts in the ground of scores of wagon trains. There's a small visitor center and a 1.6-mile paved trail around the ruins with push-button interpretation. Costumed interpreters and guided tours, including a once-a-month candlelit nighttime tour, make this park best visited in summer. Open daily summer 8 a.m. to 5 p.m. (until 6 p.m. in winter). Admission fee.

cimarron

North of Springer, the landscape sprawls into shortgrass prairie, distant mountains, and large ranches. Most are on what remains of the 1.7-million-acre Maxwell Land Grant, which was inherited through marriage by former mountain man Lucien Maxwell in 1847. Maxwell ranched here alongside his old pal Kit Carson. Much of the land grant was purchased in 1922 by Waite Phillips, founder of Phillips Oil. In 1938 he donated the land to the Boy Scouts of America as a kind of Outward Bound center for Scouts to test their backcountry skills. North of Springer, SR 21 passes through the Boy Scouts property, known as Philmont Boy

> ## springer
>
> *The unpretentious town of Springer, named for a local politician, is worth a stop for its visitor facilities and small **Santa Fe Trail Interpretive Center Museum** (606 Maxwell Ave.; 575-483-5554). Housed in the 1881 Colfax County Court House, this museum interprets the Santa Fe Trail and is a treasure trove of pioneer artifacts, trail paraphernalia, and exhibits on early railroad history. Open Memorial Day to Labor Day only, 9 a.m. to 4 p.m. Admission fee. From Springer, US 56 heads south to Clayton through scenic grasslands that were used by travelers using the Dry Cimarron Cutoff route of the Santa Fe Trail.*

Scout Ranch, and ends at Cimarron, the town that grew up around the Aztec Grist Mill operated by Maxwell on former Jicarilla Apache land. Cimarron has an authentic Wild West atmosphere. Its name (meaning "wild and unruly" in Spanish) is a reference to the Apache and Ute Indians encountered by early Spaniards. The most famous attraction is the haunted St. James Hotel, one of 14 listed structures on a historic walking tour of the town. To pick up Northeast Day Trip 06 to Taos and the Enchanted Circle, turn left and drive north through Cimarron Canyon on US 64. Angel Fire Ski Resort is 24 miles away.

where to go

Aztec Grist Mill. Downtown Cimarron, 1 mile south of the intersection of US 64 and SR 21; (575) 376-2913; cimaronnm.com. This four-story mill was built by Lucien Maxwell to supply flour to the US Army and the Jicarilla Indian Agency. It is now a small museum operated by the CS Cattle Company. Open May through Oct, Mon through Sat 9 a.m. to 5 p.m. and Sun 1 to 5 p.m. Free.

Maxwell National Wildlife Refuge. PO Box 276, Maxwell; (575) 375-2331, ext. 200; fws .gov/refuge/maxwell. This beautiful refuge is set on shortgrass prairie, lakes, and agricultural lands. It is a good place to see bison in winter, burrowing owls, and overwintering geese and ducks attracted to the irrigation dotted all around ranch country. To reach the refuge, take the Maxwell exit (exit 426) from I-25 and drive north 0.8 mile on SR 445. At the intersection of SR 445 and 505, drive 2.5 miles west. Turn north on Lake 13 Road at the entrance sign and drive 1.25 miles to the refuge headquarters. The visitor center is open only when staff are available Mon through Thurs 7:30 a.m. to 4 p.m. and Fri 7:30 a.m. to 3:30 p.m.; closed Sat and Sun. Refuge is open 24 hours a day. Free.

Philmont Boy Scout Ranch. 17 Deer Run Rd., Cimarron; (505) 376-1136; philmont-boyscoutranch.org. Much of the Boy Scout ranch is open to the public. Of particular interest are tours of Villa Philmonte, Waite Phillips's Mediterranean-style home; Philmont Museum, with its collection of paintings by artist/naturalist Ernest Thompson Seton; the Kit Carson Home and Museum at Rayado, which has living-history demonstrations; and the new National Scouting Museum, the repository for thousands of scouting history artifacts. Bison, elk, mule deer, and other wildlife graze along the highway in winter. The museums are open 8 a.m. to 5 p.m. year-round; the Kit Carson Home and Villa Philmonte are only open daily in summer, have limited hours in the shoulder seasons, and close in winter. Free.

where to stay

Casa del Gavilan. SR 21, north of Cimarron; (505) 376-2246; casadelgavilan.com. A gracious Pueblo Revival–style mountain *hacienda* built in 1912, this inn has 4 bedrooms with high ceilings, vigas, and a Southwest feel. There is also a small one-person Library Room and a two-bedroom guesthouse across the courtyard; one room has a fireplace. Gourmet breakfast is included in price. $$.

St. James Hotel. 17th and Collinson Streets; (800) 748-2694; exstjames.com. Built in 1872 by Henri Lambert, former cook to Abraham Lincoln, this hotel is the real deal. Don't miss it. It was once considered the height of luxury, the only hotel west of the Mississippi to offer running water, gourmet food, and elegant furnishings. Among its famous guests was Buffalo Bill, who planned his Wild West Show in the bar with Annie Oakley. Today, the hotel has been nicely freshened up by new owners but maintains all of its historic charm. The old bar is now Lamberts Restaurant; look for bullet holes in the tin ceiling. Be prepared to encounter ghosts if you spend the night in one of the 12 restored antique-filled rooms in the historic part of the hotel. Guests often experience a strong smell of roses in pretty room 17, which belonged to Mary Lambert, Henri's second wife. Not surprisingly, Murder Mystery Weekends are popular here. Note: The 10 rooms in the modern annex have TVs, phones, private bathrooms, and other amenities not available in the main hotel, and have a clean, rustic decor. Lamberts Restaurant serves good American and New Mexican standards and adds steak, bison, and seafood at dinner. It is open 7 a.m. to 9 p.m. TJ's Bar is open until 11 p.m. $$.

clayton

An alternative scenic loop takes you south of Springer on SR 56 through grasslands to reach Clayton, a ranch town that grew up around the railroad. You can view wagon ruts at the McKnee's Crossing section of the Santa Fe Trail, east of town. Clayton is also known for its Dinosaur Freeway: hundreds of tracks from coelurosaur, theropod, hadrosaur, and camptosaur dinosaurs that were preserved in Jurassic-era sandstone laid down on the shore of an ocean 100 million years ago.

where to go

Clayton Lake State Park. 141 Clayton Lake Rd.; (575) 374-8808. Some 500 dinosaur prints are preserved in the spillway at this fishing lake in Clayton. There is a visitor center, picnic areas, and 5 campgrounds with 26 developed sites. Open sunrise to sunset year-round. Admission fee.

Kiowa and Rita Blanca National Grasslands. 714 Main St.; (575) 374-9652; fs.usda.gov. A federal grasslands restoration project designed to bring back lands devastated by the Dust Bowl, Kiowa and Rita Blanca National Grasslands has two units off US 56. At Abbott, SR 39 heads east into the remote Mills Canyon unit, an old homestead in Canadian River Canyon. The McKnee's Crossing unit, south of Clayton, is interesting mainly for protecting a 2-mile section of the Dry Cimarron Cutoff route of the Santa Fe Trail. In the distance is Rabbit Ear Mountain, named for a Cheyenne chief who died in a fight between Indians and Hispanic settlers in 1717; it was an important landmark on the trail. These quiet, open grasslands are a great place to view pronghorn and other wildlife. Open 24 hours a day, year-round. Free.

where to stay

Eklund Hotel. 15 Main St.; (505) 374-2551, (888) 265-4683; hoteleklund.com. This classic Old West hostelry was built in 1892 and was a notorious hangout for outlaws. Its most famous resident was bank robber Tom "Blackjack" Ketchum, who was hanged here on April 26, 1901. The 26 rooms are authentically furnished and include suites with Jacuzzi tubs. The dark-paneled dining room and more-casual saloon serve mainstream New Mexico specials and locally raised beef and are open daily 10:30 a.m. to 9 p.m. $–$$.

raton

From Clayton, the loop picks up US 64 and heads north to Raton. This is a fast road, used by travelers between New Mexico and Texas, but be sure to turn off at Capulin and visit often-overlooked Capulin National Monument, which preserves the 8,000-square-mile Raton-Clayton volcanic field, the easternmost young volcanic field in the West. Raton, just south of Raton Pass and the Colorado border, is a gritty Victorian railroad town. Its historic downtown has 70 buildings listed on the National Historic Register, including the restored 1915 Shuler Theater, and has chain motels and visitor services.

where to go

Capulin Volcano National Monument. Off SR 325; (505) 278-2201; nps.gov/cavo. The historic 2-mile Volcano Road winds up to the summit of 1,400-foot Capulin Volcano for extraordinary views of Texas, Oklahoma, Colorado, and Kansas at this accessible park. At the summit, hike the short Crater Vent Trail right into the volcanic caldera, or walk the mile-long perimeter trail. It gets very chilly here off-season; the best time to visit is summer, when there are abundant wildflowers, or fall, when changing oaks flood the mountainsides with color. A visitor center has exhibits and the easy Boca, Nature, and Lava Trails, which explore the volcanic lava flows and natural history of the monument. Note: Heavy rains in 2019 washed out Volcano Road, closing it to all traffic for repairs; it reopened to the public in January 2020. Open daily 7:30 a.m. to 6:30 p.m. in summer, 8 a.m. to 4 p.m. in winter. Admission fee.

Folsom Museum. Junction of SR 325 and SR 456; (575) 278-2477; folsomvillage.com/folsommuseum. At one time the most important stockyard west of Fort Worth, tiny Folsom declined when the railroad arrived in 1880. A flood on the Dry Cimarron River in 1908 almost destroyed the town, but for an African-American cowboy named George McJunkin it yielded an important find: a beautiful fluted arrow point embedded in the ribs of a long-extinct bison, evidence of the 10,000-year-old paleo-hunter culture known as the Folsom, then thought to be the oldest on the continent. Considering its cultural significance, one would think they'd make more fuss about this claim to fame in Folsom. All you'll find, though, are a few artifacts in a dusty little museum in the 1896 mercantile store, which is only open in summer, 10 a.m. to 5 p.m. daily. Tours of the Folsom Man Site are offered several Saturdays in summer; check the website for details. Admission fee.

Sugarite Canyon State Park. 211 SR 526; (575) 445-5607; emnrd.state.nm.us/SPD/sugaritecanyonstatepark.html. Campers and hikers will enjoy Sugarite Canyon State Park, south of Raton, especially during fall color season. The park protects a former coal-mining camp and sits amid lava palisades, forests, lakes, hiking trails, and two attractive campgrounds. Open year-round. Admission fee.

day trip 03

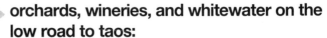

northeast

>>> **orchards, wineries, and whitewater on the low road to taos:**
españa, ohkay owingeh (san juan pueblo), alcalde, embudo, dixon, pilar

The River Road, or Low Road, through the Rio Grande Gorge is the quickest way to get to Taos from Albuquerque, about 2.5 to 3 hours, depending on your speed. Take I-25 north (you can use SR 599 to bypass Santa Fe), driving US 285/84 north to Española and then picking up SR 68, which starts out as a wide highway, then narrows to a winding two-lane road as it parallels the lush Rio Grande corridor through the volcanic gorge. The major attractions here are all pastoral: orchards, wineries, produce stands, and whitewater rafting on the river, but also included is a key historical spot—Ohkay Owingeh (San Juan Pueblo), the site of New Mexico's first Spanish capital. The arts community of Dixon, which lies in the Rio Embudo valley on SR 75, halfway between Embudo and Peñasco, is a magical place to visit—relaxing, eating local food, and meeting its creative and interesting residents. The best time to come is the first weekend in November, when the harvest is in and the community pulls out all the stops for its annual 42-studio art tour.

española

Española is a busy commercial center with a strong, gritty local cultural flavor. You'll find produce stands selling bright red chile ristras, historic exhibits at Plaza de Española mission, the quaint Saints and Sinners Bar, and a noisy Saturday-night *paseo* (parade) of brightly painted lowriders—the local art form—on the main drag. Nearby are an excellent wildlife

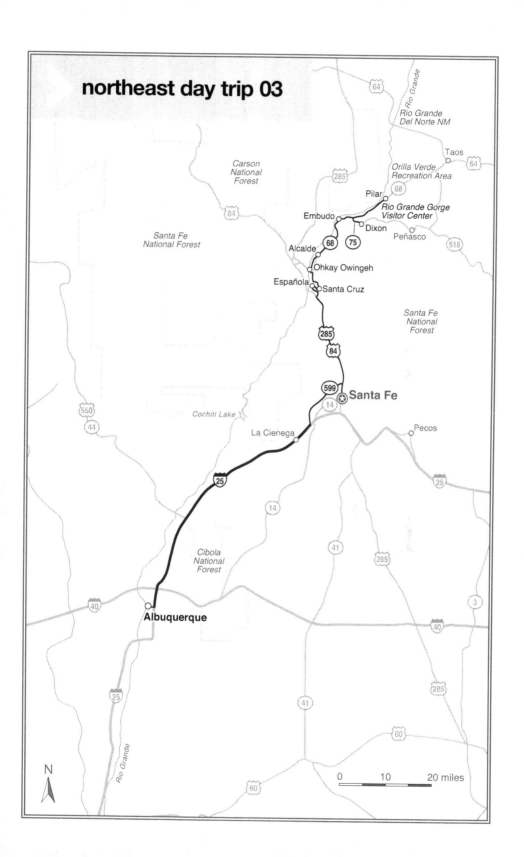

> ## santa cruz
>
> **Santa Cruz de la Cañada Church.** *The Spanish Colonial settlement of Santa Cruz, 3 miles east of Española on SR 76, was once second in size to Santa Fe. Founded in 1695, the current adobe church was built a century later and has been restored several times. Its reredos (altar screen) was painted by the Laguna Santero, who also created the lovely backdrop in San Miguel Mission ("The Oldest Church") in Santa Fe. Hours vary. Free.*

rescue center; the Spanish Colonial village of Santa Cruz; and Sikh Dharma's Hacienda de Guru Ram Das, founded by the late Yogi Bhajan (of Yogi Tea fame).

where to go

Hacienda de Guru Ram Das (Sikh Darma International). 1A Ram Das Guru Place; (505) 753-6341; espanolaashram.com. American Sikhs run many businesses in Española and Santa Fe, including healing centers, kundalini yoga classes, and property security. You are welcome to visit the ashram by appointment to see the golden-domed temple of Siri Singhasan e Khalsa Gurdwara. Call the ashram secretary at least five days ahead of time to schedule a tour; hours are Mon through Fri 12:30 to 4:30 p.m. This is the mother ashram of Sikh Darma in the US. Community vegetarian meals are served free of charge in Langar Hall, next door to the temple, every Thursday at 12:30 p.m. and after Sunday service at 1 p.m. If you wish to attend courses here, inquire about renting lodging on the ashram property.

New Mexico Wildlife Center. 19 Wheat St.; (505) 753-9505; newmexicowildlifecenter.org. Every year this reputable but often-bypassed wildlife hospital cares for some 1,400 raptors, songbirds, and reptiles, representing 120 species, and large mammals such as black bears and mountain lions. Those that cannot be released stay on as one of the 35 Ambassador Animals in the center and take part in excellent educational outreach programs. This is a great family destination. Open Mon through Sat 9 a.m. to 4 p.m. Small fee.

Plaza de Española. US 84 turnoff; (505) 747-8535; cityofespanola.org/160/plazadeespaola. Run by the San Gabriel Historical Society, this historic plaza contains a replica of the original 1598 San Gabriel Mission and church; a restored 1887 adobe mercantile, the Bond House, which serves as the town museum; and a veterans memorial, reflecting pool, and garden. Mission open Wed through Fri noon to 4 p.m. and Sat 11 a.m. to 3 p.m. Bond House open Mon through Sat, same hours. Special events in the mission include meditation classes with local Sikhs. Free.

where to eat

El Paragua. 603 Santa Cruz Rd.; (505) 753-3211; elparagua.com. Española's top restaurant is set in a distinctive stone building at the start of the High Road to Taos. Originally a roadside stand in the 1960s selling the Atencio boys' mother's tamales and tacos, El Paragua is a local success story that continues to be family-owned and serve up delicious, award-winning, authentic New Mexican food in a warm and friendly setting. The beef taco plate has won awards, and at dinner you can find good steak, lamb, and seafood. $–$$.

ohkay owingeh (san juan pueblo)

When Don Juan de Oñate and his 400 colonists arrived in 1598, they found two thriving Rio Grande pueblos—Ok'he and Yunge—which Oñate commandeered for his settlement. Only Yunge, renamed San Gabriel, proved suitable; by 1610, it had been replaced by Santa Fe. The pueblo was home to Popé, a religious leader who was flogged for practicing what the priests regarded as sorcery and went on to organize the successful Pueblo Revolt in 1680. Tewa-speaking Ohkay Owingeh's name, "Place of the Strong People," hints at its continuing leadership role. It is the administrative center for the Eight Northern Pueblos, and with 6,800 tribal residents, it is one of the largest. Colorful dances take place on the two large central plazas, with dancers emerging from rectangular kivas. Major dances take place on June 24, the tribe's feast day, and in January/February when the Deer Dance is held. An arts-and-crafts show is usually held in early July; call for details. Visitors will find a popular arts-and-crafts cooperative, a hotel/casino, an RV park, a clay-shooting club, traditional foods business, a buffalo herd, and recreation lakes and lands. To get there, take SR 68 north for 4 miles, then drive 1 mile west on SR 74.

where to go

Native Arts of the Rio Grande Gallery and Cooperative. 160 Po Pay Ave.; (505) 852-4400. Ohkay Owingeh pueblo is known for its redware pottery, weaving, and painting. You can see artisans from all of the Eight Northern Pueblos creating pottery and other crafts in the cooperative building and purchase items. Open daily 9 a.m. to 5 p.m. Free.

where to eat

El Parasol. SR 68, Ohkay Owingeh; (505) 753-8226; elparasol.com. A branch of the renowned family-run El Paragua restaurant in Española, El Parasol is a casual fast-food version of the main establishment, with six locations in northern New Mexico—two in Española, one in Pojoaque, one in Los Alamos, and two in Santa Fe. The Española North branch is located at the Ohkay Owingeh Travel Center and offers reliably good Mexican and New Mexican items as well as burgers. $.

where to stay

Ohkay Casino-Resort. SR 68 at SR 74 turnoff; (505) 747-1668, (877) 747-1668; ohkay .com. Managed by Best Western, the hotel has 100 pleasant Southwest-style hotel rooms and suites with many standard amenities. The casino has 600 slots and gaming, national acts in the conference center's Main Ballroom, and big-screen sports in the Silver Eagle Lounge. Dining options are largely mainstream fare and include the Festival Buffet, Coyote Cantina, and a coffee shop. $.

alcalde

Several small organic family farms in Alcalde, nearby Los Luceros, and Velarde, as well as New Mexico State University's Sustainable Agriculture Science Center, are open for tours by reservation. The 19th-century Los Luceros Homestead, which once belonged to Wheel-wright Museum founder Mary Cabot Wheelwright, is now a state historic site and open to the public on weekends.

where to go

Los Luceros State Historic Site. 253 CR 41; (505) 476-1165; nmhistoricsites.org/los -luceros. Picturesque 148-acre Los Luceros ranch is located north of Alcalde, along the Rio Grande, and has been home to successive generations for over 600 years, most recently Wheelwright Museum founder Mary Cabot Wheelwright in the early 20th century. The cen-terpiece of the beautiful Los Luceros property is a magnificent 5,700-square-foot renovated Territorial-style *hacienda* replete with history dating back to New Mexico's founding. There is also an 18th-century *capilla* (chapel), a Victorian cottage, a carriage house, a guesthouse, a farmyard, a visitor center, the director's residence, and a gallery. In fall, the famed apple orchards are filled with historic varieties of apples ripe for picking and the riverside bosque comes alive with flaming cottonwood trees. Seasonal special events include a Fall Harvest Festival in Oct and a Lights of Luceros Christmas event on the first Sat in Dec. Open Thurs through Mon 9 a.m. to 5 p.m. Free.

New Mexico State University Sustainable Agriculture Science Center. 371 Alcalde St., CR 40; (505) 852-4241; alcaldesc.nmsu.edu. This experimental agriculture center works to improve water management and varieties of lavender, medicinal herbs, apples, and other crops to benefit local family farms. During the 1700s, the site was part of a large land grant given by the Spanish Crown to General Juan Andres Archuleta, an officer in the Spanish army. Two buildings served as the seat of justice, which is where the name *Alcalde* originated (meaning "mayor" or "justice of the peace"), and one building was used as the courthouse. Later the property became the San Gabriel Ranch, a dude ranch that catered to well-known visitors, including the Rockefellers, Mary Cabot Wheelwright, and Georgia O'Keeffe, who moved to Abiquiu after visiting the ranch. In the 1910s the ranch came under the ownership of Florence Bartlett, who built her home here in 1923, in what is now the main office of the Science Center. Tours by appointment. Open Mon through Fri 7:30 a.m. to 4:30 p.m. Free.

where to shop

Black Mesa Winery and Tasting Room. 1502 SR 68, Velarde; (505) 852-2820, (800) 852-6372; blackmesawinery.com. Founded by Gary and Connie Andersen, this top winery continues to celebrate a renaissance in New Mexico's 400-year winemaking traditions under Oregonians Lynda and Jerry Burd. Fancifully named varietals include the improbably delicious Black Beauty Chocolate Dessert Wine, which won a gold medal at the New Mexico State Fair in 2009; among many other awards, a Viognier and a Petite Syrah won gold medals at the 2018 State Fair. Also award-winning is a hard cider called Bite Me from local Velarde apples, available in growlers in the taproom. The wine store also sells olive oil, olives, and other gifts. The pretty tasting room samples 30 wines, hard cider, and local beer; a walking trail around the vineyard is kid- and pet-friendly and takes you to some ancient petroglyphs in the rocks. Open Mon through Sat 11 a.m. to 6 p.m. and Sun noon to 5 p.m.

Ice's Organic Farm. Route 1097, #33, Alcalde; (505) 852-2589; icesorganicfarm.com. Santa Fe Farmers' Market regulars Ron and Gayle Ice left professional careers to farm lettuce, radishes, garlic, snap peas, strawberries, blackberries, herbs, and other produce in Alcalde. You can arrange to visit the farm for a tour and buy organic jams and jellies and other items made on the farm in the gift shop. To get to the farm, turn on CR 48 at the sign for Los Luceros (see entry above), drive to the end, and turn onto the dirt Route 1097 on the right and continue to the farm. Hours of opening vary; call to make arrangements before driving out to the farm.

embudo

In the early 1900s, the Chile Line, a narrow-gauge railway, transported freight to and from Colorado through the Rio Grande Gorge to Santa Fe's historic railyard district. It got its name because it carried chiles from Chimayó to Colorado. Sadly, the trains are long gone—the only narrow-gauge train still in service in New Mexico is the tourist train between Chama and Antonito (see Northwest Day Trip 05). A popular riverside restaurant used to occupy the old train station in Embudo, an apple-growing village where the Rio Embudo meets the Rio Grande. It's closed now, but it's still a lovely location.

where to shop

Vivác Winery and Gallery (Dixon Tasting Room). 2075 SR 68; (505) 579-4441; vivac winery.com. Owned by local brothers Chris and Jesse Padberg and their wives Liliana and Michele, this up-and-coming winery at the Dixon turnoff is an interesting addition to northern New Mexico's wineries. Inspired by Italian winemaking traditions, the brothers make aromatic dry wines such as Sangiovese and Dolcetto that are unusual for the area. The adjoining gallery sells original wine-label artwork by Jim Vogel, Randall LaGro, and Barbara Zaring, as well as contemporary art and jewelry by Michele and homemade chocolate and black-and-white photography by Liliana. There is live music on the patio. The tasting room is open Mon through Sat 10 a.m. to 7 p.m. and Sun 11 a.m. to 7 p.m. in summer, closes at 6 p.m. the rest of the year. A satellite tasting room is located in Santa Fe in the Farmers' Market Pavilion and is open year-round during market hours on Sat from 8 a.m. to 2 p.m. There is a fee for tasting.

where to eat

Sugar's BBQ and Burgers. 1799 SR 68; (505) 852-0604. This scenic roadside barbecue joint, named for the owner's deceased bulldog, occupies an inconspicuous shack but has legions of fans who come for the cooked-to-order smoked brisket with green chile and the Sugar Burger. Eat under a shady apple tree and enjoy the "gorge-ous" views. Open year-round for lunch; call for specific hours. $$.

dixon

Its enchanting setting in the Rio Embudo valley has made Dixon popular with artists, many of whom have built or converted adobe buildings into homes and also farm and make wine. Dixon's most famous resident is award-winning author Stanley Crawford, whose nonfiction books *Mayordomo: Chronicle of an Acequia in Northern New Mexico, A Garlic Testament: Seasons on a Small New Mexico Farm, A River in Winter, and* 2019's *The Garlic Papers*, about a remarkable feud among local garlic growers, chronicle life in the traditional Hispanic farming village where he and his artist wife Rosemary have lived and raised garlic for four decades. The popular 42-stop Dixon Studio Tour (dixonarts.org) is the oldest in northern New Mexico and takes place the first weekend in November. Lodgings are available with locals operating independently or through Airbnb or VRBO and book up fast, so plan ahead.

where to shop

Dixon Co-op Market. 215 SR 75; (505) 579-5625; dixonmarket.com. This community hangout is the only grocery store in Dixon, a good place to buy delicious breakfast burritos, pizza, soup, and sandwiches in the deli; stock up on supplies; and take the local pulse. You can even purchase bags of good red chile powder here (highly recommended). Some 50 vendors sell everything from handmade tortillas and tamales to jams and local produce at a farmers' market in front of the co-op every Wed 3 to 6 p.m., Apr through Oct. Regular co-op market hours are Mon through Fri 9 a.m. to 7 p.m., Sat and Sun 10 a.m. to 6 p.m.

La Chiripada Winery. 3 miles east on SR 75 from SR 68; (505) 579-4437, (800) 528-7801; lachiripada.com. With sandy loam soil, warm days, and cool nights, Dixon is perfect for growing grapes. This award-winning winery run by the Johnson brothers makes premium wines in a beautiful location. Signature regional wines include Special Reserve Riesling, Rio Embudo Red, Rio Embudo Red Reserve Selection, and Primavera, a blend of muscat and Seyval Blanc that pairs well with chile, poultry, and fish. Tasting room open Mon through Sat 10 a.m. to 5 p.m. and Sun noon to 5 p.m.

where to eat

Zuly's Café. 234 SR 75; (505) 579-4001. This locally run cafe in an adobe building surrounded by a coyote fence serves hearty New Mexican food in a cozy village setting. Try the justly famous red chile on anything, particularly tacos or enchiladas, and the bison burger and fries. Picnic tables are set up on the patio to eat outside in good weather. Open Tues through Thurs 7:30 a.m. to 3 p.m., Fri 7:30 a.m. to 8 p.m., and Sat 9 a.m. to 8 p.m. $.

where to stay

The Tower Guest House at El Bosque Garlic Farm. (505) 579-4288; vrbo.com/118083. This hand-built two-story adobe rental cottage is surrounded by Stanley and Rosemary Crawford's garlic farm, and guests may pick produce for meals in season. It has a lovely view from the deck, a downstairs bedroom with double bed and shower, and an upstairs living room with sofa sleeper and kitchen. Satellite TV, phone, CD/DVD player. No pets/smoking. Buy groceries at Dixon Co-op; free Wi-Fi at Dixon Library next to the store. $.

pilar

Hispanic farmers were granted land here on the Rio Grande in 1795. They joined Jicarilla Apaches, who had settled Pilar, been scattered by de Vargas in 1694, and later returned. The Apaches and Hispanics spent decades fighting one another, but the Apaches signed a peace treaty in the 1800s and were forced to relocate to a new reservation in northwestern New Mexico. The Rio Grande through the Upper and Lower Gorge was originally part of a state park that included the state's best whitewater, a 17-mile section north of Taos with Class III and IV rapids dubbed "the Taos Box." The Box and Upper Gorge, accessed from Questa, are now managed by the Bureau of Land Management as part of Rio Grande del Norte National Monument (see Northeast Day Trip 06). Within the national monument, the 14 miles of river between Pilar and Velarde are designated Wild and Scenic and managed as Orilla Verde Recreation Area. They have small rapids and, with easy access from SR 68, are a perfect place to float the river in rafts, canoes, and kayaks.

where to go

Rio Grande del Norte National Monument (Orilla Verde Recreation Area/Rio Grande Gorge Visitor Center). Intersection of SR 68 and SR 570; (575) 758-8851; blm.gov/visit/orilla-verde-recreation-area. Orilla Verde has 6 campgrounds along the Rio Grande, 3 hiking trails, fishing opportunities, and put-ins and take-outs for those wishing to run the Rio Grande, either privately or with outfitters. Stop at the Rio Grande Gorge Visitor Center in Pilar for information and camping, hiking, and river-running permits. Open daily 8:30 a.m. to 4:30 p.m. in summer, 10 a.m. to 2 p.m. in winter.

worth more time

Outfitters in Santa Fe and Taos organize half- and full-day rafting trips on the Rio Grande's Upper and Lower Gorges. Two of the oldest and best known are **Los Rios River Runners** in Taos (575-776-8854; losriosriverrunners.com) and **New Mexico River Adventures** in Santa Fe (800-983-7756; newmexicoriveradventures.com). Minimum age 13 years. $$$–$$$$.

day trip 04

northeast

>>>

sacred architecture and pilgrims on the high road to taos:
nambé pueblo, chimayó, cordova, truchas, las trampas, picurís pueblo, ranchos de taos

Built in the early 1700s when Hispanics and Rio Grande Pueblos united to repel raids by Comanches and Jicarilla Apaches, the adobe villages in the rugged foothills of the Sangre de Cristos reflect the heart and soul of the state's rich Hispanic culture: *familia y fé* (family and faith). Fortified villages feature interconnected *placitas* (neighborhoods) of family *haciendas* (compounds) built around small defensible plazas; devotion to the Catholic Church; livestock grazing on *potreros* (family pastures); short-season farming of corn, squash, chiles, apples, and other crops irrigated by the *acequia* (community ditch); weaving, woodworking, tinwork and tinsmithing, carving, straw inlay, pottery, needlework, and other arts; and traditional fiddle music, dance, and *cuentos* (folktales) told in ancient Spanish dialects unique to each village.

To reach the bottom of the High Road, drive north from Albuquerque on I-25 and either take NM 599 to US 285/84, bypassing Santa Fe or go through Santa Fe, and then continue north on US 285/84. Just after Pojoaque, about two hours from Albuquerque, turn right onto SR 503 to reach the start of the High Road. The drive is best done on the last two weekends in September to coincide with the popular annual High Road Artisan Studio Tour (highroadnewmexico.com), when you can meet artisans at 33 studios, art centers, and galleries and enjoy spectacular fall vistas. It's usually done as part of a weekend trip to Taos, but for a shorter trip, consider a day or overnight trip to Chimayó, known for its world-famous

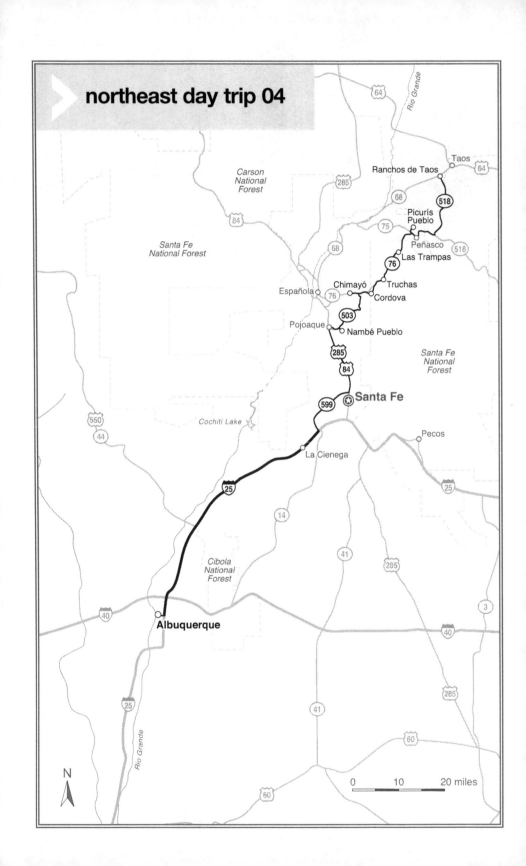

Santuario de Chimayó healing shrine, historic plaza and museum, weaving shops, traditional cuisine using the superb locally grown red chile, and charming bed-and-breakfasts.

nambé pueblo

The road winds through the Hispanic village of Nambé (named for the pueblo), along the riverbank lined with lush bottomlands of cottonwoods, willows, and alders, to reach the Pueblo of Nambé, one of six Tewa-speaking pueblos in northern New Mexico. Once a major religious center, Nambé, or *Nanbé Owingeh* in the Tewa language, which translates to "The Place of the Rounded Earth," is listed on the National Register of Historic Places. About 1,100 tribal residents, many of whom make pottery and jewelry, live here. The tribe has a small buffalo herd and operates a recreation area on its 1,900 acres.

where to go

Nambé Falls and Lake Recreation Area. 15A NP 102 West, Santa Fe; (505) 455-4410; nambepueblo.org. This picturesque 20,000-acre area is popular with local residents for its scenery and outdoors activities. It has trails, three waterfalls, and a lake, where you can picnic, hike, camp, fish, and swim. Indian dances are held here on October 3, the day before the pueblo's feast day, and on the Fourth of July, when there is a big celebration with food vendors and arts and crafts. Several movies have been filmed at Nambé Falls, including *City Slickers*, starring Billy Crystal. Open Thurs through Sun 7 a.m. to 7 p.m. Apr through Oct. Separate fees for admission, camping, and fishing.

chimayó

Stay on SR 503 and then turn left onto SR 76 to reach Chimayó, named for an earlier Tewa village, *Tsi Mayoh*, "Hill of the East." Following the 1680 Pueblo Revolt, Spain granted this land to the Ortega and Trujillos families on the condition they built their homes around fortified *placitas* to repel Indian raids. Chimayó's reputation as a religious center came about in 1814, when Padre Bernard Abeyta, a priest from the parish church at Santa Cruz, is said to have repeatedly found the same distinctive cross—displaying the Black Christ of Guatemala—in a pasture in Chimayó, despite removing it to Santa Cruz. He was eventually given permission to build a shrine around the well of soil in which it was found. The simple yet beautiful Santuario de Chimayó, quite possibly the most spiritual place in America, is one of my favorite spots in northern New Mexico, a place I visit regularly myself and always take visitors.

where to go

Chimayó Museum. (505) 351-0945. This charming community museum on Plaza del Cerro is housed in the former adobe home of José Ramon Ortega and his wife Petra Mestas

pilgrimage to el santuario

Every year some 300,000 people make a pilgrimage to this tiny church in a for-mer family chapel on the south end of Chimayó. Most come during Holy Week, when hundreds of New Mexico's Catholics travel here on foot, some carrying crosses, to atone for the sins of the previous year. Many make the trip annually, walking all night to arrive in Chimayó in time for Good Friday mass. The first Eas-ter pilgrimage began when US soldiers and sailors prayed to Santo Niño de Ato-cha for safe passage during the Bataan Death March and, after being delivered safely, made an annual pilgrimage to give thanks.

Ortega, who raised 14 children here. The museum's mission is to preserve local culture through programs such as Los Maestros de Norte, a program designed to teach youngsters traditional Hispanic arts. It has revolving exhibits on village history and information on walking tours around the village, and it hosts lectures, book signings, and other special events. Author Don Usner, who married into a Chimayó family, is closely involved with the museum. He has been documenting this disappearing way of life through photographs and interviews with elders, published in books like *Sabino's Map: Life in the Old Chimayó Plaza* (Museum of New Mexico Press, 1996). Open Wed through Sat 10 a.m. to 4 p.m. Apr through Oct; Fri only 10 a.m. to 4 p.m. the rest of the year. Admission fee.

El Santuario de Chimayó. 15 Santuario Dr.; (505) 351-9961; holychimayo.us. You don't have to be Catholic to be deeply affected by this peaceful spot, sanctified by the faith of generations of New Mexicans. Doves coo under the eaves of Our Lord of Esquipulas Cha-pel, where people sit in reflection in front of the altar with its lovely hand-painted *retablo* (altar backdrop) created by famed *santero* Mollero. A tiny room houses El Pozo, the holy well where the miraculous cross was found; visitors line up to scoop blessed dirt from the hole in the floor into a plastic bag. Next door, you understand why this shrine has been dubbed the "Lourdes of America." Scores of prayers and testaments of healing line the walls, and people leave shoes, photos, crutches, and other items in front of a statue of Santo Niño de Atocha, the Spanish child saint who is said to wear out his shoes nightly traveling to aid villagers. A nearby chapel is dedicated to Santo Niño, and a third chapel to the Holy Family. Open summer 9 a.m. to 6 p.m., winter 9 a.m. to 5 p.m. Daily mass 11 a.m.; Sunday mass 10:30 a.m. and noon. Free.

Plaza del Cerro. Plaza del Cerro, Chimayó's main plaza, is one of the best-preserved Spanish Colonial plazas in New Mexico. Both crumbling and restored adobes surround the plaza, and there is a *torreon*, or watchtower, in the southwestern corner, once used as a lookout against raids. On the west side is an old *capilla* (chapel), owned by the Ortega family, which served parishioners unable to travel to the main church in Santa Cruz. The former Ortega mercantile store and residence is now a lovely inn on the south side of the plaza, Rancho Manzana.

where to shop

El Potrero Trading Post. 17 Santuario Dr., next to El Santuario; (505) 351-4112. A good place to buy traditional *santos*, *retablos*, rugs, silver jewelry, and *milagros* (small tin charms from Mexico shaped like body parts that are popularly worn as pendants to protect against illness). One essential item is a bag of Chimayó red chile powder. Chimayó red chiles ripen later than Hatch chiles from southern New Mexico. Once dried and ground, the powder has a complex, sweet, wine-like taste that is the essential ingredient for red chile and mole sauces, marinades, and spicing everything from breakfast eggs to fries. It is the quintessential New Mexico gift—and it won't break the bank. Open daily 9 a.m. to 5 p.m.

Ortega's Weaving Shop. Junction of SR 520 and SR 76; (505) 351-4215, (877) 351-4215; ortegasweaving.com. The distinctive Rio Grande style of weaving, which uses bright stripes and diamond patterns, grew out of the intermingling of Hispanic and Indian cultures. Eight generations of Ortegas have perfected the craft, using wool from Churro sheep introduced from Spain. You can buy both small and large weavings and watch family members at this popular shop, in business since 1900, weave Rio Grande–style rugs on large looms. For men, an Ortega vest serves as the New Mexico equivalent of business casual, paired with a bolo tie, jeans, and cowboy boots, and women will love the colorful jackets. Open Mon through Sat 9 a.m. to 5 p.m.

where to eat

Note: If you are going to drive the entire High Road (at least half a day), plan on eating a substantial breakfast or lunch in Chimayó. There are no restaurants to speak of until you get to the other end of the High Road, about 106 miles.

Rancho de Chimayó. 300 Juan Medina Rd., off CR 98; (505) 354-0444; ranchodechimayo .com. In business since 1965, this restaurant in the converted Jaramillo family *hacienda* serves good traditional northern New Mexican food in a romantic setting, complete with hardwoods, fireplaces, and a courtyard. Try the carne adovada or green chile stew, but everything here is good, and made better by the addition of delicious chile sauce made from Chimayó red chile. Note: *The Rancho de Chimayó Cookbook: The Traditional Cooking of New Mexico* (Lyons Press, 2014), written by Cheryl Alters Jamison and Bill Jamison and updated for the restaurant's 50th anniversary, makes an excellent souvenir (my original 1991 edition is now thoroughly dog-eared from use). The gift shop also sells jars of the restaurant's delicious salsa. Lunch and dinner Tues through Sun 11:30 a.m. to 8:30 p.m. (open several Mondays in Oct and Dec, call for details); breakfast Sat and Sun 8:30 to 10:30 a.m. Be sure to make a reservation; it's popular with tour groups in summer. $$–$$$.

where to stay

Hacienda Rancho de Chimayó. 297 Juan Medina Rd., off CR 98; (505) 351-2222, (888) 270-2320; ranchodechimayo.com/hacienda. Epifanio and Adelaida Jaramillo's former home has been beautifully converted to an 8-room bed-and-breakfast that offers gorgeous rooms and friendly hospitality at a really good price. All rooms have antiques, hardwood floors, views, baths, and fireplaces. Continental breakfast included. Located near the popular restaurant under the same ownership. $.

Rancho Manzana. 26 Camino de Mision; (888) 505-2277; ranchomanzana.com. This eco-friendly country inn has been owned by Jody Kent since 1995 and is in the 18th-century Ortega mercantile building on the south side of Plaza del Cerro. Accommodations are in 2 casitas and a large loft that are all light and airy with mud walls, high ceilings, private baths, and down comforters on the beds. They are all located near a hot tub and fire pit. Farmhouse-style breakfasts made from organic ingredients, such as free-range eggs from on-site chickens, set you up for a day of touring, although with 4 acres of lush orchards to explore, you may not want to leave. No pets; the owner's dogs, cats, and hens already live on part of the property. Budget-friendly. Two-night minimum for casitas and 3-night minimum for adobe loft. $.

cordova

Cordova is a sleepy village in its own valley off SR 76. It has a celebrated historic adobe church and many traditional wood-carving studios.

where to go

Saint Anthony Church. 185 CR 80; (505) 587-2111. This 1832 church is on the National Register of Historic Places and significant for its large *reredos* (altar screen), which was painted by famed *santero* Rafael Aragon, and many other fine examples of this historic tradition. The church is only open for mass at noon the second and fourth Sundays of the month and in June, July, and Aug. Special state-run tours of several of the historic churches of the Taos High Road that are not typically open are offered from time to time through a special state-run project called Nuevo Mexico Profundo. For more information, visit nuevo-mexico-profundo.com.

truchas

From Cordova, SR 76 climbs steeply to Truchas (named for the plentiful trout in local streams). Founded in 1754 by settlers from Chimayó, Truchas is perched on an 8,000-foot plateau beneath 13,102-foot Truchas Peak, the state's second-tallest mountain; it has stupendous views across the Rio Grande valley all the way to Pedernal, near Abiquiu. The lovely setting has always inspired artists. In the 1700s, Truchas was home to famed *santero* Antonio Fresquis, known as the Truchas Master, and it continues to attract creative and counterculture types who treasure its beauty, authenticity, and remoteness. It is famous as the location for Robert Redford's 1987 film adaptation of John Nichols's popular novel *The Milagro Beanfield War*. Plan on stopping here for a bit longer if you enjoy meeting artists — there are a number of worthwhile art galleries here, and nearby Ojo Sarco is a tiny settlement in a lovely valley.

where to shop

Hand Artes Gallery. 137 CR 75; (505) 689-2443; handartesgallery.com. This attractive contemporary art gallery in a home owned by William Franke was one of the first in Truchas and is still a great place to head for folk art, paintings, art glass, and sculptures by New Mexico and out-of-state contemporary artists. There is a piano in the West Gallery. Open daily sunrise to sunset.

High Road Art Gallery. 1642 SR 76; (505) 689-2689; highroadnewmexico.com. You can't miss this nonprofit artists' co-op, just past the dogleg in SR 76 in the village. Approximately 70 local artists are represented, making this a good place to get a feel for the work being done all along the High Road. Open 10 a.m. to 5 p.m. daily, until 4 p.m. in winter.

las trampas

About 7 miles north of Truchas on SR 76, just south of Peñasco, Las Trampas ("the Traps") is another land-grant settlement founded in 1751 by families from Santa Fe. Its main attraction is its very photogenic 1760 adobe church.

where to go

San José de Gracia Church. 2377-81 SR 76; (505) 351-4360. This church, located on the north side of the village right off SR 76, is worth a stop to take a closer look at its spectacular exterior. With its huge buttressed walls, carved wooden doors, twin bell towers, and *canales* (gutters), the church is one of the best examples still standing of monumental adobe mission architecture. Due to population decline locally, the church was closed up until early 2019 when, at residents' request, priests from the Holy Family Parish in Chimayó began holding mass here again regularly on the first and third Sunday of the month, as well as Christmas and on the feast day of St. Joseph on March 19. If the church does happen to be open when you pass, it's worth stepping inside to view the interior, which boasts magnificent woodwork by master carpenters Nicolas de Apodaca and Juan Manual Romero. If you wish to photograph the church (as many people do), try to get here either early in the morning or late in the day; midday light will flatten out the image.

where to eat

Sugar Nymphs Bistro. 15046 N. SR 75, Peñasco; (575) 587-0311; sugarnymphs.com. Located on SR 75, not far from Picurís Pueblo, you'll find this unexpectedly wonderful rustic bistro. Owner Ki is a trained pastry chef and art framer, and partner Kai is an artist and meditation teacher who learned to cook at the San Francisco Zen Center restaurant Greens, and both escaped California to live the artistic life. They describe their restaurant as "Country Atmosphere, City Cuisine," and as you might expect, the menu focuses on fresh, local, seasonal produce; locally raised meat and eggs; and fresh trout caught in the high-country streams. At Sunday brunch, there are egg dishes such as quiche or hash accompanied by homemade scones; for lunch, you can't go wrong with the famed green chile cheeseburger, soup and salad, or a BLT. Vegetarians will find plenty here: a veggie burger, a grilled farmers' veggie plate, and salads with fresh goat cheese accompanied by fresh focaccia bread. At dinner, don't pass up the opportunity to try the fresh grilled trout or a local rib eye steak. It goes without saying that dessert is a highlight—everything from a gluten-free fruit crisp to a variety of delicious homemade cakes, from chocolate to carrot, which would go nicely with a cup of tea if you get here at teatime on the weekend. Note: This restaurant would make a good destination if you do the High Road Art Tour in late Sept or the Dixon Studio Tour the first week in Nov; both routes go straight up to Peñasco. Open in summer for lunch Sat through Thurs 11 a.m. to 3 p.m.; dinner Fri and Sat 11 a.m. to 8:30 p.m.; and brunch Sun 10 a.m. to 3 p.m. Restricted hours at other times of the year. $–$$.

picurís pueblo

Surrounded by spectacular alpine scenery, traditional Picurís Pueblo was once one of the largest and remotest pueblos in New Mexico; now it is the smallest, with just 100 tribal members living on the quiet pueblo. The tribe's main moneymaking operations are far away in Santa Fe, tied up in its majority ownership and active involvement in the lovely Hotel Santa Fe (see North Day Trip 03), as well as on tribal lands, raising its 50-strong bison herd as both a food source and spiritual nourishment for tribal members. It's worth stopping by to view the bison herd, picnic by the fishing pond, and visit the tribe's historic church, which has been beautifully restored inside and out; there's a smoke shop on-site where you can pick up tobacco products. Traditional Buffalo and Corn Dances are held in June and August (August 10 is the tribe's feast day), a good time to make the trip. *Picurís* means "Those Who Paint," and the pueblo is known for its utilitarian but glittery micaceous pottery and other arts and crafts, on sale in the gallery at Hotel Santa Fe. Stop at tribal headquarters and ask the custodian to open the church for you. For a small fee, he will be happy to give you a personal guided tour of the ruins behind the main pueblo and share stories about tribal history and life as a pueblo. Such personal encounters are one of the joys of a road trip and worth seeking out. The pueblo is open Mon through Fri 8 a.m. to 5 p.m.

where to go

San Lorenzo de Picurís Mission Church. (575) 587-2519; picurispueblo.org. The first mission church at Picurís was built in 1621, destroyed in the Pueblo Revolt, and replaced in the 1700s with the current structure. With the help of volunteers, it underwent a massive restoration in recent years and is now once more a beautiful and functional space used for regular services. There is a lovely statue of San Lorenzo next to the altar; the *reredos* includes a red, white, and blue banner, commemorating the many tribal members who have served in recent wars in the Middle East. The church is now listed on the National Register of Historic Places.

ranchos de taos

From the pueblo, continue through Peñasco to SR 518, then turn left. The road starts to drop in elevation as you come down from the High Road, passing Fort Burgwin, a reconstructed 19th-century fort and museum, and joining SR 68 at Ranchos de Taos, a few miles south of Taos proper. Taos Pueblo farmers founded this small community, which is now occupied mainly by artists. You'll find a few good galleries, restaurants, and a historic bed-and-breakfast here, but it is mainly known for its 1730 church on the old plaza, without doubt the most painted and photographed mission church in New Mexico.

where to go

La Hacienda de los Martinez. 708 Hacienda Way; (575) 758-1000; taoshistoricmuseums .org. This atmospheric frontier *hacienda* was built as a fortified home by Severino Martinez and his family in 1804 and became an important ranching and trading operation at the north end of El Camino Real. Twenty-one thick-walled adobe rooms surround two neighborhoods built around small central plazas, or *placitas*. The main *placita* includes family bedrooms, trade rooms, a chapel, a dispensary, and a *sala,* or family room, with a wooden floor. Weaving rooms, storerooms, and a kitchen with an unusual shepherd's bed over the fireplace surround the servants' *placita*. Padre Antonio Martinez, the eldest son, is an important Taos figure. He founded Taos's first coed school and its newspaper and became a local hero when he opposed Archbishop Lamy and advocated to preserve the folk character of New Mexico's Catholic religion. Living-history demonstrations weekly. Open Mon, Tues, Fri, and Sat 11 a.m. to 4 p.m. and Sun noon to 4 p.m. Admission fee.

San Francisco de Asís Church. 60 St. Francis Plaza; (575) 751-0518. Built between 1772 and 1816, this soaring mission church is, quite simply, stunning. Viewed aerially, it is clear that it has been built in a cruciform, recalling Christ on the cross, with massive buttresses and sensuously curving adobe walls that have become iconic through inspired renderings by painter Georgia O'Keeffe and photographer Ansel Adams, among others. Inside the church is a less well-known attraction: an 1896 painting by Canadian Henri Ault called *The Shadow of the Cross*, which depicts Christ walking along the Sea of Galilee. It has come to be known as the "mystery painting" because, when viewed in total darkness, the figure of Christ seems to double in size, the shadow of a cross appears over his left shoulder and the keel of a boat by his right knee, and the waters become wild. No one knows why. Open Mon through Sat 9 a.m. to 4 p.m.

where to eat

Trading Post Café and Gallery. 4179 SR 68; (575) 758-5089; tradingpostcafe.com. This little gem features great Italian food in an art gallery atmosphere in an old trading post near the Taos High Road junction. Excellent pasta dishes include penne arrabbiata and fettuccine alla carbonara, and they make a good Caesar salad and minestrone soup, too. Open Tues through Sat for lunch 11 a.m. to 3:30 p.m. and dinner 4 to 9 p.m.; Sunday brunch 10 a.m. to 2 p.m. Budget prix fixe three-course early bird dinner Tues through Thurs 4 to 6 p.m. $–$$$.

where to stay

Adobe & Pines Inn Bed and Breakfast. 4107 SR 68; (575) 751-0947, (855) 828-7872; adobepines.com. This inn near Ranchos de Taos Plaza is built around a tranquil 1832 adobe *hacienda* that was home to arts patron Mrs. Paul Griffin in the 1930s. The grand portal has a wall fresco by noted Taos Pueblo artist Juan Mirabal. Mrs. Griffin was also responsible for donating the famous "mystery painting" in the nearby San Francisco de Asís Church after finding it in Canada. The inn has 8 unique art-filled Southwest rooms with kiva fireplaces, bathrooms, sitting areas, and TVs with CD/DVD players. The hearty, three-course, all-organic hot breakfast accommodates all diets and will set you up for the day. It features anything from eggs Benedict to migas to waffles and frittata, and is available as a sit-down meal (prepared early if you have to leave), in your room, or as a packed meal to go, with prior notice. Wi-Fi throughout. $$–$$$.

worth more time

Sipapu Ski Area. 5224 SR 518; (800) 587-2240 (info and lodging reservations); sipapu .ski. To explore more of the Carson National Forest and the Sangre de Cristo Mountains, instead of heading west on SR 518 as you leave Peñasco, turn east toward Mora and Las Vegas. Not far along the road, you'll come to 200-acre Sipapu Ski Area, 22 miles southeast of Taos. In summer, this high-country setting is popular for hiking and camping. In winter, it's an old-fashioned family-operated ski resort popular with telemark skiers, snowboarders, and others skiers, who all enjoy the uncrowded conditions. There are 41 runs—20 percent classified beginner, 40 percent designated intermediate, 25 percent advanced, and 15 percent expert—and the 6 lifts can handle 2,900 skiers per hour. Three terrain parks for snowboarders offer beginner and advanced lines, rails, boxes, jumps, and a huge teeter-totter. There's a folksy ski lodge with a big fireplace, a riverside cafe, and shops and a wide array of other accommodations available, from rustic lodge rooms and cabins to casitas, duplexes, mobile homes, and seasonal campground on the Rio Pueblo.

day trip 05

northeast

>>> iconoclasts, indian dances, and après ski:
taos

historic taos

"This Taos myth, it is just unbelievable," wrote artist Georgia O'Keeffe, after her first visit in 1929. "One perfect day after another, everyone going like mad after something." A visit to this remote mountain town—130 miles north of Albuquerque via I-25, NM 599, US 285/84, and SR 68—tends to have that effect. Taos has a spirit and energy so great for its tiny size (pop. 6,000) that it feels wild and uncontained. Throughout its long, colorful history, it has erupted at every opportunity into creative expression in art, architecture, music, acting, cuisine, extreme sports, healing modalities, and experimental communal living. There are seven excellent museums (most occupying the homes of early settlers and artists), an Indian pueblo so old and intact it is a recognized World Heritage Site, a world-class ski resort, a hundred art galleries, and numerous reasonably priced lodging and dining options, many in historic buildings. Don't plan on a day trip—plan on a whole weekend.

Taos's unique setting is key to its allure. It perches on a 7,000-foot sagebrush plateau, halfway between the state's highest peak—13,161-foot Mount Wheeler—and the 650-foot-deep Rio Grande Gorge, a narrow, dark, volcanic rift zone created by the constant pulling apart of tectonic plates and now occupied by a raging river. The result is a palpably brooding landscape, numerous hot springs, and the exciting sensation of energy gathering and funneling repeatedly as you penetrate the gorge, wind up onto the plateau, then drive the narrow roads through the three small communities of Taos: Ranchos de Taos, the town of Taos, and Taos Pueblo.

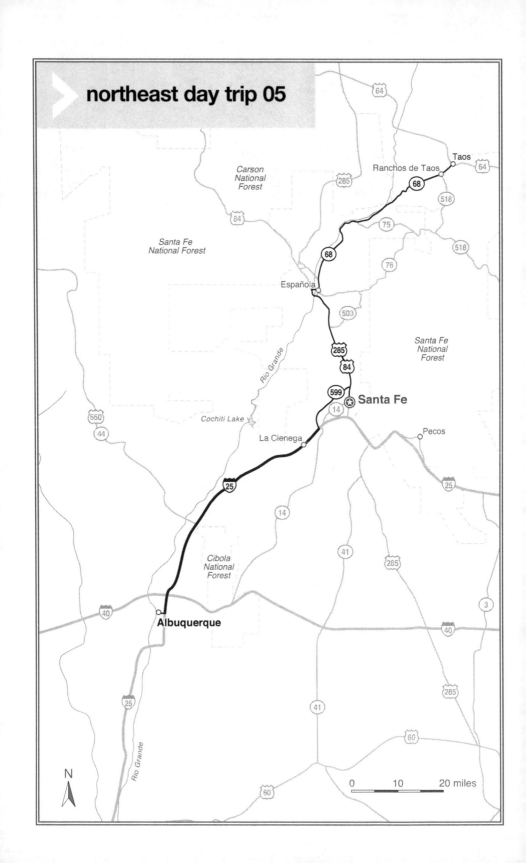

northeast day trip 05

where to go

Blumenschein Home and Museum. 222 Ledoux St.; (575) 758-0505; taoshistoricmuseums .org. Ernest "Blumy" Blumenschein, one of the two founders of the celebrated Taos Society of Artists, spent only summers in Taos until 1919, when he, wife Mary Greene, and daughter Helen—all accomplished artists—bought this 1797 adobe and moved here full-time. The home expanded organically as the family acquired adjoining rooms and converted them. Of all the attractions, don't miss this one. The home has an authentic 1920s feel, with its fireplaces, traditional local wood furniture, murals by Mary, family artwork on the walls, cozy library, and old-fashioned kitchen and garden. Open Mon, Tues, Fri, Sat 11 a.m. to 4 p.m. and Sun noon to 4 p.m. Admission fee.

Couse-Sharp Historic Site. 146 Kit Carson Rd.; (575) 751-0369; couse-sharp.org. The newest museum in Taos is only open to the public for tours by appointment, but for anyone interested in the Taos Society of Artists, it's a necessity. The home and studios of two of the six founding members of the Taos Society of Artists—E. I. Couse and Joseph Henry Sharp—are on the National and State Registers of Historic Places and, to mark the centenary of the founding of the Taos Society of Artists, were designated a historic site and opened to visitors. The property on Kit Carson Road includes the Couse home, studio, and gardens; the workshops of Couse's son; and the two neighboring studios of fellow artist Joseph Henry Sharp. Full tours by appointment only May through Oct, Mon through Sat

taos super ticket museum pass

The **Museum Association of Taos** (MAT) is a nonprofit association of five separate museums whose unique historic buildings and exceptional collections present the art, history, and culture of Taos and northern New Mexico: the Taos Art Museum at Fechin House, the Millicent Rogers Museum, the Harwood Museum of Art, and the Taos Historic Museums, comprising the E. L. Blumenschein Home and La Hacienda de los Martinez. Entrance for the individual museums is $8, but for just $25, you can purchase a discounted combination pass good for one visit to each of MAT's five Taos museums honored for one full year from the date of purchase (note: the Governor Bent House and Museum, Kit Carson Home, and Couse Historic Site are not included in this discounted pass). MAT Super Tickets can be purchased at any of the five museums or by email at MAT@taosmuseums.org. Opening hours vary for each of the five museums: Mon, Tues, Fri, and Sat 11 a.m. to 4 p.m. and Sun noon to 4 p.m.

9 a.m. to 5 p.m.; limited tours by appointment Nov through Apr, Tues through Fri 10 a.m. to 4 p.m. Admission fee.

Governor Bent House and Museum. 117 Bent St.; (575) 758-2376. Privately run, this old adobe, a block north of the plaza, is the former home of renowned trader Charles Bent, who was installed as the first US governor of New Mexico in 1846. Bent and other Americans were murdered in 1847 by a group of disgruntled Hispanic settlers and Taos Indians; his wife and children managed to escape through a hole in the wall of the house. The museum is a little dusty but worth a visit for its period artifacts and paintings by Taos Society artists. Open daily 9 a.m. to 5 p.m. in summer, 10 a.m. to 4 p.m. the rest of the year. Admission fee.

Harwood Museum of Art. 238 Ledoux St.; (575) 758-9826; harwoodmuseum.org. The elegant Harwood Museum was founded in the family adobe of Taos artist Burt Harwood; it is the second-oldest museum in the state. The University of New Mexico took over its administration in 1936 and, fortunately for visitors, hired famed Santa Fe style architect John Gaw Meem to design an attractive, luminous expansion to showcase Taos artists. The best examples of Taos Society art in town occupy a downstairs room. A second room is dedicated to minimalist Agnes Martin's white-on-white canvases. Upstairs you'll find examples of traditional Hispanic wood carving, including unique *bultos* (carved saint statues) by Patricio Barela, a master *santero* from the 1940s. Open Tues through Fri 10 a.m. to 5 p.m. and Sat and Sun noon to 5 p.m. Admission fee.

Kit Carson Home and Museum. 113 Kit Carson Rd.; (575) 758-4945; kitcarsonmuseum .org. One of Taos's most famous residents, trapper, mountain man, translator, scout, and army officer Christopher "Kit" Carson moved here in 1826 and stayed for 42 years. Carson bought this modest, four-room 1825 adobe as a wedding present for his young wife, Maria Josefa Jaramillo, in 1843, and the couple raised seven children here. Exhibits celebrate the trappings of Carson's adventurous life, including fine examples of guns and a typical camp that kids can walk through. Two of the costumed interpreters are distant relatives of Josefa Jaramillo. The Masonic Order Bent Lodge #42 of Taos, founded by Carson and fellow mountain men Charles Bent and Ceran St. Vrain, runs the museum. Open daily May through Oct 10 a.m. to 5 p.m., Nov through Apr noon to 4:30 p.m. Admission fee.

Millicent Rogers Museum. 1504 Millicent Rogers Rd.; (575) 758-2462; millicentrogers .org. Beautiful and artistically gifted, oil heiress Millicent Rogers packed a lot into the five years she lived in Taos before her untimely death in 1952 at the age of 50. She befriended Native artists and amassed one of the premier collections of Southwestern art in the region, 7,000 pieces, now displayed in her former home just north of town. Highlights are rooms full of Navajo rugs and silver, Hopi kachinas, and sculptures by R. C. Gorman. Top of my list is the collection of pottery by and memorabilia of famed San Ildefonso Pueblo potter Maria Martinez and her family, donated to the museum. Comprising letters, family photos, and awards, as well as many secrets of Maria's techniques, it offers a remarkably intimate look at the potter's life and the development of the Pueblo pottery tradition through succeeding

taos society of artists

Taos became an artist colony in 1898, when New York artists Bert Phillips and Ernest Blumenschein traveled to New Mexico to sketch. They broke a wagon wheel in Taos Canyon and fell in love with Taos while waiting for the wheel to be repaired. The two men organized the Taos Society of Artists in 1912, which also included Bert Dunton, Joseph Sharp, Victor Higgins, John Marin, Marsden Hartley, and Dorothy Brett. Examples of art by the Taos Society of Artists can be found in many Taos museums.

generations. Rogers herself was an artistic original: model thin, she designed and wore Indian-inspired clothing and jewelry that, like everything else in her life, made a strong statement. Replicas of her jewelry are on sale in the excellent museum store. Open daily 10 a.m. to 5 p.m. Admission fee.

Taos Art Museum at Fechin House. 227 Paseo del Pueblo Norte; (575) 758-2690; taosartmuseum.org. The Taos Art Museum is located in the fabulous home of renowned Russian immigrant artist Nicholai Fechin. The son of a wood-carver, Fechin found a spiritual home among New Mexico's traditional artisans, taking woodworking to dizzying heights when he converted this traditional adobe between 1924 and 1927. Everything in the sunny home is hand carved, from beds, chests, chairs, and other furniture to barley-sugar twisted posts and corbel beams. The woodwork perfectly complements Fechin's vibrant paintings downstairs and the works by other Taos artists upstairs. Fechin left the house in 1933 when he divorced. Daughter Eya later lived in the studio behind the house and worked with the City of Taos to preserve her father's legacy. Open Tues through Sun 11 a.m. to 4 p.m. Docent tours at 11 a.m. on Sat and Sun. Admission fee. Taos County residents free every Sun.

Taos Pueblo. 120 Veterans Hwy.; (575) 758-1028; taospueblo.com. Built between AD 1000 and 1450, Taos Pueblo is one of the oldest continuously occupied pueblos in the Southwest and both a National Historic Landmark and UNESCO World Heritage Site. It is recognized worldwide for its distinctive stacked architecture, photogenic setting below Taos Mountain, historic San Geronimo mission church, and talented artisans known for their micaceous pottery, beadwork, moccasins, drums, flutes, music, art, and other handicrafts that reflect the unique synthesis of both Pueblo and Plains Indian artistic traditions. About 150 tribal members live in the old pueblo, which has no running water, electricity, or plumbing; most of the 1,800 other tribal members are decidedly modern, living in contemporary homes on surrounding pueblo land and working regular jobs. The pueblo is open to visitors Mon through Sat 8 a.m. to 4:30 p.m. and Sun 8:30 a.m. to 4:30 p.m., except for 10 weeks in spring, when it closes for ceremonial purposes. Traditional dances, held year-round, are usually open to the public: Christmas and the tribe's feast day of San Geronimo on September 30 are the most popular. Fees are charged for entrance, photography, videotaping, and sketching.

Taos Ski Valley. 116 Sutton Place, Taos Ski Valley, SR 150; (888) 569-1756 (reservations), (844) 828-5601 (snowphone); skitaos.com. *Outside* magazine ranked Taos Ski Valley, 18 miles northeast of Taos at the end of SR 150, as one of the top 15 ski resorts in North America. Founded in 1956 by Swiss skier and entrepreneur Ernie Blake, the 1,294-acre, European-style resort is renowned for its average 300 inches of perfect powder, steep runs, top-ranked ski school, and children's programs. The 14 lifts can handle more than 15,000 skiers an hour, and of the 110 named runs, 24 percent are beginner, 25 percent intermediate, and 51 percent expert—meaning that there is more than enough here for everyone. Snowboarding is now permitted. The ski valley has a noncorporate feel and numerous options for lodging and dining, including The Blake at Taos Ski Valley, an 80-room alpine guesthouse in a green building adjacent to Lift 1. The compact village also offers also condos, B&Bs, restaurants, and shopping. Lifts operate 9 a.m. to 4 p.m. in season.

where to shop

Desert Blends of Taos. PO Box 2126, Ranchos de Taos; (575) 758-4000; desertblends .com. These lovely organic Ayurvedic skin care and body lotions are professionally formulated from local desert sage and other herbs and are found in several local lodgings. They can be bought at stores in Taos, Santa Fe, and Albuquerque or online.

Las Comadres Gallery. 120 Bent St., Ste. G; (575) 737-5323; lascomadresgallery.com. This women-owned-and-operated artists' cooperative offers a wide selection of pastels, oils, watercolors, print and mixed media, silver jewelry and beadwork, tinwork, weaving, ceramics, mosaics, glass, and photography at reasonable prices. The professional artists have exhibited at the New Mexico Art Museum in Santa Fe and other major New Mexico venues. Open 10 a.m. to 6 p.m. daily.

Mirabal Music Flutes and Native Gifts. Two locations: 216 Paseo del Pueblo Norte, in Yucca Plaza opposite Kit Carson Park in downtown Taos, and in the village at Taos Pueblo; (575) 751-1143. Grammy Award–winning Taos Pueblo musician and storyteller Robert Mirabal's entrancing contemporary sound is woven around his haunting flute music, rock instruments, and vocals sung in English and Tiwa. CDs, DVDs, books, flutes designed by Mirabal, rattles, drums, Indian jewelry, and apparel are on sale at both locations. Downtown shop open daily 10 a.m. to 6 p.m. spring and summer, 9 a.m. to 5 p.m. fall and winter; pueblo shop open May through Nov only, 8:30 a.m. to 4:30 p.m.

Op Cit Books. 124A Bent St., #6 Dunn House; (575) 751-1999; opcit.com. Step into Op Cit Books in the former Moby Dickens Bookstore and see why independent bookstores like this still thrive. You'll find new and used titles and regular author readings and signings. There is a second branch in Santa Fe in De Vargas Mall. Open daily 10 a.m. to 6 p.m.

R. C. Gorman Navajo Gallery. 104 S. Plaza; (575) 758-3250; rcgormannavajogallery.com. The late R. C. Gorman's elegant depictions of Navajo women are instantly recognizable. The gallery and store, once in his former home and studio but now on Taos Plaza near the La Fonda Hotel, sells original paintings, signed posters and limited-edition prints, and sculptures. Open Mon through Sat 11 a.m. to 5 p.m.

Taos Drum Company. 3956 SR 68, 5 miles south of Taos Plaza; (575) 758-3786; taos drums.com. The sound of drums can be heard throughout Taos—buy one to take home at this factory south of town. Handmade drums of all sizes hand-painted in traditional Native American style are for sale. Open daily 10 a.m. to 5 p.m.

Taos Healing Arts. 308B Paseo del Pueblo Norte at Duane Street; (575) 758-7975; taoshealingarts.com. The therapists at this well-regarded massage practice have decades of experience in healing bodywork. Modalities include deep tissue, hot stone, facials, craniosacral therapy, and Ayurvedic shirodara hot-oil treatments. Hours vary; call for appointment.

where to eat

Gutiz. 812B Paseo del Pueblo Norte; (575) 758-1226; gutiztaos.com. This Latin American–French country restaurant on the north side suffers not a jot from its lowly setting next to an oil lube spot. That's because there's a passionate chef-owner in the kitchen, confidently creating clean, fresh-tasting food that makes your taste buds sigh with pleasure. At breakfast, try a French crepe, a Spanish tortilla, or a breakfast bean bowl with beans, potatoes, rice, red and green chile, cheese, and an egg on top or andouille sausage. At lunch, there are a variety of tapas for lighter appetites and entrees that range from the novel, such as Drunken Chicken, to classic salade Niçoise and croque monsieur or madame. Homemade mint lemonade is refreshing, or try the house hot chocolate on a chilly day. Open Tues through Sun 8 a.m. to 3 p.m. $–$$.

Love Apple. 803 Paseo del Pueblo Norte, El Prado; (575) 751-0050; theloveapple.net. Proving that good food is, indeed, a religious experience, this tiny restaurant in an old church in El Prado serves regional food that honors both its origins and spirit. The food is 70 percent local and organic, including Shepherd's lamb, Pecos Valley grass-fed beef, and Taos-raised produce and honey, all of it prepared with a lot of heart and reasonably priced. Try a salad of local greens to start, followed by Love Apple tacos or a tamale with Oaxacan mole sauce. This is where the chefs eat out. No credit cards. Open for dinner only Tues through Sat 5 p.m. to close; reservations recommended. $$.

Orlando's New Mexican Cafe. 1114 Juan Valdez Ln., El Prado; (575) 751-1450; orlandos taos.com. This family-run spot has a pretty courtyard and is THE place for authentic New

Mexican food. Try Los Colores: three blue corn tortilla enchiladas—chicken, beef, and cheese—served with beans and posole (hominy stew), a regional dish that is easier to find in Taos than elsewhere in northern New Mexico. A friendly, upbeat place that won't break the bank. Open daily 10:30 a.m. to 3 p.m.; dinner Fri through Mon 5 to 9 p.m. $.

Wild Leaven Bakery. 216 Paseo del Pueblo Norte; (575) 758-4453; facebook.com/wild leavenbakery. Andre Kempton started on his bread-making journey in Santa Fe under the tutelage of Buddhist master baker Willem Malten at famed Cloud Cliff Bakery. Going solo, he began grinding his own flour and using sourdough techniques to create delicious, wholesome German-style breads and now has his own bakery in Taos. In addition to hand-sliced loaves of sourdough wheat, rye, quinoa/sunflower, buckwheat, and nutty brot-style breads, he offers a tasty daily homemade soup with choice of bread, healthy little pizzas, and unusual stuffed croissants, so you can eat a spot of lunch here while picking up bakery items. Andre sells at the Taos Farmers Market in Kit Carson Park on Saturday mornings in summer, and the bread is sold in Santa Fe at Natural Grocers and La Montanita Coop. The store is set back a bit, just north of the park on the other side of the road. Open Tues through Fri 9 a.m. to 3 p.m. and Sat 9 a.m. to 1 p.m. $.

where to stay

El Monte Sagrado Living Resort and Spa. 317 Kit Carson Rd.; (855) 846-8267; elmonte sagrado.com. This chic eco-resort raised the bar on sustainability when it was built in 2003. Buildings occupy a small footprint and are made from recycled materials. An elaborate water purification system recycles water through lush plantings and rock waterfalls, offering the soothing sound of water throughout the hotel. Each of the 89 guest rooms, suites, and casitas feels like a sanctuary, with an aesthetic drawn from around the world. Amenities include gas-fired kiva fireplaces, soaking tubs, Desert Blends organic toiletries, BOSE radio/CD players, free Wi-Fi, patios or private courtyards, and luxury linens. The spa offers special-ized treatments such as oxygenating, remineralizing, and remoisturizing facials; de-stressing massages; and craniosacral therapy. The lovely De La Tierra Restaurant offers New Mexi-can and American favorites at breakfast and lunch, and for dinner, a sophisticated Modern Western menu that includes elk short ribs, lobster bucatini, tea-smoked duck, Berkshire pork belly, and salmon with a prickly pear glaze. $$$–$$$$.

Historic Taos Inn. 125 Paseo del Pueblo Norte; (575) 758-2233, (888) 518-8627; taosinn .com. Opened in 1936, this Pueblo Revival–style inn incorporates 19th-century family ado-bes on a historic *placita* and is also famous as the place where the Taos Society of Artists was founded. The 45 guest rooms exude New Mexico style, and many have kiva fireplaces. The cozy on-site restaurant, Doc Martin's, is reliably good. It has an award-winning wine list and offers locally sourced fare such as bison and elk, house-grown greens, and wild Alaskan salmon in season, all at a reasonable price. The Adobe Bar in the lobby is the best place in town to meet locals and hear live music by talented Taos musicians. $–$$.

Mabel Dodge Luhan House and Conference Center. 240 Morada Ln., off Kit Carson Road; (575) 751-9686; mabeldodgeluhan.com. A must for creatives, this atmospheric historic *hacienda* near downtown Taos is not so much a bed-and-breakfast as a full-blown experience. It was built by New York salon hostess Mabel Dodge Luhan and her Taos Pueblo husband, Tony, between 1918 and 1922, and over 40 years some of the world's most celebrated artists, writers, and social reformers stayed here, including Georgia O'Keeffe, Carl Jung, and D. H. Lawrence. The 21 spartan but classic rooms these luminaries occupied are available to overnight guests and those attending popular residential workshops on meditation, writing, and art. Mabel and Tony's quarters, in a solarium atop the house, include use of a unique bathroom with claw-foot tub and windows painted by D. H. Lawrence. For privacy to read, write, and reflect, consider the lovely high-ceiling Robinson Jeffers Room or the Ansel Adams Room, which was commandeered by *Easy Rider* director Dennis Hopper, who bought the property when he moved here as part of Taos's counterculture movement in the 1960s. Mabel's spirit is most evident at breakfast, when guests unite in the original dining room for conversation over gourmet breakfasts lovingly created by resident cook Melody Sayre; workshop participants also enjoy fabulous lunches and dinners, an added incentive to sign up for a weekend retreat here. Rooms have private or shared bathrooms and some have fireplaces. A cottage has a kitchenette; newer rooms are available in the conference center. No phones, TVs, or radios; Wi-Fi in lobby only. Well-stocked on-site bookstore. $–$$.

day trip 06

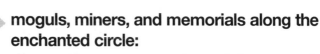
northeast

>>>

moguls, miners, and memorials along the enchanted circle:
rio grande gorge, questa, red river, angel fire, taos canyon

The 86-mile scenic loop via SR 522, SR 38, and US 64 around Mount Wheeler, New Mexico's highest mountain, offers a long, quiet drive through spectacular alpine scenery. The route takes in the Upper Gorge of the Rio Grande; the Red River and Angel Fire ski resorts; Elizabethtown, a mining ghost town; historic high-country vistas; and narrow, winding Taos Canyon, a haven for artists. The two attractions you shouldn't miss are memorials. The D. H. Lawrence Memorial sits on the beautiful Lawrence Ranch above San Cristobal. Four decades before the Summer of Love brought Dennis Hopper and other hippies to Taos, Lawrence and four others experimented with communal living here. Lawrence never got over his time in New Mexico and wrote about it in several novels and essays. "There is something savage and unbreakable in the spirit of the place out here," he wrote. "It is good to be alone and responsible. But it is also very hard living up against these savage Rockies." The elegant Vietnam Veterans Memorial State Park, near Angel Fire, was also built privately—by the grief-stricken father of a young man killed in the Vietnam War. For very different reasons, these simple memorials deserve a special pilgrimage.

rio grande gorge

The Rio Grande rises in Colorado's San Juan Mountains and journeys 1,900 miles through central New Mexico en route to the Gulf of Mexico. Its most dramatic expression may well

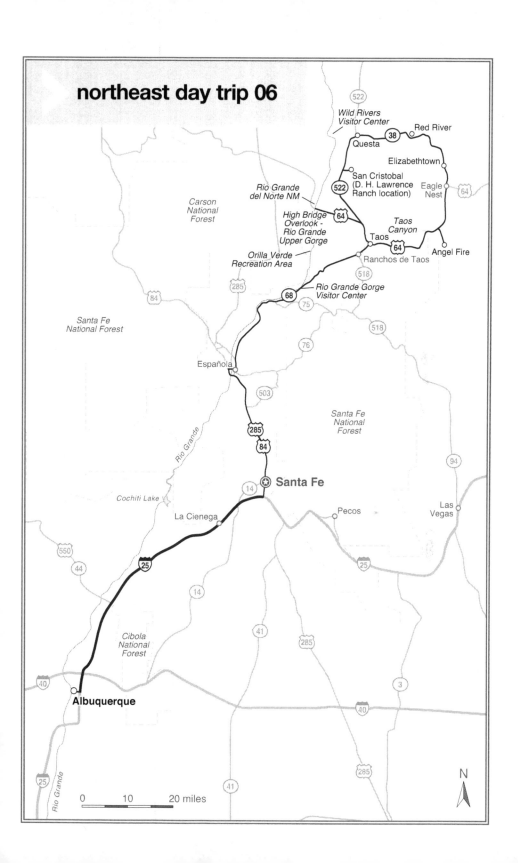

northeast day trip 06

522

Wild Rivers
Visitor Center

Red River

38

Questa

Elizabethtown

Rio Grande
del Norte NM

San Cristobal
(D. H. Lawrence
Ranch location)

Eagle
Nest

522

64

High Bridge
Overlook -
Rio Grande
Upper Gorge

Taos
Canyon

Orilla Verde
Recreation Area

Taos

Ranchos de Taos

64

Angel Fire

285

68

Rio Grande Gorge
Visitor Center

75

518

Carson
National
Forest

84

Santa Fe
National Forest

Española

503

76

518

Rio Grande

285

84

Santa Fe
National
Forest

94

14

Santa Fe

Cochiti Lake

La Cienega

Pecos

Las
Vegas

550

44

25

25

14

41

285

Cibola
National
Forest

40

Albuquerque

94

41

3

40

25

Rio Grande

285

N

0   10   20 miles

> ## d. h. lawrence ranch

Drive north from Taos for 20 miles on SR 522 to San Cristobal, then make a right and drive a few miles up Lobo Mountain to reach the Lawrence Ranch. The 160-acre former Kiowa Ranch was given to D. H. Lawrence by his patron Mabel Dodge Luhan in 1924, after he returned to Taos to start a utopian community called Rananim. Over the next 14 months, Lawrence, his wife Frieda, and their only convert, painter Lady Dorothy Brett, together with Trinidad Archuleta (the nephew of Mabel's Taos Pueblo husband, Tony Luhan) and his wife, attempted a back-to-the-land experiment in these beautiful forested foothills. It ended when Lawrence was diagnosed with tuberculosis and returned to Europe, where he died in Vence, France, in 1930. The ranch was willed to the University of New Mexico by Frieda Lawrence and remains an oasis of natural calm in a busy world. People make pilgrimages here from all over the world and leave moving personal poems, letters, flowers, and comments in a small visitor book inside the memorial.

In 2014 the university reached an agreement with the D. H. Lawrence Alliance to restore and reopen the ranch to visitors after an extended closure. The alliance is part of the Taos Community Foundation and is a multicultural group of local residents and Lawrence admirers wishing to see Lawrence's legacy continued in Taos; a grant from the foundation has allowed for a docent program to begin and tours to be given on the property, as well as restoration of certain buildings. The

be in the volcanic gorge that pierces the high Taos Plateau, where the river occupies a geological rift 800 feet deep. Most people drive west a little way on US 64 to the vertiginous High Bridge Overlook over the Upper Gorge to view the lively river dancing through this dark slash in the earth. With more time, you can hike, camp, and raft the Taos Box at Wild Rivers Recreation Area, part of Rio Grande del Norte National Monument, west of Questa.

where to go

High Bridge Overlook. The 650-foot-high bridge over the gorge, the second-highest suspension bridge in the nation, was dubbed the "Bridge to Nowhere" when it was built in 1965 because the road ended on the other side of the gorge. Today, US 64 continues across the plateau to Tres Piedras and Tierra Amarilla into Georgia O'Keeffe Country (Northwest Day Trip 05) around Abiquiu and Ojo Caliente Hot Springs. Be careful walking on the footbridge; winds really whip here. Parking available on the east end.

ranch is now open year-round Thurs and Fri from 10 a.m. to 2 p.m. and Sat from 10 a.m. to 4 p.m., weather permitting; there is no admission charge; (575) 770-4830; dhlawrenceranch.unm.edu.

The Lawrence Memorial. *Park in the designated area next to the corral, and take a self-guided tour (information plaques are situated around the property). A winding pathway leads up to the Lawrence shrine, a charming whitewashed building at a natural break in the forest, which offers spectacular views of the Rio Grande Plateau. Frieda's lover Angelo Ravagli buried her outside the memorial. Lawrence's ashes are interred inside. Frieda claimed to have mixed them into the concrete she used to create the altar to stop fans from stealing them (the misadventures of bringing Lawrence's ashes back from Vence is a story in itself). Note Lawrence's trademark phoenix on the roof and sunflowers on the altar.*

Lawrence Cabin. *The rough homesteader cabins in which "Brett" and Frieda and D. H. Lawrence lived are behind the caretaker's cabin. A painting of a buffalo by Trinidad Archuleta adorns the exterior of the Lawrence Cabin; it is shaded by a huge, gnarled ponderosa pine under which Lawrence wrote at a wooden table. The tree was later the subject of one of Georgia O'Keeffe's most famous paintings: 1929's The Lawrence Tree. The Lawrence Cabin is closed to visitors, but you can go inside the tiny cabin where the profoundly deaf Brett typed Lawrence's manuscripts. She stayed in Taos and became a beloved founding member of the Taos Society of Artists.*

questa

The quiet artsy village of Questa is in a naturally lovely spot near the conjunction of the Rio Grande and Red River. These rivers were among the first in the nation to be designated "Wild and Scenic Rivers" in 1968. Wild Rivers Recreation Area, now folded into Rio Grande del Norte National Monument, one of the state's newest national monuments, is a popular destination for hiking, camping, river rafting, and its scenic drive.

where to go

Wild Rivers Recreation Area, Rio Grande del Norte National Monument. 1120 Cerro Rd., Cerro; (575) 758-8851; blm.gov/visit/wild-rivers-recreation-area. Wild Rivers Backcountry Byway follows the rim of the gorge for 22 miles and offers great scenery and photo and wildlife-viewing opportunities as well as access to 5 developed campgrounds, primitive hike-in campsites within the gorge, and 10 hiking and mountain-biking rim and river trails. Rafting in the whitewater conditions is dangerous; it should only be undertaken with an outfitter (see

Northeast Day Trip 03). Rim trails are best for beginners; hiking in and out of the 800-foot-deep gorge is only for the very fit. The visitor center in Cerro has information, permits, and exhibits on the geology. To reach it, drive 3 miles north of Questa on SR 522, turn west on SR 378, and continue for 17 miles. The visitor center is open Memorial Day to Labor Day, 9 a.m. to 6 p.m. Call for hours off-season. The recreation area is open for day use 6 a.m. to 10 p.m. Low use fees for camping and other activities.

red river

Red River was founded as a mining town in 1892, and the community reinvented itself as an old-fashioned family-oriented ski resort in 1959. There's a fun, theme-park, Old West meets Switzerland flavor to Main Street, which features plenty of homegrown saloon bars and cafes, steakhouses, and entertainments. In summer, there are scenic chairlift rides, jeep tours, horseback riding, camping, hiking, biking, fishing, and a Hot Blues and Cold Brews Festival that features great blues music and microbrew beer. Red River has plenty of parking, lodgings are all within walking distance of the ski slopes, and best of all, it's much less expensive than other ski resorts in the Rockies.

where to go

Enchanted Forest Cross Country Ski and Snowshoe Area. 29 Sangre de Cristo Dr., off SR 38; (575) 754-6112; enchantedforestxc.com. You'll find 17 miles of beautifully groomed cross-country trails at Enchanted Forest, a 5-minute drive east of Red River. Trails are groomed for both classic and freestyle cross-country skiing, and there is a separate area for snowshoeing. Special events include a Christmas Eve Luminaria Ski Tour, a magical skiing experience amid glowing candle lanterns. Yurt rentals are available in summer. Open 9 a.m. to 4:30 p.m. daily, Thanksgiving to Apr. Admission fee.

Red River Ski and Snowboard Area. 400 Pioneer Rd., off SR 38; (575) 754-2223; redriver skiarea.com. This folksy ski resort on Black Mountain has been voted New Mexico's best ski area for families. It has 64 trails—evenly divided among expert, intermediate, and beginner—and 3 mountain restaurants. Seven lifts have a capacity of 7,920 per hour, second only to Taos. There's a separate terrain park for snowboarders. Kids have their own ski and other chaperoned activities, including a ski-in miners' camp complete with cabin and tepee. Open 9 a.m. to 4 p.m. daily, Thanksgiving to the third week in March. Admission fee.

where to eat

Capo's Corner. 110 Pioneer Rd.; (575) 754-6297. This longtime favorite Italian restaurant serves pasta with homemade green chile and other sauces and steak and seafood. For a light bite, try a bowl of fresh minestrone and a sandwich, pizza, or calzone. Open daily for lunch 11:30 a.m. to 2 p.m. and dinner 5 to 9 p.m. during fall, winter, and summer seasons; during slow spring season, Apr and May, open Wed through Mon for dinner only. $–$$$.

Texas Reds Steakhouse. 400 E. Main St.; (575) 754-2922; texasreds.com. Steak is the highlight of this Red River classic restaurant, which has been in business 47 years, but you can also find good poultry, fish, and game meats like bison and elk. After a fire burned down its historic building in 2004, the restaurant moved across the street into the Lodge at Red River; however, its down-home flavor, complete with gingham tablecloths, still reigns. Open for lunch from 11:30 a.m. on and dinner 4:30 to 9 p.m. during fall, winter, and summer seasons and spring break. $$–$$$.

where to stay

Three Bears Lodge. 301 E. Main; (575) 754-2272, (800) 548-5713; 3bearsrr.com. This quaint budget resort offers traditional pine-clad cabins. One-bedroom efficiencies have bathrooms and fridges, microwaves, and coffeemakers; two- and three-bedroom cabins have living rooms, fireplaces, kitchens, and futon couches. Rooms have flat-screen TVs with cable and Wi-Fi. Fire pit. $.

angel fire

The beautiful high country around the 15-mile-long Moreno Valley was originally part of the 1.7-million-acre Maxwell Land Grant, given to mountain man and trader Lucien Maxwell in 1864 on former Moache Ute and Jicarilla Apache territory (see Northeast Day Trip 02). When gold was discovered by prospectors in 1867, thousands of illegal homesteaders flooded into the area and founded Elizabethtown, a typical rowdy mining boomtown. Charles and Frank Springer, owners of the CS Ranch, harnessed the wild Cimarron River for irrigation purposes in 1918, creating Eagle Nest Lake. The lake adjoins the small village of Eagle Nest, which has food, lodging, and visitor services. The LeBus brothers from Texas bought the 9,000-acre Monte Verde Ranch in 1954, and 10 years later began converting it to a ski resort community called Angel Fire, a name Kit Carson gave the area.

where to go

Angel Fire Ski Resort. 10 Miller Ln., off SR 434; (800) 633-7463; angelfireresort.com. This resort has 80 runs and 3 terrain parks for skiers and snowboarders as well as a half-pipe—21 percent beginner, 56 percent intermediate, and 23 percent advanced. Of the 7 lifts, 2 are high-speed detachable quad chairlifts, the fastest in New Mexico. Angel Fire offers a money-back guarantee to skiers for both lift tickets and lessons: If you don't like conditions, report back within an hour of buying your ticket and you'll get a free return ticket. Golf, fishing, mountain biking, tennis, boating, and other special events are available in summer at this year-round resort.

> ## elizabethtown

Elizabethtown *is a mining ghost town, 4.8 miles north of Eagle Nest. It once had a population of 7,000 but has now fallen into ruin, with few residents. After the wooden town burned down in 1903, residents rebuilt it using brick, but it was never the same again. The most intact building is the Mutz Hotel, visible from SR 38. You can stop and wander around anytime. A descendant of one of the early "E-Town" residents has established a small museum (575-377-3420) near the hotel. It displays artifacts, a video about the town, and a gift store. Gold Rush Days takes place July 3–5 annually and includes a trade fair and entertainment. The museum is open daily Memorial Day to Labor Day 10 a.m. to 5 p.m. and by appointment thereafter.*

Eagle Nest Lake State Park. 42 Marina Way; (575) 377-1594; emnrd.state.nm.us/SPD/EaglesNest.htm. This 2,200-acre high-country lake is brimming with kokanee salmon and rainbow trout and popular with anglers (including for winter ice fishing), boaters, campers, winter snowmobilers, and wildlife enthusiasts who come here to view elk, deer, bald eagles, and other wildlife. A state-of-the-art "green" visitor center has interpretive exhibits, a classroom, and patio overlooking the lake. The campground has 19 campsites, a vault toilet, and water; 6 sites are reservable and the rest are first come, first served. Boat ramps open in season. Open for day use only, 6 a.m. to 9 p.m.

where to eat

The following restaurants are all at Angel Fire Resort (angelfireresort.com/dining). They cover the bases of just about anything you might be in the mood to eat.

Chianti's Buffet. (575) 377-4203. Located on the second level of the lodge, Chianti's offers a revolving variety of buffet options, including Asian, Italian, and Texan. Open Fri and Sat 4 to 9 p.m. $–$$.

Elements Fine Dining at the Country Club. (575) 377-3055. Steak, game, poultry, seafood, and vegetarian dishes sourced locally are on the menu at Angel Fire Lodge's main sit-down restaurant upstairs. It has a nice contemporary feel and is a good place for a celebratory meal. Nightly specials include prime rib and dry-rubbed steaks as well as elk. Reservations suggested. The more affordable bar and lounge menu features upscale pub food, such as truffle fries, crab cakes, pot stickers, fish-and-chips, steak frites, gourmet burgers, and chili made from slow-cooked Wagyu beef spare ribs. Award-winning wine list. Open year-round Tues through Sat 5 to 9 p.m. $–$$$.

The Lift Café. Open for breakfast, lunch, and dinner, this local meeting spot is in the lobby of the lodge. It serves hot drinks and ice cream, as well as breakfast burritos, bagels, and pastries, and quiches, soups, and salads for lunch and dinner. Open daily 7:30 a.m. to lodge closing. $.

The Summit Haus. (575) 377-4371. Located by the Chile Express Chair Lift on the summit, this eatery serves burgers, sausages, and other standards. Full bar and patio. Open 10 a.m. to 3:30 p.m. Dec to Mar. $.

The Village Haus. (575) 377-4242. This family-friendly cafeteria-style restaurant at the Mountain Base Area is open for breakfast and lunch daily 8 a.m. to 4 p.m. Dec to Mar. $.

where to stay

The Lodge at Angel Fire Resort. 10 Miller Ln., off SR 434; (800) 633-7463; angelfireresort .com. This beautiful glass-and-timber ski lodge has rooms and suites mere steps from the chairlift. Each attractive New Mexico–style room has two queen-size beds, a refrigerator, coffeemaker, and pay-per-view cable TV; suites have sitting areas with couches and fireplaces, robes, and other luxury extras. Indoor pool, hot tub, fitness classes, restaurants, and shops. Free Wi-Fi. Pet-friendly. $$–$$$$.

vietnam memorial

Vietnam Veterans Memorial State Park. *Angel Fire turnoff; (575) 377-6900; angelfirememorial.com. This poignant memorial was funded and built by Dr. Victor and Jeanne Westphall in 1971 to honor the memory of their son David, who was killed with 15 comrades in Vietnam in 1968. Although modern, it has a lot in common with the Lawrence Memorial: It's in a haunting whitewashed building whose design references the stunning natural beauty of its site and is shaped like a dove's folded wings. The Peace and Brotherhood Chapel, with its small altar, photos of the deceased, and meditation cushions, invites contemplation. The newly renovated visitor center has a state-of-the-art museum, which offers a timeline of events, information on the Westphalls, and a multimedia presentation that tells both sides of the conflict and elegantly presents a pacifist message. Make time to watch the excellent PBS documentary about the Vietnamese experience. It uses home movies, soldiers' letters home, and contemporary music to pack a powerful punch. Free. Open daily 9 a.m. to 5 p.m.*

Rental Condominiums and Homes at Angel Fire Resort. (800) 633-7463; angel fireresort.com. Slopeside and nearby rental units, from studios to beautifully furnished Southwest-style homes, may be rented through the resort. Guests check in at the lodge's front desk and have full access to all lodge amenities. $–$$$$.

taos canyon

US 64 continues east through beautiful forested high country. It descends through steep Cimarron Canyon, with its Wild West feel and nature reserves, to pick up I-25 between Las Vegas and Raton (see Northeast Day Trip 02). Returning west to Taos on US 64, the highway winds through narrow Taos Canyon, following the Rio Fernando de Taos. Parts of the route are in Carson National Forest, and you'll find primitive campgrounds, hiking trails, and good birding. This is the place where Taos Society of Artists founders Bert Phillips and Ernest Blumenschein broke a wagon wheel while visiting the area. A number of artists live in Taos Canyon and are part of the annual Labor Day weekend Taos Studio Tour sponsored by the Taos Artist Organization.

where to shop

Dawn Chandler, Taos Dawn Designs Gallery. US 64, #26068; (575) 737-9293; taos dawn.com. Dawn Chandler's meditative paintings evoke connections between the feminine and the land and are very peaceful, reflecting the artist's use of painting as daily meditative practice. She exhibits at local venues and sells online and at her gallery. Her studio is usually part of the Taos Studio Tour. Call ahead for gallery hours.

Ron Cline, Enchanted Mountain Woodworks Gallery and Workshop. US 64, #26558; (575) 751-7223; taosartistorg.org. Ron Cline produces gorgeous, highly polished carved-wood sculptural forms, including containers and furniture. His work has won many awards, including Best of Furniture in the 2003 Taos Open and Third Place in the 2007 Taos Invites Taos art competitions. He, too, is usually part of the Taos Studio Tour. Open daily 8 a.m. to 6 p.m.

east

day trip 01

east

>>> **from clovis man to buddy holly on route 66:**
edgewood, clines corners, santa rosa,
fort sumner, clovis, portales, tucumcari

This day trip follows Historic Route 66 east along I-40, over the mountains and onto the dusty plains. It's flat, featureless ranch country, with big skies and dramatic storms in summer (sometimes with tornadoes). The endless highway and monotony of the desert encourage daydreams. Along with tough realists eking a living from the land, you may meet a few dreamers on Route 66—friendly folks who are determined to keep alive the unpretentious hometown hospitality and roadside attractions of the Mother Road. At Fort Sumner (Bosque Redondo) on US 60, you can visit the grave of Billy the Kid and learn about the fort's sad history as a prison camp for Navajos and Apaches during the Long Walk period (1863–68). For music buffs, the town of Clovis is better known as the hometown of Norman Petty, the local musician who discovered Buddy Holly, Roy Orbison, and other musicians and recorded them in his home studio in the '50s. Eastern New Mexico University in Portales is known for its archeology program, after the oldest evidence of early man in North America, the Clovis culture, was found at Blackwater Draw in the 1930s. Route 66 buffs will want to visit Tucumcari, famous for its classic Route 66 motels and neon.

edgewood

Edgewood is off I-40 on the other side of the Sandia Mountains, about 20 minutes east of Albuquerque. Its main attraction is Wildlife West Nature Park, a 122-acre sanctuary that cares for injured and problem animals that cannot be released back into the wild.

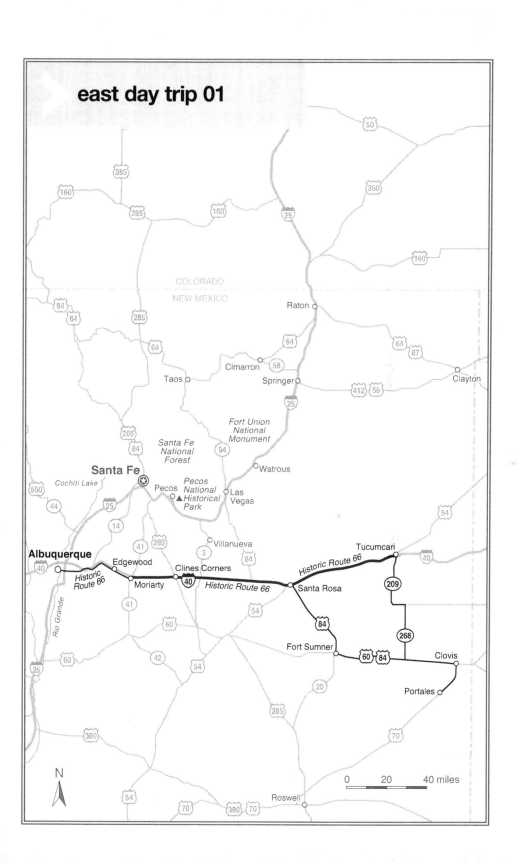

east day trip 01

> ## moriarty
>
> *The longest remaining stretch of Route 66 in New Mexico ran right through the center of the Estancia Basin community of Moriarty, hopefully nicknamed the "Crossroads of Opportunity." Nostalgic reminders of the Mother Road (the name first appeared in John Steinbeck's Depression-era story of dustbowl migrants, The Grapes of Wrath) include a Whiting Brothers Gas Station and the huge 1960s "rotosphere" rotating neon Sputnik sign on top of the building housing El Comedor de Anayas, a restaurant run for 60 years by the Anayas family (now sadly closed). Moriarty is 35 miles east of Albuquerque and south of the junction with NM 14, the Turquoise Trail (see Northeast Day Trip 01). Rotospheres were created and produced by Warren Milks between 1960 and 1971, and there are only 264 of them in the country. The one atop the former El Comedor de Anayas is one of nine vintage neon signs to has been restored in 2003 using grant money. It is thought to be the only working rotosphere on Route 66 but rotates no more.*

where to go

Wildlife West Nature Park. 87 North Frontage Rd.; (505) 281-7655, (877) 981-9453; wildlifewest.org. Wildlife West's residents include black bears, pronghorn, elk, bobcats, mountain lions, coyotes, Mexican wolves, and a variety of raptors. Many animals take part in educational presentations, and there are special programs such as Zookeeper for the Day, docent and keeper training, bird handling, and wildlife field trips to the nearby Manzano Mountains. The 30 exhibits are connected by 2 miles of trails. An amphitheater hosts concerts, fairs, and special events such as chuckwagon suppers offered every Sat in summer. Open mid-Mar through Oct 10 a.m. to 6 p.m., Nov through mid-Mar noon to 4 p.m. Admission fee.

clines corners

Located at the junction of I-40 with US 285, Clines Corners is an eye-catching historic roadside attraction built in 1937 by entrepreneur Roy Clines. It's 50 miles in any direction to the next main town from here, making this a popular place to stop and get gas.

where to shop

Clines Corners Retail Center. 1 Yacht Club Dr.; (505) 472-5488; clinescorners.com. Originally a filling station and cafe selling curios on Historic Route 66, Clines Corners is typical of the kind of smorgasbord retail emporium you see all along I-40/Route 66 out West. The retail area is huge and has a convenience store, a Subway sandwich shop, and a homemade fudge counter. Its curio shop is the largest in New Mexico and sells everything from Indian art, buckskin clothing, and toy guns to kitsch snow globes and Kokopellis (the humpbacked traveling flute player so ubiquitous throughout the Southwest). Phillips 66 gas and diesel pumps are in the forecourt.

santa rosa

Santa Rosa is on the Pecos River, 122 miles from Albuquerque. Built in 1824 on a Spanish land grant and known as the "City of Natural Lakes" for its 12 spring-fed lakes, it makes a good place to cool off in summer. Blue Hole's clear, deep, and blue waters have made it a mecca for divers. Park Lake, the town swimming pool, was constructed in the 1930s under the Works Progress Administration (WPA) program. Santa Rosa Lake State Park has developed camping. With its classic Thunderbirds and Corvettes, Route 66 Auto Museum is one of the town's biggest draws. A Route 66 Festival is held here every September.

where to go

Blue Hole. 1085 Blue Hole Rd.; (575) 472-3763 (on-site dive shop); visitsantarosanm.com. Reminiscent of Mexico's beguiling *cenotes*, the flooded limestone sinkholes on the Yucatán Peninsula, Blue Hole is famous for its diving. Aquifer springs pumping out 3,000 gallons of freshwater per day keep this 80-foot-deep hole topped up with unbelievably clear 64-degree water, and it's just really cool to dive in the desert. Blue Hole is in Santa Rosa, off Route 66, just minutes from downtown, and open 24 hours a day. A dive shop on the premises sells permits and rents gear; you can also get a permit in advance through **Santa Rosa Visitor Center** (244 S. 4th St.; 575-472-3763; visitsantarosanm.org) or, in the same building, through **Santa Rosa City Hall** (575-472-3404; srnm.org). Note: You must have current dive certification and insurance to dive at Blue Hole. The dive shop is open Mon through Fri 8 a.m. to 5 p.m., 7 a.m. to 3 p.m. on weekends.

Route 66 Auto Museum. 2436 Route 66; (575) 472-1966; route66automuseum.net. There are 30 classic, vintage, and hot-rod cars on display and an array of Route 66 memorabilia at this fun hometown homage to the Mother Road owned by the Cordova family, who also restore and sell classic cars. Gift shop and snack bar on premises. Open daily 7:30 a.m. to 6 p.m. Admission fee.

Santa Rosa Lake State Park. SR 91; (575) 472-3110; emnrd.state.nm.us/SPD/santarosa lakestatepark.html. This 3,800-acre reservoir, created by damming the Pecos River for flood-control purposes, has sailing, motorboating, fishing, waterskiing, swimming, hiking, and camping. Visitor center, children's playground, restrooms, water, and a campground with 52 developed campsites and 17 primitive campsites; 13 may be reserved online. Admission fee.

where to eat

Encino Firehouse Mercantile and Deli. 121 W. US 285, Encino; (575) 584-9111; facebook.com/theencinofirehouse. Located 54 miles southwest of Santa Rosa, but a straight shot south on US 285 from Clines Corners, near Vaughn, this back-road family-run place is a nice find in the sticks if you decide to take a shortcut southeast across the Estancia Basin. They specialize in fresh comfort food using locally sourced ingredients at a bargain price in a converted firehouse setting, and what's not to love about that? The menu features burgers, pizza, barbecue, sandwiches, handmade tamales and tacos, and fresh pie. Try the barbecue brisket sandwich or perhaps the taco plate with pulled pork. Note: The eatery is up for sale at the time of this writing, so check for updates. Open Tues through Fri 11 a.m. to 3 p.m.

Joseph's Bar and Grill. 865 Route 66; (575) 472-3361. They serve big helpings of American and Mexican food at this historic joint, which has been run by the Campos family since 1956. It's the perfect choice for fajitas or a burger and fries while touring the Mother Road. Check out the historic "fat man" sign above the door. It was moved here from the nearby Club Cafe, a Route 66 landmark since 1935 that closed its doors in 1991. There's also a curio shop and bar/lounge. Things move a bit slowly here; expect a wait. Open Sun through Thurs 11 a.m. to 9 p.m., Fri and Sat 11 a.m. to 10 p.m. $–$$.

fort sumner

From Santa Rosa, take exit 277 off I-40 and head south on US 84 to Fort Sumner. Located on the banks of the Pecos River, Fort Sumner was the administrative center for the million-acre Bosque Redondo Indian Reservation, where 9,000 Navajos and Mescalero Apaches were forcibly held by the US Army between 1863 and 1868. It was a concentration camp in all but name. If they survived death and slave traders on the 300-mile Long Walk, Navajos were required to scrabble for survival, living in holes in the ground, drinking non-potable water from the river, and trying to farm non-friable land and clothe themselves using old flour sacks and materials given to them by army wives. Appalled by the conditions, most of the 400 Apaches had escaped by 1865. Of the remaining Navajo captives, one-third died of starvation and illness before the army admitted it had made a serious error and allowed them to return home to a newly created reservation.

Fort Sumner also held another famous captive: Lincoln County outlaw William Bonney, aka Billy the Kid, who was kept in a variety of jails before he escaped near Fort Sumner in July 1881 and was shot down by Sheriff Pat Garrett. Fort Sumner has thrown in its lot with Billy the Kid. The Billy the Kid Museum has Kid memorabilia, and the Kid's grave is behind the former Fort Sumner Museum, 7 miles southeast of town.

where to go

Billy the Kid Gravesite. 3501 Billy the Kid Rd.; (575) 355-2942. We're led to believe that the grave out back of the former Fort Sumner Museum was Billy the Kid's, although numerous stories say that he may have escaped and a flood destroyed the original grave. The headstone has been stolen so often that the grave is now enclosed by a huge, very unphotogenic cage. It's all a bit forlorn.

Billy the Kid Museum. 1435 Sumner Ave.; (575) 355-2380; billythekidmuseumfortsumner .com. This family-run roadside attraction from the 1950s houses all kinds of dusty memorabilia collected by the Sweet family. Among its advertised "60,000 relics of the historic past" are Billy the Kid's rifle (with documentation). Open 8:30 a.m. to 5 p.m. daily; closed Sun in winter. Admission fee.

Fort Sumner Historic Site/Bosque Redondo Memorial. Billy the Kid Rd.; (575) 355-2573; bosqueredondomemorial.com. This state historic site has exhibits about the army fort, and you can walk the Old Fort Site Trail and 0.75-mile River Walk Trail. More importantly, though, a fitting memorial to the Navajos and Mescalero Apaches who were held here has now been built, in the form of a museum designed by Navajo architect David Sloan and shaped like a traditional Navajo hogan and Apache tepee. Inside, a film and interpretive exhibits tell the story of the Long Walk, and guides offer tours. Don't miss the large pile of stones outside the museum; they were carried from the Navajo reservation by relatives who have never forgotten what their ancestors endured and continue to keep their memory alive. Open Wed through Sun 8:30 a.m. to 4:30 p.m. Admission fee.

clovis

From Fort Sumner, continue east on US 84/60 to Clovis. This unremarkable town (pop. 39,000) is famous for two things: the Clovis culture archeological site at Blackwater Draw near Portales (see next section), which in the 1930s yielded the oldest arrowheads and water-control features ever discovered in North America, and the Norman Petty Recording Studios, which helped launch the career of Texas musician Buddy Holly in 1958.

where to go

Norman Petty Recording Studios. 1313 W. 7th St.; (575) 356-6422; norvajakmusic.com. Over one remarkable year—1958—Norman Petty launched the career of an unknown musician from Lubbock, Texas, named Buddy Holly with recordings like "That'll Be the Day," "Peggy Sue," and "Every Day." Petty and wife Vi were local musicians who began a recording studio in their Clovis home. With Holly's rise to fame, Petty also became his manager. It was while touring in 1959 that Holly was killed in an air crash. Petty went on to discover Roy Orbison, Roger Williams, Buddy Knox, and other musicians who recorded with him until his death in 1984. Kenneth Broad runs tours of the studio (there are no recording sessions here anymore) from his Portales home; call to book with him two weeks ahead of time. You'll see original equipment, musical instruments, and music awards; hear master recordings; and usually meet a musician who played with Holly. Reissues of Petty Productions through the Nor-Va-Jak Music label are available, as well as a documentary about the studios. Admission fee.

portales

Portales, a short drive south from Clovis on US 70, is the county seat of Roosevelt County, an area known for its Valencia peanuts. Its main cultural institution is Eastern New Mexico University, which serves local students and runs six good museums, five on its pleasant campus. The town has a seasonal farmers' market and a few bed-and-breakfasts. Nearby Oasis State Park is a lovely place to hike and camp.

where to go

Blackwater Draw National Historic Landmark and Museum. 508 SR 467; (575) 356-5235; bwdarchaeology.com. In the 1930s the finely worked arrowheads that were unearthed amid bones at this old gravel pit pushed back the date of early man in North America to 9,000–11,000 BC. Now a designated National Historic Landmark, 7 miles north of Portales, Blackwater Draw is open seasonally and has a visitor center with short films, dioramas, a timeline, and examples of Clovis spearpoints and bones. You can also visit a nearby excavation site. Blackwater Draw Museum (1500 S. Avenue K, Lea Hall, Rm. 163; 575-562-2202) is on the Eastern New Mexico University and contains artifacts from the excavation. During the ENMU semester, the campus museum is open Tues through Sat 10 a.m. to 5 p.m. and Sun noon to 5 p.m. The National Historic Landmark is open Memorial Day to the beginning of the semester Tues through Sun 9 a.m. to 4 p.m.; it is open Sat and Sun only Apr through May and Sept through Oct; closed Nov through Mar. Admission fee.

Eastern New Mexico University. 1500 S. Avenue K; (575) 562-1011; enmu.edu. ENMU opened in 1934 as a junior college serving this rural area. It was accredited as a four-year college in 1947 and is now the third-largest university in New Mexico. In addition to the off-site Blackwater Draw National Historic Landmark, ENMU's on-campus museums include the Blackwater Draw Museum, a history museum, geology museum, natural history museum, and science fiction library. Campus museums are open Mon through Fri 8 a.m. to 5 p.m. The Roosevelt County Historical Museum is also open Sat 10 a.m. to 4 p.m. and Sun 1 to 4 p.m. Free.

Oasis State Park. 1891 Oasis Rd.; (575) 356-5331; emnrd.state.nm.us/SPD/Oasis statepark.html. Located very close to Blackwater Draw on SR 467, this state park has a 3-acre pond among sandy dunes and cottonwoods and is a great spot for relaxing, hiking, picnicking, and fishing. The campground has 26 shady developed sites, 9 of which may be reserved. Admission fee.

where to eat

Cattle Baron Restaurant. 1600 S. Avenue D; (575) 356-5587. Within a stone's throw of the Texas border, this old-fashioned steakhouse is the original location in a chain of steakhouses in southeast New Mexico and west Texas. It is primarily geared toward those with a hankering for huge steaks and all the fixings, but you'll also find chicken, seafood, and pasta entrees for those with lighter appetites. Open Mon through Thurs 11 a.m. to 9 p.m., Fri and Sat 11 a.m. to 10 p.m., and Sun 11 a.m. to 9 p.m. $$.

Roosevelt Brewing Company. 201 S. Main St.; (575) 226-2739; rooseveltbrewing.com. This family-run brewpub is located in a century-old brick building downtown and offers good microbrews and pub food, including light snacks such as chile queso and truffle fries, beer-infused artisan cupcakes, wood-fired sourdough pizzas, handmade beef and bison burgers infused with beer, salads, and specialty sandwiches featuring slow-cooked and house-smoked meats. $–$$.

where to stay

Casa del Sol Bed and Breakfast. 1401 W. 17th St.; (575) 356-5966. Designed by Santa Fe style architect John Gaw Meem for Bartlett and Evelyn Dewey in the 1940s, this adobe *hacienda* is an authentic historic gem in Portales. Guest quarters are either a private suite in the main house or a lovely casita on the grounds; both have private baths, TVs, and Wi-Fi. Full breakfast included in the reasonable overnight rate. $.

tucumcari

After Portales, you can either continue south on US 70 to Roswell and make a long weekend of it, or head back to Albuquerque on I-40. Route 66 buffs won't want to leave the area, though, without visiting Tucumcari, famous for its classic Route 66 motels and neon. Tucumcari bills itself as having over 1,000 rooms, so you can be sure of finding somewhere to spend the night. It's known, though, for the Blue Swallow Motel, a classic motor-court motel that is famous for its hospitality and its large neon-lit sign. Now a National Historic Landmark, it was built in 1939 by W. A. Huggins and has had several owners. The best known is Lillian Redman, who was given the motel as an engagement present in 1958 and ran it for 40 years. The current owners have run the motel since 2004 and have renovated the rooms and maintain the tradition of friendly hospitality. To reach Tucumcari from Portales, travel north on US 70 back to Clovis, then follow US 84/60 west to SR 268 North. Follow SR 268 North to SR 209 North until you reach Tucumcari near I-40.

where to eat

Del's Restaurant and Gifts. 1201 E. Route 66; (575) 461-1740; delsrestaurant.com. Del's has been a popular local destination for steaks, seafood, pasta, and Mexican food since 1956. The chicken-fried steak is typical of the kind of home-cooked food that keeps the lines out the door. Open 11 a.m. to 9 p.m. daily. $–$$.

where to stay

Blue Swallow Motel. 815 E. Route 66; (575) 461-9899; blueswallowmotel.com. Rooms at this classic family-run motor-court motel on Route 66 are small and retro but authentically kitted out and full of ambiance. Each has a queen-size or double bed with candlewick bedspread, antique Southwest furnishings, shower, desk, and adjoining garage; suites have sitting areas. There are blue-painted rocking chairs out front. If you love Route 66, you'll want to stop here and swap stories with other travelers. Free Wi-Fi. Pet-friendly. $–$$.

southeast

day trip 01

southeast

the salt missions trail:
tijeras, tajique, manzano mountains, punta del agua, mountainair, belen, isleta pueblo

The quiet Estancia Basin is named for its ranches but was once better known for another important resource: salt. During the last ice age, the basin held a large lake frequented by mammoth and other big game that attracted paleo hunters. By the early Christian era, people of the Mogollon culture were living in pit houses here, followed 1,000 years later by Tiwa- and Tompiro-speaking Pueblo people from the north who built masonry villages and traded with Mogollon and Plains people along the southern cultural frontier. In the early 1600s, Spanish priests and colonists took over the pueblos for missions, using free Indian labor to build churches and to mine salt for trading with Mexico along El Camino Real. Drought, European diseases, overwork, famine, and Apache raiding doomed the whole enterprise. By 1677 the pueblos were empty, their residents dead or moved to Isleta Pueblo.

The highlights of this trip are great scenery, wildlife watching, and the pueblo missions of Quarai, Abó, and Gran Quivira, which are together protected as Salinas Pueblo Missions National Historical Park. The park headquarters and visitor center is in the ranch town of Mountainair. Mountainair is known for its pinto beans and the 1923 Shaffer Hotel, a classic of Pueblo Deco style—a brightly painted Southwestern take on stylized Art Deco, with Spanish Mission and Indian art influences—created by folk artist Pop Shaffer. To start the tour, drive east on I-40 and then turn south on SR 337, east of the Manzano Mountains, passing through Tijeras and Chilili. SR 337 seamlessly changes to SR 55, the main route west from Estancia, and continues to Tajique, Punta del Agua, and Mountainair, a major junction of SR

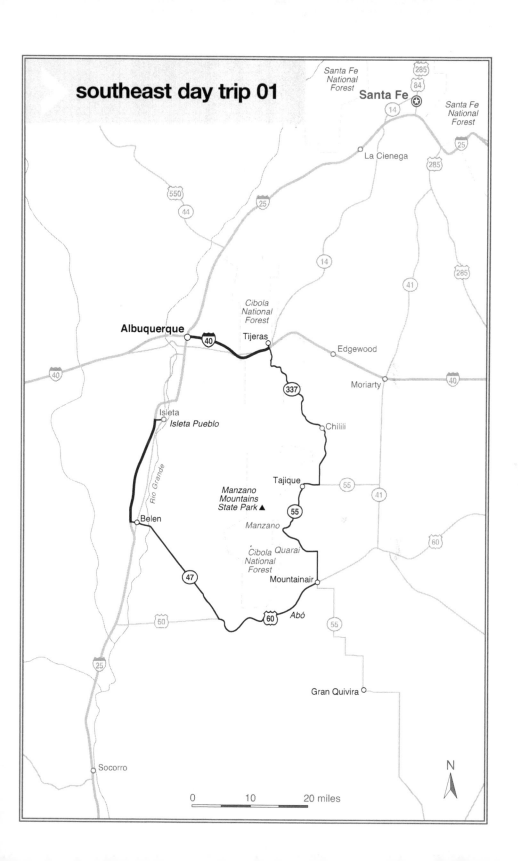

55 and US 60. The trip is best done as an overnight getaway, using Mountainair as a base from which to visit the Salt Missions, each of which tells a slightly different tale.

tijeras

Located astride the Sandia and Manzano Mountains, Tijeras was the site of an important 80-room gateway pueblo occupied between AD 1313 and 1425, which served as an important trading center. One-third of the pueblo was excavated by University of New Mexico (UNM) archeologist Linda Cordell in the 1970s. Cordell remains involved with Tijeras Pueblo, using ceramic artifacts housed at UNM's Maxwell Museum to research prehistoric pottery manufacture.

where to go

Tijeras Pueblo Archeological Site. 1776 SR 337; (505) 281-3304; friendsoftijeraspueblo .org. The archeological site is managed by the US Forest Service and Friends of Tijeras, which have built a nice little museum with exhibits about the Ancestral Pueblo people who occupied this site. They offer a number of interesting family programs, including kids' archeology worksheets, special Archeology Days, and monthly lectures. The 1/3-mile self-guided trail through the pueblo site offers a look at how Pueblo people lived here and is open sunrise to sunset daily. The museum is only open May through Oct, Fri, Sat, and Sun 10 a.m. to 4 p.m.; to schedule a tour at other times, call the Sandia Ranger Station Mon through Fri 8:30 a.m. to 4:30 p.m. Donation suggested.

tajique

Continue south on SR 337. About 19 miles south of Tijeras, you pass through the village of Chilili and then pick up SR 55, which goes west a short way then drops south through the villages of Tajique and Torreon. These three villages have a similar feel to them—each one only has about 100 residents and is popular with artists and retirees. Originally a Tigua pueblo, Tajique is a typical Spanish Colonial village with church, plaza, and a few adobe homes.

manzano mountains

The Manzanita and Manzano Mountains (*manzano* means "apple" in Spanish) attract a rich mix of wildlife, including large numbers of migratory raptors that use the mountains as a flyway, sometimes flying up to 200 miles a day along this corridor. Every winter HawkWatch International conducts a count of the raptors. Volunteers are stationed at a remote lookout in the Manzanos in the Cibola National Forest, reached via Manzano Mountains State Park, a great base for outdoor activities.

where to go

Manzano Mountains HawkWatch. (505) 255-7622; hawkwatch.org. If you like the idea of watching and counting raptors in Cibola National Forest in the Manzanos, contact Hawk-Watch International to find out more. You can either take part in the daily count 9 a.m. to 5 p.m. between Aug 27 and Nov 5 or simply visit and learn more from volunteers. Typically, 5,000 to 7,000 raptors representing 18 species migrate along the corridor each season, and peak migration period is Sept 10 to Oct 26. Bring food, drink, binoculars, bird field guide, protective glasses, and warm layers, as weather changes at this elevation, and check the weather forecast before setting out, as no counts take place during inclement weather. To get here, continue south on SR 55 after the village of Torreon, then turn right onto CR B066 at Manzano and continue for 9 miles up to Capilla Peak (follow the signs to Capilla Peak Campground). The trailhead is on the west side of the road; from here, it's a 0.7-mile hike to the observation area with moderate elevation gain.

Manzano Mountains State Park. MM 3, SR 131; (505) 469-7608; emnrd.state.nm.us/SPD/Manzanomountainsstatepark.html. At 7,600 feet, this 160-acre park is a terrific spot for hiking, camping, fishing, photography, picnicking, and wildlife viewing when it's warm at lower elevations. In winter it has cross-country skiing and snowshoeing and is a good place to see migrating raptors. Visitor center, trails, campground with 42 developed sites. Open 24 hours year-round. Admission fee.

where to stay

Casa Manzano Bed and Breakfast. 103 FR 321, Estancia; (505) 384-9767; facebook .com/casamanzanobandb. Located on a dirt road, 25 minutes from the Quarai ruins of Salinas Pueblo Missions National Historical Park, this pretty rural adobe was lovingly built and furnished by author Bert Herrman and retired educator Guy Seiler, both involved in the local arts scene. Bert died in 2013, but Guy continues to run the B&B on a seasonal basis. It has traditional Saltillo tile floors, plaster walls, and Southwest ranch–style furnishings. Four fresh-feeling and comfy rooms open onto a courtyard with terrific views. Two have shared bathrooms, two have private baths, with a choice of queen-size beds or platform futon beds. Hot tub. Kid- and pet-friendly. Full-cooked breakfast with homemade pastries included, but bring your own food for other meals, as you are miles from anywhere. Open May through Nov; closed rest of the year. $$.

punta del agua

This lush valley is notable mainly for its ruins of Quarai, one of the three 17th-century Spanish pueblo missions protected under the aegis of Salinas Pueblo Missions National Historical Park. Using this itinerary, you will reach Quarai 15 minutes before you get to Mountainair, the main park headquarters, so I have provided information here.

where to go

Quarai Ruins. SR 55, 1 mile east of Punta del Agua, 8 miles north of Mountainair; (505) 847-2290; nps.gov/sapu. Nuestra Señora de la Purísima Concepción at Quarai was founded in 1626 atop the Tewa-speaking pueblo of Cuarac, now just a memory under grassy hummocks in the ruined church grounds. A typical church mission, Quarai has a particularly photogenic church of red sandstone built with wall-and-lintel construction, tapering walls, a long nave, transepts, a choir loft, and clerestory windows. The *convento* next door was the living quarters for the monks. It has a *porteria* (waiting room), patios, *ambulatarios* (walkways), cells, kitchens, and livestock corrals. An interesting tidbit: Quarai was the base for the local branch of the Spanish Inquisition, which collected evidence of impropriety against the Church by colonists. One poor man, a German settler named Bernard Gruber, was jailed without trial on charges of heresy. He escaped, but unluckily for him, he perished in the scorching desert of the Llano Estacado, or *La Jornada del Muerto*—Dead Man's Way. There is a trail through the ruins and an on-site visitor center (the main park visitor center and HQ is in downtown Mountainair). Free annual classical concert by local musicians De Profundis in Sept. Ruins open daily 9 a.m. to 5 p.m.; visitor center as staffing allows. Admission fee.

mountainair

The ranch settlement of Mountainair (pop. 863), at the crossroads of SR 55 and US 60, was founded in 1903 and sits at the geographic center of the state. The location seems like a state of mind as well. Mountainair feels like it got stuck in the early 20th century and never left, with its motor-court motels, folksy hometown coffee shop, sleepy Main Street, feed stores, bric-a-brac stores, arts-and-crafts festivals, rodeos, and community potlucks. Its one genuine historic attraction is the 1923 Shaffer Hotel, a National Historic Landmark that is only open for dining now but retains much of its funky charm. Until the 1950s, Mountainair was known as the "Pinto Bean Capital of the World." It had the world's largest bean-processing plant, and bean shipments from Mountainair helped soldiers fight two world wars. A 10-year drought hit in the mid-1940s, making irrigated dryland farming impossible. Folks shifted to ranching, but the railroad closed its depot here, and when I-25 was built, US 60 no longer brought travelers through town. The designation of Salinas Pueblo Missions National Historical Park in 1980, and with it the construction of the park's visitor center and the museum in town, attracted more tourists. Things are still pretty laid-back around here, but as more artists, retirees, and others in search of slow-paced country living move here, Mountainair is trying on a new identity as an authentic art town, with an annual art show in summer, a family-run coffeehouse that is a popular local hangout, and an eclectic art gallery featuring work by members of the local Manzano Mountain Art Council (manzanomountainartcouncil .org).

where to go

Abó Ruins. 9 miles west of Mountainair on US 60; (505) 847-2400. Like Quarai, Abó is sited on a natural spring and was a farming pueblo that was eventually taken over by Spanish missionaries, who built a typical mission church and *convento* here. But like Gran Quivira, it was an important gateway pueblo on a cultural frontier. Its small church of San Gregorio de Abó was the first to be built in the area in 1622; it was later replaced by a much larger church in 1651 and its priests served the *visitas*, or satellite parishes, of neighboring Tenabo and Tabira and Gran Quivira to the south. There is a small visitor center open when staffing allows and a trail through the ruins but no other services. Open daily 9 a.m. to 6 p.m. (until 5 p.m. in winter). Admission fee.

Gran Quivira Ruins. 26 miles south of Mountainair on SR 55; (505) 847-2770; nps.gov/sapu. Unlike Quarai and Abó, Pueblo de las Humanas ("Pueblo of People with Stripe-Painted Faces") was never suitable for farming. By the 1400s it had made itself into a major trading center between the Rio Grande Pueblos to the north, the Plains Indians to the east, the Pacific cultures to the west, and the Mesoamerican cultures to the south. It was the last to accept missionization in 1630, when Fray Francisco Letrado oversaw the construction of the church and *convento* of San Isidro. The limestone structure was left incomplete when Letrado moved to Zuni Pueblo and was subsequently martyred. A new church was begun in 1659, named for San Buenaventura, but it too was never completed before environmental and man-made disasters killed most of the residents. This is a large, hauntingly beautiful pueblo. Of the three, on no account should you miss this one. There's a small visitor center open when staffing allows and a ruins trail but no other facilities. Open 9 a.m. to 6 p.m. daily (until 5 p.m. in winter). Admission fee.

Salinas Pueblo Missions National Historical Park Main Visitor Center. Ripley and Broadway, Mountainair; (505) 847-2585; nps.gov/sapu. Pay your entrance fee for all three missions, get information and maps, and view exhibits at the park headquarters. There's a small bookstore. Open daily 9 a.m. to 6 p.m. (until 5 p.m. in winter).

where to eat

Alpine Alley Cafe. 210 N. Summit Ave.; (505) 847-2478; alpinealley.com. Begun in 2007 as a community coffee shop/art gallery and run by artists, this popular hometown cafe was bought by new owners in 2017 who have continued to offer New Mexican and American home cooking, pastries, and hot drinks. Custom coffee drinks, breakfast burritos, pastries, soups, salads, and customized sandwiches and wraps for breakfast or lunch. Wi-Fi. Open Tues through Thurs 6 a.m. to 2 p.m., Fri 6 a.m. to 3 p.m., and Sat and Sun 8 a.m. to 3 p.m. $.

Shaffer Dining Room. 103 W. Main St.; (505) 847-2888. Industrial artist Clem "Pop" Shaffer moved to Mountainair in 1908 and built this reinforced and highly decorated cast-concrete hotel in 1923. It is considered one of the best examples of Pueblo Deco style—a brightly painted Southwestern take on stylized Art Deco, with Spanish Mission and Indian art influences. The extraordinary decor is visible in the ceiling of the dining room, now the only part of the former hotel open, and you really should stop in and check it out. It has been featured in a number of movies. The menu in the cafe features New Mexican and American diner food served in plentiful quantities. Open Mon 8 a.m. to 6 p.m., Thurs through Sat 9 a.m. to 6 p.m., and Sun 10 a.m. to 6 p.m. $.

where to stay

Two Ponyz Ranch. 100-198 Old Abo Trail, Mountainair; (505) 847-0245; twoponzyranch .com. Located off US 60 west of Mountainair, near the Abó ruins preserved as part of Salinas Pueblo Missions National Historical Park, this lovely green-built one-bedroom casita and adjoining stable makes a nice base for visiting the area, whether on foot or horseback. It can accommodate 4 and has a kitchen, fireplace, portal, and hot tub. Bring your own food. The owner was in the music business for years and escaped to this area. Two-night minimum. $$.

Turner Inn and RV Park. 303 E. US 60; (505) 847-0248, turnerinnandrvpark.com. The former Tillie's is a classic motor-court motel with 14 sweet, unpretentious rooms and 2 cabins for rent, in addition to an RV park. All rooms and cabins have fridges, microwaves, coffeemakers, satellite TV, and Wi-Fi. Pet-friendly. $.

belen

Belen ("Bethlehem") was founded in 1740. A farming and sheep ranching village, it became an important stop on El Camino Real and, after railroads and paved highway links were built, has remained a busy commercial center. It's linked to Albuquerque by I-25 and the Rail Runner Express train.

where to go

Belen Harvey House Museum. 104 N. First St.; (505) 861-0581; harveyhousemuseum .org. This museum in a 1910 building commemorates the grand era of railroad hotels created by British immigrant Fred Harvey at the turn of the 20th century and is part of the renaissance of Harvey Houses taking place with the recent restoration of La Posada in Winslow, Arizona, and the Hotel Castañeda in Las Vegas, New Mexico. The museum has costumed Harvey Girl volunteers, exhibits, and a research archive and puts on regular lectures and Harvey events, as well as a popular Christmas illuminations display. Open Tues through Fri noon to 5 p.m. and Sat 10 a.m. to 5 p.m. Admission fee.

isleta pueblo

One of the pueblos that accepted refugees from the Salt Missions in the late 1600s, Tiwa-speaking Isleta has taken in refugees several times (and been in that situation itself). It was initially founded around AD 1300, but during the Pueblo Revolt, Isleta people fled to Arizona's Hopi Mesas, intermarrying with Hopi Pueblo people and returning later with their Hopi relatives. Acoma and Laguna people joined the pueblo in the 1800s, but friction led to the pueblo separating into three villages: the satellite villages of Oraibi (named for the Hopi village) and Chicale and the main pueblo. Historic St. Augustine Church, built in 1612, is in the main plaza. Just off I-25, the tribe runs an eye-catching casino-and-resort complex, 27-hole golf course, and lake recreation area.

where to go

Isleta Lakes Recreational Complex. (505) 244-8102. The tribe has two well-stocked lakes for fishing, camping, and picnicking. You can angle for catfish in spring and summer and rainbow trout in fall and winter. Stop at the convenience store to pay for permits and purchase supplies and tackle. Fish cleaning station, 44 picnic shelters, restrooms, and volleyball court. Complex open 6:30 a.m. to 6:30 p.m. (until 8 p.m. in summer). Admission fee.

where to stay

Isleta Casino and Resort. 11000 Broadway SE; (877) 7ISLETA; isleta-casino.com. Hotel rooms and suites in this comfortably modern and spacious resort are all luxurious and decorated in soothing dark browns and creams. Flat-screen TVs, high-thread-count linens, soaking tubs and showers with rain-head fixtures, minibars, and Wi-Fi are standard. The resort has five dining options, from casual coffeehouse and sports bar to steakhouse gourmet and nightclub bites. On-site spa, fitness center, golf, casino, and concerts. You won't find a better deal in the area. $.

day trip 02

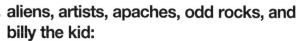

aliens, artists, apaches, odd rocks, and billy the kid:
roswell, ruidoso, mescalero apache reservation, capitan, lincoln, alamogordo, cloudcroft, carlsbad

You'll need at least three days to visit the basin-and-range desert of southeastern New Mexico, where expanses of desiccated former seas yielding minerals, oil, and gas nudge up to lava fields, white gypsum dunes, and "sky island" mountain ranges. Rising to 12,000 feet, the cool, forested Sacramento Mountains are a magnet for recreation and home to artists, the Mescalero Apache Indian reservation, and the southernmost ski resort in New Mexico. Anglo pioneers joined the Apache in 1898, logging high-elevation forests and farming pistachios around Alamogordo, as well as crossing from Texas to drill oil in the Permian Basin. Technological advances during World War II attracted international scientific pioneers. Early rockets, atomic bomb testing, modern weaponry, astronomy advances, deep-space exploration, and even contact with aliens have galvanized public opinion ever since. Controversy also swirls around a trigger-happy young cowboy named Billy the Kid, at the forefront of Lincoln's bloody range wars in 1878. The Kid, whose exploits in his adopted hometown of Lincoln led the entire village to be preserved as a state historic site, played cat and mouse with lawmen for months until he was shot by Sheriff Pat Garrett at Fort Sumner (see East Day Trip 01) in 1881.

From Albuquerque, the quickest way to reach Roswell is to drive east on I-40, then take US 285 south, a trip of just over four hours. I have set up some of the day trips in this book, however, as interlinked trips, so you might consider extending your trip and taking in

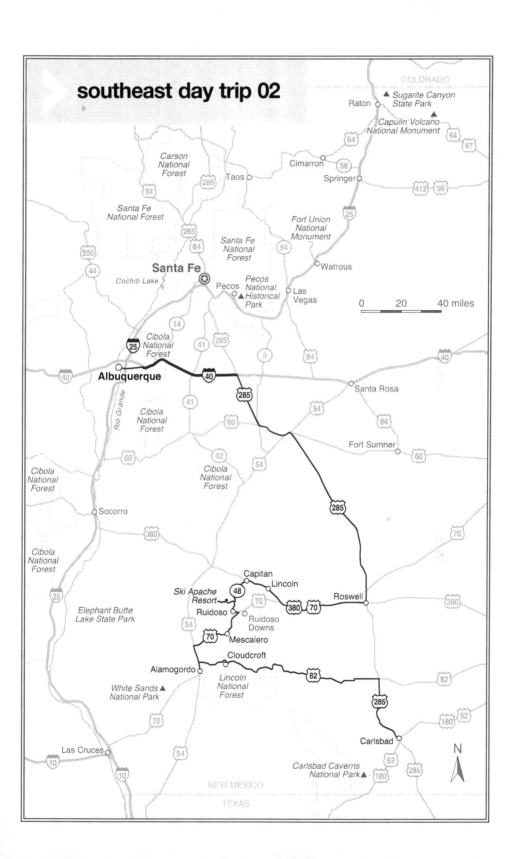

southeast day trip 02

some of the sights on those day trips. For example, if you do East Day Trip 01, you could continue south on US 70 from Portales to Roswell and Alamogordo, with side trips on US 380 to Ruidoso and Lincoln and southeast to Carlsbad Caverns on US 82/285; drive east on US 380 from I-25, just south of Socorro (South Day Trip 01); or drive west on US 70 to Las Cruces to visit the new Organ Mountains–Desert Peaks National Monument (South Day Trip 02). It's entirely up to you; I'm just offering some options, as this is the way I like to explore.

roswell

Homely Roswell feels stuck in the 1940s, around the time alien remains were allegedly found here. It ought to be known more for its art than its UFO controversy, which isn't helped by a hokey downtown museum that is strictly for fans of kitsch. Roswell's terrific 1937 art museum is one of my favorite small museums in the state. It holds the largest collection of works by Roswell native Peter Hurd and wife Henriette Wyeth, among many other world-class pieces of art by New Mexican artists. The museum functions as a community art center. Its well-regarded Roswell Artist-in-Residence (RAiR) program has graduated such famous alumni as the late Mexican-American sculptor Luis Jimenez and Chiricahua Apache sculptor Bob Haozous, son of famed sculptor Allan Houser. Many artists live in the lush Hondo Valley, 50 miles west of Roswell, a good place to visit art studios and spend a couple of nights exploring the area.

where to go

Anderson Museum of Contemporary Art. 409 E. College Blvd.; (575) 623-5600; rair.org/about-amoca. Artist Donald Anderson, creator of the RAiR Foundation program at Roswell Museum and Art Center, founded this elegant contemporary museum in 1994 to display the artwork of former RAiR alumni. Today, the collection has grown to include more than 500 photos, paintings, prints, drawings, and sculptures on display in 12 galleries; oversize public sculptures by Bob Haozous and Luis Jimenez are among the delights. Open Mon through Fri 9 a.m. to 4 p.m. and Sat and Sun 1 to 5 p.m. Free.

Bitter Lake National Wildlife Refuge. 4200 E. Pine Lodge Rd.; (575) 625-4011; fws.gov/refuge/Bitter_Lake. One of a number of natural limestone-sinkhole lakes located 9 miles northeast of town, this 25,000-acre refuge is one of the most biologically significant wetland areas in the Pecos River watershed. It attracts migratory geese, ducks, and sandhill cranes in fall and winter and is also a haven for over 100 species of dragonflies and damselflies, one of the most diverse arrays of odonates in the US. A Dragonfly Festival is held in spring. The refuge receives government funds to eradicate nonnative species like tamarisk and restore the wetland. The Joseph R. Skeen Visitor Center has exhibits and information and is open Mon through Fri 8 a.m. to 4 p.m. and sporadically on Sat. The refuge has 4 short trails and 2 longer trails for hiking and wildlife watching, an 8-mile gravel Wildlife Drive for auto touring, and a paved 4-mile loop for bicycling. Note: Hunting of waterfowl, deer, hogs, and rabbits takes place on the refuge from Sept 1 to Feb 15. The refuge is open Mon through Fri 24 hours a day. Free.

Bottomless Lakes State Park. 545A Bottomless Lakes Rd.; (575) 624-6058; emnrd.state .nm.us/SPD/Bottomlesslakesstatepark.html. Cowboys passing through the once-booming ghost town of Seven Rivers may have named these lakes 14 miles southeast of Roswell in the 1880s. They aren't bottomless, but they are a good place to cool down in summer and are surrounded by attractive red bluffs. Lea Lake is a popular swimming hole and has a nice campground. Activities include camping, fishing, boating, sailing, scuba diving, picnicking, hiking, and wildlife viewing. To reach the park from Roswell, drive east on US 380 for 12 miles and then south on SR 409 for 2 miles.. Admission fee.

International UFO Museum and Research Center. 114 N. Main St.; (575) 625-9495; roswellufomuseum.com. This hokey roadside attraction in downtown Roswell is laid out like an old-fashioned classroom, with yellowing newspaper articles on the walls, posters, films, and videotapes of military personnel and local ranchers recounting what they saw amid the wreckage of a crashed spaceship in a nearby field in the 1940s. There's real evidence amid the schlock, if you take the time to pull it apart. Open daily 9 a.m. to 5 p.m. Admission fee.

Roswell Museum and Art Center. 1011 N. Richardson Ave.; (575) 624-6744; roswell-nm .gov/308/Roswell-Museum-Art-Center. Housed in a beautiful 1937 building, the Roswell Museum is one of only a handful of WPA-era art centers still in operation nationwide. Twelve galleries display the extraordinary Aston Collection of Plains Indian, Pueblo, Spanish Colonial, and early American artifacts, as well as traditional New Mexican arts and crafts made by local artists who were funded by WPA programs during the New Deal era. Georgia O'Keeffe's painting *Ram's Skull with Brown Leaves* was a favorite of the artist herself, a sign of the caliber of art here. While this museum is a must for art lovers, it is also interesting for the work of pioneer rocket scientist Robert Goddard, who conducted experiments with rocket propulsion in Roswell in the '20s and '30s; the Robert Goddard Planetarium is located in a separate wing of the museum, dedicated to Goddard and funded by his widow and the local Rotary Club. Among the exhibits is a re-creation of Goddard's workshop. Open Tues through Sat 9 a.m. to 5 p.m., Sun and holidays 1 to 5 p.m. Free.

where to eat

Tinnie Silver Dollar. 28842 US 70; (575) 653-4425; facebook.com/tinnie.dollar. This sprawling historic roadside property has gone through a number of changes over the years, but has been a mainstay in the Hondo Valley since 1892, where it has been variously a general mercantile, a post office, and a popular destination restaurant/bar. In the 1950s it was run by Robert O. Anderson, owner of the Lincoln County Livestock Company, and then the wealthiest landowner in New Mexico. He spared no expense in fixing up the Victorian property, installing the porch, the famous Tinnie tower, and the store and restaurant/bar. He purchased the handcrafted bar from Al Capone's establishment in Chicago, half of which he installed in the Silver Dollar and half in the Lodge at Cloudcroft, which he also owned (along with the historic Double Eagle in Mesilla and Legal Tender in Lamy). In July 2019 the elegant steakhouse, beer and wine bar, and boutique, along with two modern guest suites, reopened under the management of the owner of popular Big D's Downtown Dive in Roswell, and locals could not be more pleased. The menu features steak, poultry, seafood, burgers, soups, sandwiches, and its popular crepes, all of it beautifully presented and much of it sourced locally, including the coffee, which is roasted in Roswell and served in the mercantile and restaurant. Lunch and dinner are served Fri and Sat only 11 a.m. to 9 p.m. (8 p.m. winter) and Sunday brunch 11 a.m. to 2 p.m. Space in the dining room is limited, so be sure to make reservations. Lodging is in two suites and available nightly through Airbnb.

where to stay

Hurd La Rinconada Gallery and Guest Homes. 105 La Rinconada, San Patricio; guesthouse reservations (800) 658-6912, art gallery (575) 653-4331; hurdgallery.com. Peter Hurd and Henriette Wyeth's son Michael is an accomplished artist in his own right. He still makes his home on his parents' lovely Sentinel Ranch in the Hondo Valley, using it as a home studio and art gallery, displaying his work and that of his family and others. Several of the buildings once used by ranch hands (Billy the Kid and his Regulators were regulars in Hondo Valley) have been converted to delightful guesthouses. Limited dining in San Patricio; the best choice of restaurants is in Ruidoso, 20 miles away, your best bet as a base with abundant food and lodging. Two-night minimum. Gallery open Mon through Sat 9 a.m. to 5 p.m.. $$–$$$$.

ruidoso

Ruidoso is named for the "very noisy" river that pours out of the Sacramento Mountains. This lovely mountain town is surrounded by 1.1 million acres of Lincoln National Forest and adjoins Ski Apache Resort. It is a haven for West Texans, who come here to escape the heat at lower elevations; many have stayed and helped fund cultural institutions like the Spencer Performing Arts Center, designed by famed architect Antoine Predock, and the Hubbard Museum of the American West, founded by entrepreneur R. D. Hubbard, a horse lover who also owns neighboring Ruidoso Downs. You'll find a number of decent restaurants and lodgings here, so Ruidoso makes a logical base from which you can make day trips to the nearby historic villages of Lincoln and Capitan and Mescalero Apache Reservation.

where to go

Billy the Kid National Scenic Byway Visitors Center. 791 US 70; (575) 378-5318; billybyway.com/bywaycenter.html. Adjoining Ruidoso Downs, this little visitor center has information about the area and second-tier exhibits about Billy the Kid. The scenic byway explores Kid-related haunts along a very enjoyable 84-mile loop between Ruidoso, Capitan, Lincoln, Roswell, and the Hondo Valley. Open daily 10 a.m. to 5 p.m.

Hubbard Museum of the American West. 841 US 70; (575) 378-4142; hubbardmuseum .org. Horse lover Ann Stradling's bequest of 10,000 equine items to R. D. Hubbard led him to found this museum in 1992; the museum was given to the City of Ruidoso in 2005. Now an affiliate of the Smithsonian Institution, the hangar-like structure also displays wagons, stagecoaches, Hollywood Western movie memorabilia, and the Race Track Hall of Fame. Fun for families. Open Thurs through Mon 9 a.m. to 5 p.m. Admission fee.

Ruidoso Downs Race Track and Casino. 1461 US 70; (575) 378-4431; raceruidoso .com. One of the most popular racecourses in the West, Ruidoso Downs hosts both thoroughbred and quarter horse racing, including the $2 million purse All-American Futurity quarter horse race, the richest quarter horse race in the world. Races every weekend between Memorial Day and Labor Day.

Spencer Theater for the Performing Arts. 108 Spencer Rd., Alto; (575) 336-4800, (888) 818-7872; spencertheater.com. Designed by renowned architect Antoine Predock, the Spencer Theater is housed in a fascinating trapezoidal building with clear sight lines to, and inspiration from, 12,003-foot Sierra Blanca, the peak that is sacred to the Apache. The 514-seat theater is well known for its Broadway shows and big-name music acts. Open Mon through Fri 9 a.m. to 5 p.m. Tours on Tues and Thurs at 10 a.m. and 2 p.m. Call for information.

mescalero apache reservation

The Mescalero have lived in the Sacramento Mountains for centuries, and like the Navajo, they trace their ancestry to the Dineh, the prehistoric nomadic hunter-gatherers of northwest Canada who began migrating to this region perhaps as early as AD 1000, according to new evidence in northern New Mexico. Apaches learned ranching and horsemanship from Spanish and Anglo settlers and are today skilled stockmen and cowboys. The annual Fourth of July Rodeo is the highlight of the year and includes bull riding and other cowboying competitions; a powwow; dances featuring spectacularly costumed *gaan*, or mountain spirit dancers; and the important three-day puberty ritual that every young Apache girl undergoes. The tribe gets its name from its use of mescal, made from maguey, an agave plant native to Mexico, which is still collected in the desert and used in ceremonies. Tribal headquarters is in Mescalero (mescaleroapachetribe.com), on the other side of the mountains, where there is a beautiful old church mission and a small cultural center. The tribe's main tourist facilities are on the east side of the 40,000-acre reservation at Ski Apache and Inn of the Mountain Gods, adjoining Ruidoso.

where to go

Ski Apache Resort. 1286 Ski Run Rd., Alto; (575) 464-3600; skiapache.com. With an average snowfall of 15 feet a year and 11 ski lifts (including the state's only passenger gondola) serving 55 runs, Ski Apache, 11 miles north of Ruidoso, is not only a beautiful place to ski, but its Apache ownership offers an exotic element that you won't find at many mainstream ski resorts. Snowboarding is permitted on all runs. Ski runs are 20 percent beginner, 60 percent intermediate, and 20 percent expert. Ski rental shops, cafeterias, and snack bars. **Lincoln County Tours** (505-257-6069) offers a shuttle from Ruidoso.

where to stay

Inn of the Mountain Gods. 287 Carrizzo Canyon Rd., Ruidoso; (800) 545-9011; innofthe mountaingods.com. Completely rebuilt in 2004, this spectacular lakeside resort has 273 luxurious rooms and suites and several good restaurants, including a popular steakhouse. Guided hunting, fishing, and other outdoor pursuits. On-site 18-hole golf course. $$–$$$.

capitan

From Ruidoso, head north on SR 48 to reach the little village of Capitan. Capitan is nestled below the Capitan Mountains, where the real Smokey Bear, the US Forest Service's beloved fire-prevention mascot, was rescued from a forest fire. Smokey is a VIP in Capitan and the subject of a delightful state park that offers some fascinating insights into forest fire management and ecology.

where to go

Smokey Bear Historical State Park. 118 Smokey Bear Blvd.; (575) 354-2748; emnrd .state.nm.us/SPD/SmokeyBear/SmokeyBearPark.html. This tiny state park has a really worthwhile little museum, with fascinating exhibits on firefighting, fire prevention, and Smokey Bear (note the name; it's not Smokey the Bear). Smokey was originally christened "Hotfoot Teddy" by the firefighters who rescued him. He is buried on the grounds, where you will also find a useful life zones exhibit that allows you to learn about which plants live at which elevation. A joy for adults as well as kids, this state park is one of my favorite southern New Mexico haunts and recommended for everybody. Open daily 9 a.m. to 4:30 p.m. Admission fee.

where to eat

Che Palle. 433 Smokey Bear Blvd.; (575) 973-0933; reneesrealfood.weebly.com. Formerly known as Renee's Real Food, this chef-owned cafe near the state park features a small, changing menu of pizzas, meat loaf, pastrami, po'boy and grinder sandwiches, fish-and-chips, and brunch items like home-baked bagels, crème brûlée French toast, and the crowd favorite, chicken and waffles. You'll also find some lovely baked items for dessert, such as chocolate cupcakes, so save room. Everything is beautifully plated and made from scratch daily using local sources, including organic produce from the hydroponic greenhouse of a former Capitan chef and restaurant owner (amazingly, this village has attracted some world-class chefs). Open for lunch and dinner Wed through Sat 11 a.m. to 9 p.m. and Sun noon to 6 p.m. $–$$.

lincoln

From Capitan, drive 12 miles east on US 380 to Lincoln, one of the most storied small towns in New Mexico. The February 13, 1878, shooting of young English cattleman John Henry Tunstall by a member of the local Murphy-Dolan ranch syndicate at Tunstall's ranch near Lincoln triggered a series of tragic events. First, Billy the Kid, Alexander McSween, and other Tunstall loyalists avenged the death of their friend by killing Sheriff Bill Brady. They then returned for a final showdown on July 14, holing up in buildings all over Lincoln for what came to be known as the Five Day Battle between the Kid and his Regulators, the Murphy-Dolan faction, and, at one point, soldiers from nearby Fort Stanton. The Kid escaped, then was captured and held in the Lincoln County Courthouse and various private homes, then escaped again, only to be shot at Fort Sumner by Sheriff Pat Garrett. Lincoln, a tiny one-horse town, is now protected as a state historic site, managed by the state and the Hubbard Museum in Ruidoso. Old Lincoln Days in August celebrates Billy the Kid's exploits.

where to go

Anderson-Freeman Museum. Main Street (US 380); (575) 653-4025. The Hubbard Museum runs this Lincoln County historical museum. It's very attractive, with a timeline and extensive exhibits on the so-called Lincoln County War. Gift shop and walking tour maps. Open daily 8:30 a.m. to 4:30 p.m. Admission fee.

Lincoln Historic Site. PO Box 36, Lincoln; (575) 653-4372; nmmonuments.org. Housed in the Tunstall Store, on Main Street (US 380), Lincoln is the most popular state historic site in the system. Its monument headquarters displays some 1,000 items from Tunstall's original inventory; the other half of the store was the bank. Stop here for a walking tour map; a 22-minute video about the Lincoln County War and Lincoln is shown every half hour. The admission fee allows entrance to 9 buildings, including the Tunstall Store, Dr. Wood's Mansion, Gallegos House, Lincoln County Courthouse, Montano Store, and Anderson-Freeman Museum. Open daily 9 a.m. to 5 p.m. Admission fee.

where to stay

The Wortley Hotel. 585 Calle La Placita; (575) 653-4300; wortleyhotel.com. Right at the western end of Main Street, you'll find the historic Wortley Hotel ("No guests gunned down in over 100 years"), now a delightful bed-and-breakfast. The original 1874 structure burned to the ground in the 1930s and has been reconstructed but feels quite authentic. Under new ownership since 2016, the 7 remodeled rooms are simply but freshly done, with clean white paint on the walls and period furnishings reflecting Lincoln's heyday. Each has an antique brass bed with a new mattress, fireplace, and private bath. Settle into one of the many old rockers on the porch wrapping around the Wortley's facade, and you can almost imagine yourself back in Lincoln's colorful past as wild turkeys strut by. The hotel restaurant is open daily for breakfast for guests only (included in the room rate) and features farm eggs cooked to order by Troy, the owner. Lunch is served Wed and Thurs only, from 11 a.m. to 3 p.m., and features classic American and New Mexican comfort foods. $$.

alamogordo

US 70 joins US 54 in the Tularosa Basin, a few miles north of Alamogordo, amid the pecan and pistachio orchards that provide the principal crops in this area. To the west is Holloman Air Force Base and White Sands Missile Range; its Trinity Site was chosen to test the world's first atomic bomb in July 1945. White Sands National Park, set aside to protect blinding-white gypsum sediments washed out from nearby mountains and blown into shifting dunes, is one of the strangest sights in the world. Alamogordo itself feels a bit like another deliberately anonymous government-contractor town: Los Alamos. The New Mexico Museum of Space History, commemorating the history of space exploration, is its main attraction.

where to go

New Mexico Museum of Space History. SR 2001; (575) 437-2840; nmspacemuseum .org. Located behind the campus of New Mexico State University, this modern glass cube is a must for space fans. It traces rocketry all the way from pioneer Robert Goddard's first jet-fuel propulsion experiments on the plains east of Roswell to the Apollo and Skylab missions and more recent milestones in the space program. The **New Horizons Dome Theater** features the world's first Spitz Scidome 4K Laser full-dome planetarium projection system and is named after the NASA spacecraft that flew by Pluto in 2018. IMAX films and live star shows are offered several times a day. Outside are the **Astronaut Memorial Garden,** a tribute to the *Apollo 1* and space shuttle *Challenger* and *Columbia* astronauts, and the **John P. Stapp Air and Space Park,** which is filled with space hardware and rocket equipment. The **Daisy Track** commemorates tests that were crucial in developing elements of NASA's Project Mercury orbital tests and Apollo moon landings. Open Wed through Mon 10 a.m. to 5 p.m. Admission fee.

Oliver M. Lee Memorial State Park. 409 Dog Canyon Rd.; (575) 437-8284; emnrd.state .nm.us/SPD/oliverleestatepark.html. Historic Dog Canyon Ranch and House was built in 1898 by Oliver Lee, a prominent local cattle rancher and Republican state senator who is credited with attracting the railroad to Alamogordo, which led to its prosperity. A rocky 5.5-mile trail leads into pretty Dog Canyon, a longtime Apache haunt. The 50-site developed campground has great views and is your best bet for camping in the area. The ranch house opens for guided tours on select weekends throughout the year, usually Sat 10 a.m. and Sun 3 p.m. Call for current information. The state park is open 24 hours. Admission fee.

Three Rivers Petroglyph Site. Three Rivers Road, Tularosa, off CR B30; (575) 525-4300; blm.gov/visit/three-rivers-petroglyph-site. At this remote desert location near Tularosa, a rugged 0.5-mile trail leads from a visitor shelter past 21,000 petroglyphs (some badly vandalized) carved onto volcanic basaltic rocks by the Jornada Mogollon people from AD 900 to 1400. A second trail leads to a partially excavated pit house and pueblo village. The site has 5 picnic shelters. Camping is available in Three Rivers Campground, at the edge of Lincoln National Forest, where you will find a group site, 2 RV sites, and 5 tent sites. Water and a restroom are available. Note: Summer temperatures reach into the 100s and the petroglyphs are in very exposed location, so plan accordingly and cover up. Open daily Apr through Oct 8 a.m. to 7 p.m. and Nov through Mar 8 a.m. to 5 p.m. Admission fee.

Trinity Site. (575) 678-1134; wsmr.army.mil/Trinity/Pages/Home.aspx. Now a National Historical Landmark, the site of the detonation of the world's first atomic bomb may be visited twice a year, the first Sat in Apr and Oct, with a military escort. On open days, visitors may enter Trinity Site at the Stallion Gate off SR 380 between 8 a.m. and 2 p.m.; exit must be by 3:30 p.m. For directions, contact White Sands Missile Range Public Affairs Office at the number listed. Free.

White Sands National Park. PO Box 1086, Holloman AFB (off US 70); (575) 479-6124; nps.gov.whsa. This national monument upgraded to a national park in 2019 is a wonderful place to pull off and let your inner child play in the world's oddest dunes. There's a 16-mile scenic loop, picnic areas, interpretive signs, and a visitor center in an attractive Pueblo Revival historic building from the 1930s WPA era in the park's historic district. Moonlight hikes are offered once a month. The site adjoins White Sands Missile Range, and missile testing may occasionally close the park and US 70; dates are posted on the park website, so check before coming. Open daily 8 a.m. to 4:30 p.m. Admission fee.

where to shop

Heart of the Desert at Eagle Ranch. 7288 US 54/70; (575) 434-0035, (800) 432-0999; heartofthedesert.com. Four miles north of Alamogordo, you'll find the state's oldest and largest pistachio grower, which offers tours of the shady groves and samples of pistachios flavored with garlic, green and red chiles, and other seasonings year-round. Sept through May, the 45-minute tours take place Mon through Fri at 1:30 p.m.; June through Aug, tours are Mon through Fri 10 a.m. and 1:30 p.m. Groups of 10 or more may call and arrange a special tour in advance. The Eagle Ranch store sells pistachios and other Southwestern food and gift items and is open Mon through Sat 8 a.m. to 6 p.m. and Sun 9 a.m. to 6 p.m. Wine tastings are also held in the store. Free.

cloudcroft

The drive up to Cloudcroft on US 82 from Alamogordo, about 19 miles with an elevation gain of 4,300 feet, is spectacular, allowing you views across the Tularosa Basin and, in summer, blessed relief from white-hot valley temperatures. Indeed, the quaint mountain village of Cloudcroft was founded by the owners of the railroad that passed through as a cool forest getaway for desert dwellers. It's known for its forest hiking and the nearby National Solar Observatory. The Bavarian-style Lodge at Cloudcroft, built in 1909, remains the most luxurious place to stay amid a sea of cabin resorts.

where to go

National Solar Observatory. SR 6563, Sunspot; (575) 434-7190; sunspot.solar or nso .edu. The tiny forest community of Sunspot, 16 miles south of Cloudcroft, is home to this distinctive observatory atop 9,200-foot Sacramento Peak, where astronomers safely observe the sun through the Dunn Solar Telescope. The observatory's visitor center, a co-venture of the NSO, neighboring Apache Point Observatory, and the US Forest Service, has astronomy exhibits, a gift shop, vending machines, water fountains, and restrooms, and the observatory grounds are open for self-guided tours on a half-mile loop daily from sunrise to sunset. Be sure to check in at the visitor center to receive a walking tour booklet; all other tours are currently suspended. Note: Apache Point Observatory is closed to visitors. Admission fee.

where to stay

Lodge at Cloudcroft. 601 Corona Place; (575) 682-2566, (800) 395-6343; thelodgeresort .com. Since 1909, the year it was built to replace the old pavilion that housed earlier guests, this alpine-fantasy lodge has hosted all of New Mexico's governors, Mexican revolutionary Pancho Villa, and Hollywood stars like Judy Garland and Clark Gable, who carved their names in the tower. The fine-dining restaurant, Rebecca's, has good food and views. It is named for the hotel's resident ghost, a maid who died at the hands of her lover in the 1930s, and believe me, as someone who has stayed in that room, she exists. Spa and croquet. $$.

carlsbad

From Cloudcroft, it's a long 150-mile drive on US 82 through the mountains, then south on US 285 to reach Carlsbad in the expansive Permian Basin. This area is aptly called "Little Texas," and oil pumps, windmills, cattle, antelope, and far-flung ranches do indeed blur the

how carlsbad caverns formed

Carlsbad Caverns was formed in a 400-mile, horseshoe-shaped reef growing on an offshore shelf of the shallow Permian Sea. When the sea became landlocked, it dried and evaporated, trapping the reef under layers of gypsum, salt, and potash, which are now mined in the area. Later geological uplift elevated the Guadalupe Mountains and erosion uncovered the reef, which gradually was dissolved by a mild sulfuric acid created by a mixture of hydrogen sulfide gas seeping up from the oil-rich shales and oxygen-rich water, leaving behind large caves. When groundwater moving down through cracks in the rocks encountered drier air in the caves, it dropped its carbon dioxide load and evaporated, leaving behind crystalline calcite formations that decorate the cave interior. Exposure to dry air has stopped the formation of new decorations on the cave walls; however, there are several wild caves at Carlsbad where conditions remain perfect for new decorations to form. They are only open to seasoned cavers with permits for research.

boundaries between the states. Texas cattle baron John Chisum blazed the first trail through the Pecos River valley in the 1860s and built huge ranches south of Roswell. The discovery of artesian water in the early 1900s ushered in irrigated agriculture, but it was the recovery of oil—trapped in the old seabed of the 250-million-year-old Permian Sea—that made the fortunes of billionaires like Robert Anderson. Carlsbad is nothing much to look at on the surface; its treasures lie 750 feet deep underground, among 30 miles of highly "decorated" limestone caves preserved at Carlsbad Caverns National Park, south of town at one of New Mexico's top visitor attractions. Incidentally, the caverns are part of the same formation as Guadalupe Mountains National Park, just over the border in Texas. The Guadalupe Mountains are Texas's highest mountains and a great place to hike and camp, especially in fall, when the Texas madrone trees in scenic McKittrick Canyon turn bright red.

where to go

Carlsbad Caverns National Park. 727 Carlsbad Caverns Hwy.; (575) 785-2232 (information), (877) 444-6777 (guided cave tour reservations); nps.gov/cave (information), recreation .gov (reservations). All visitors start with a self-guided tour of the Big Room, one of the world's largest chambers and the centerpiece of Carlsbad. You can take an elevator down, but if you are fit enough, it's more fun to enter via the 1-mile paved Natural Entrance, the original opening to the caves discovered by cowboy Jim White. Wild cave tours through undeveloped caves guided by park rangers are not to be missed if you're comfortable doing minor crawling, squeezing, and ladder and rope work. The 3-hour Lower Cave tour takes you along the route used by a National Geographic Society exploratory party in 1924. The 2-hour Lefthand Tunnel tour by candle lantern highlights Carlsbad's early history, geology, cave pools, and Permian age fossils. The most popular off-trail tour is the Slaughter Canyon Cave tour, a rugged hike into a cave containing the Monarch; at 89 feet, it is one of the world's largest limestone columns. Make advance reservations for wild cave tours; they are limited and very popular. Open daily 8 a.m. to 7 p.m. in summer, until 5 p.m. in winter. Admission fee.

Living Desert Zoo and Gardens State Park. 1504 Miehls Drive N.; (575) 887-5516; emnrd.state.nm.us/SPD/livingdesertstatepark.html. Learn all about the natural history of the Chihuahuan Desert at this terrific nature park. The zoo cares for more than 200 species of animals that have been rescued and rehabilitated after injury in the wild, including mountain lions, bobcats, and black bears. Endangered Mexican wolves raised here are part of a captive breeding program designed to reintroduce wolves into the Southwest. The 4-day Apache Mescal Roast powwow takes place here in May. Camping is available at both developed and primitive sites. Open daily 8 a.m. to 5 p.m. Memorial Day to Labor Day, 9 a.m. to 5 p.m. the rest of the year. Admission fee.

where to eat

Blue House Bakery and Café. 609 N. Canyon St.; (575) 628-0555; facebook.com/Blue HouseBakeryAndCafe. This breakfast and brunch bakery cafe is a good find in unpromising Carlsbad. The menu features homemade granola, breakfast burritos, breakfast bagel or croissant sandwiches, waffles, French toast, and a variety of homemade muffins, scones, sticky buns, and coffee drinks. Open Mon through Sat 6 a.m. to noon. $.

where to stay

Fiddler's Inn Bed and Breakfast. 705 N. Canyon St.; (575) 303-0755; fiddlersinnbb .com. Located near the Blue House Bakery, this delightful B&B is owned by a pair of local bluegrass musicians with an artful touch and down-home-on-the-ranch friendliness. The 6 rooms can sleep from 2 to 5 people, depending on size, and are elegantly furnished with king or queen four-poster and futon beds, quilts, Turkish robes, and sitting areas, and have minifridges, microwaves, coffeemakers, flat-screen TVs, and Wi-Fi; some have fireplaces. Rate includes vouchers for made-to-order breakfast at the Blue House Bakery Mon through Sat and breakfast in bed at the inn on Sun. $$–$$$.

south

day trip 01

south

birds, bosque, and hot springs:
socorro and truth or consequences

This drive down I-25 into the Chihuahuan Desert is popular with outdoors lovers in the winter, when temperatures are mild at lower elevations and waterfowl overwinter on the wetlands surrounding the Rio Grande. Two towns offer a good base for explorations in the area: Socorro, known for its mining institute, Fort Craig National Historic Site, and Bosque del Apache National Wildlife Refuge, and the funky desert hot springs town of Truth or Consequences, whose many historic, rustic resorts attract snowbirds and artists.

socorro

Socorro received its name, meaning "help," in 1598 from Spanish colonist Juan de Oñate, who found an ally in the Piro Pueblo people of this area during his expedition north to settle New Mexico. In fact, during the Pueblo Revolt, the Piros fled with Spaniards into El Paso, Texas, and never returned. When Spanish rule resumed, Socorro became an important stop on El Camino Real. El Camino Real International Heritage Center is 35 miles south of town, near the ruins of historic Fort Craig. In the 1880s, Socorro was mobbed on weekends by silver miners blowing off steam in its 44 saloons. Things are pretty boring around here now, but love of rocks keeps people coming. Students at New Mexico Institute of Mining and Technology study the volcanic landscape of the surrounding Magdalena and San Mateo Mountains. New Mexico Tech runs a popular campus geology museum and also administers the Very Large Array, a cluster of 27 telescopes on the Plains of San Agustin about 50 miles west of town (see Southwest Day Trip 01).

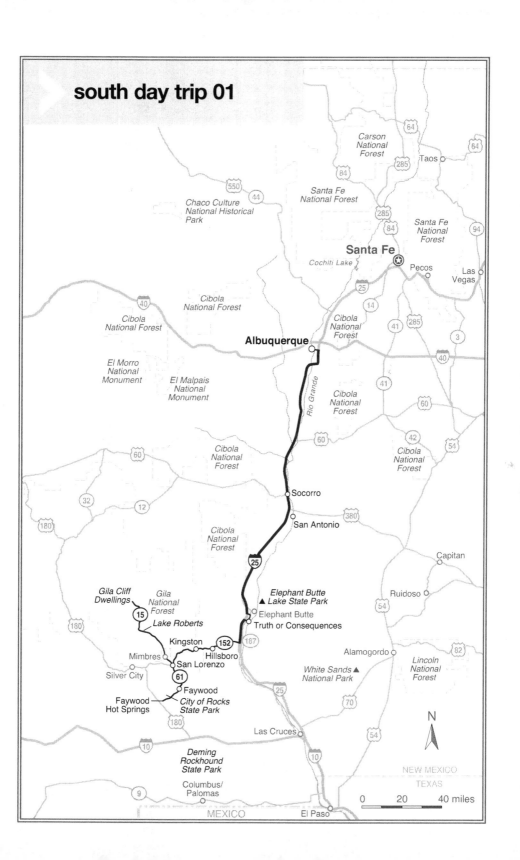

south day trip 01

Note: The main drag of Socorro is a dispiriting succession of gas stations and chain restaurants and lodgings. Take heart, though: A couple of popular bed-and-breakfasts in nearby San Antonio, the closest community to Bosque del Apache, offer good lodging options close to the refuge, allowing you to rise early to view the mass ascension of birds at the refuge in winter. If you want to visit during the popular Festival of the Cranes in November, book well ahead; they are very popular.

where to go

Bosque del Apache National Wildlife Refuge. SR 1, San Antonio; (575) 835-1828; friendsofthebosquedelapache.org. This 57,000-acre wildlife sanctuary sits on a bend in the Rio Grande and includes ponds and marshes. It is one of the nation's major stopovers for migratory waterfowl every fall. Photographers flock here to witness the mesmerizing dawn takeoffs and dusk landings of 15,000 sandhill cranes and thousands of Arctic and snow geese, ducks, and shorebirds—one of the great wildlife sights in the world. Information about birding tours, photography workshops, lectures, and the popular November Festival of the Cranes weekend is available at the visitor center and on their website. Visitor center open Sept through May 8 a.m. to 4 p.m.; closed Tues and Wed June, July, and Aug. Tour loop daily, one hour before sunrise, one hour after sunset. Admission fee.

Fort Craig National Historic Site. I-25, exit 124; 901 S. US 85, Socorro; (575) 835-0412; blm.gov/visit/fort-craig-historic-site. In the mid-1800s, this ruined fort was one of eight forts protecting citizens of the Rio Grande valley. It played an important role in Indian campaigns (buffalo soldiers—African Americans who served in the military—were stationed here) and in repelling Confederate advances during the Civil War. It has self-guided hikes and occasional Civil War reenactments. Free.

New Mexico Bureau of Geology and Mineral Resources Mineral Museum at New Mexico Tech. 801 Leroy Place, Socorro; (575) 835-5620; geoinfo.nmt.edu/museum/home.html. New Mexico Tech was founded in 1889 and is one of the leading undergraduate and graduate institutions for science, engineering, and mining in the West. Programs include earth sciences, astrophysics, petroleum recovery, and hydrology. In recent years, it has received additional funding from the federal Department of Homeland Security for its research programs. Over 5,000 geological specimens from around New Mexico, including silver and turquoise, are displayed in the Mineral Museum, a true treasure trove with its extraordinary large-size gems. Open Mon through Fri 9 a.m. to 5 p.m. and weekends 10 a.m. to 3 p.m. Free.

where to eat

M Mountain Coffee. 110 W. Manzanares St., Socorro; (575) 838-0809. This laid-back student hangout sits right on the plaza in Socorro and offers stuffed croissants, paninis, baked goods, and other light cafe fare. It's a good place to stop to check your email, cool down with a homemade gelato on a hot day, or get a coffee and sandwich for the road. The owner is a professor at New Mexico Tech. Open daily 7 a.m. to 6 p.m. $.

Owl Bar and Cafe. 77 US 380, San Antonio; (575) 835-9946; sanantonioowl.com. Mecca for burger lovers on the Green Chile Cheeseburger Trail through New Mexico, the Owl serves up one of the best in the West, attracting burger pilgrims from across the country. San Antonio is a tiny Hispanic village, but it is also famous for having the first vineyard in New Mexico and as the birthplace of hotelier Conrad Hilton. The spit-and-sawdust Owl is the place to eat after a day birding at Bosque del Apache. Open Mon through Sat 8 a.m. to 8 p.m. $.

Socorro Springs Restaurant and Brewery. 1012 N. California St., Socorro; (575) 838-0650. This brewery is pretty much your only bet for decent substantial casual food on the main drag in Socorro. They serve Colorado microbrewed ale and a selection of wood-fired pizzas and other grilled foods, as well as soup, sandwiches, and salads. Open daily 10:30 a.m. to 10 p.m. $.

where to stay

Casa Blanca Bed and Breakfast. 13 Montoya St., San Antonio; (575) 835-3027; casablancabedandbreakfast.com. This homespun B&B was built in 1880 by Eutimio Montoya, a well-known territorial representative to the government in Santa Fe. Built of double adobe (24-inch-thick walls) with a typical tin roof and a large veranda, it was one of the largest Victorian farmhouses in the area. Stay in either the Heron, Crane, or Egret rooms. The assistant innkeeper is a former Bosque del Apache refuge manager, so you're in good hands. $–$$.

Fite Ranch Bed and Breakfast. CR A153 (Fite Ranch Road), San Antonio; (575) 838-0958; fiteranchbedandbreakfast.com. This working cattle ranch offers 3 charming guest-room options for overnight guests. Each room has an interesting family story attached to it. The Evelyn Fite room, for example, is named after the Fite matriarch who moved to the ranch to marry her cowboy husband and lived here for 64 years, building up the ranch house from its humble beginnings in an old railroad boxcar to the beautiful spread you see today. There's also an attractive "bunkhouse" made from old stalls with 4 queen-size beds. An authentic cowboy experience. No pets allowed. $$.

truth or consequences

Before it changed its name to Truth or Consequences in a 1950 publicity stunt to mark the 10th anniversary of the eponymous TV show, this funny little town in southern New Mexico—near Elephant Butte Reservoir—had a name more in keeping with its main attraction: Hot Springs. Local Indians, including Apache leader Geronimo, and achy cowboys frequented the mineral springs, and by the early 1900s rustic resorts had appeared. The town has been popular with snowbirds for decades, and many of the original historic resorts and RV parks that sprang up to accommodate them are still in business, giving the whole town the air of another era. Perhaps because everyone soaks regularly, it's very laid-back here, with nothing much to distract you from the healing waters and just relaxing. T or C, as it's known locally, attracts artists and entrepreneurs who enjoy rubbing shoulders with the mix of folks who live in this small town. Several art galleries, healthy eating restaurants, and spiritual centers have opened, and more recently CNN founder and rancher Ted Turner has taken over the elegant Sierra Grande Lodge and Spa in a 1929 building in town and is operating tours of his nearby ranches from there. In addition, the opening of the New Mexico Spaceport in the desert nearby—a joint venture of the state and Virgin Airlines founder Richard Branson—has brought new jobs and tourism. The main visitor center for the Spaceport is in downtown T or C, the jumping-off point for four-hour tours of the facility.

where to go

Caballo Lake State Park. SR 187, Caballo; (575) 743-3942; emnrd.state.nm.us/SPD/Caballostatepark.html. Caballo Lake is 16 miles south of T or C, via exit 59 and SR 187. It is well known for its nesting bald and gold eagles in winter. Activities include boating, fishing, camping, waterskiing, and wildlife viewing. There is a 170-site campground with restrooms and water. A visitor center has exhibits on natural history. Open 24 hours. Admission fee.

Elephant Butte Lake State Park. 101 SR 195, Elephant Butte; (575) 744-5923; emnrd.state.nm.us/SPD/elephantbuttestatepark.html. The eroded core of an extinct volcano forms an island in the lake in the shape of an elephant, giving this park its name. The reservoir is a big draw for bass fishermen, boaters, windsurfers, and swimmers. There's also developed camping and hiking. Park headquarters is 5 miles north of T or C, via exit 83 off I-25. The visitor center has exhibits and information. There is a 132-site campground with restrooms, showers, water, and a marina. Open 24 hours. Admission fee.

Geronimo Springs Museum. 211 Main St.; (575) 894-6600; geronimospringsmuseum.com. This "Grandma's attic" type of place is on the site of the original springs and has an outdoor ceramic-mosaic fountain that commemorates the Apache leader's link with the town. Inside, Sierra County's Indian, Hispanic, and frontier ranching history is told through interesting artifacts, including pottery and an old log cabin. Open Mon through Sat 9 a.m. to 5 p.m. and Sun noon to 5 p.m. Admission fee.

Spaceport America Experience Tour. 301 S. Foch St.; (575) 267-8888, (844) 7-2SPACE; spaceportamericatour.com. After years of anticipation, Spaceport America, the world's first commercial spaceport, is now open to the public for tours by advance reservation. For security reasons it is a closed facility, which means that you must be accompanied as part of an official tour, so plan ahead. Tours leave from the Spaceport America Visitor Center in a historic adobe building in downtown T or C, which offers exhibits before visitors board the shuttle out to the desert to the Spaceport. On arrival, you will walk up the Astronaut Walk into the Gateway Gallery, featuring hands-on multimedia exhibits as well as the G-Shock

Simulator, which allows you to experience the same type of acceleration as astronauts do on launch into space. After this, Spaceport personnel are available to discuss their work in the Spaceport Operations Center (SOC). The entire tour lasts 4 hours. Note: The operator of the official Spaceport America Experience Tour, Final Frontier Tours, also offers Fri departures from the Visit Las Cruces visitor center (336 S. Main St., Las Cruces; lascrucescvb.org/explore/spaceport-america), should this be more convenient for you. Open daily 8:30 a.m. to 4:30 p.m.

where to shop

Black Cat Books and Coffee. 128 Broadway; (575) 894-7070; facebook.com/blackcat booksandcoffee. This quirky book lover's paradise is located near the Rio Grande and Ralph Edwards Park. After being started by longtime owner Rhonda Brittain, it is now operating as a trust run by volunteers and remains a popular community hangout. It's just the place to curl up with a used or newly published tome, a cup of locally roasted organic coffee from the carafe, and a homemade pastry. They host regular author readings and live music. A good place to stop off before or after visiting the Saturday farmers' market in the park (May through Oct). Open year-round Fri through Mon 8 a.m. to 4 p.m. and for morning coffee Tues through Thurs 7:30 to 10:30 a.m.

Rio Bravo Fine Art. 110 E. Broadway; (575) 894-0972; riobravofineart.com. The studio and gallery of the late T or C artist H. Joe Waldrum, located next door to Black Cat Books, has been run by his daughter as a contemporary art gallery since 2000. It shows work by other well-known local artists, including Delmas Howe, famous for his gay cowboy erotic art, but focuses on the art of H. Joe Waldrum. Open Wed through Sun, noon to 5 p.m., or by appointment. This gallery opens as part of the second Saturday T or C Art Hop, a monthly evening art walk through town from 6 to 9 p.m.

where to eat

Latitude 33 Brewing. 304 S. Pershing St.; (575) 740-7804; latitude33.sierracountynm.org. This brightly painted little cafe is flooded with sun late in the day and makes a good place to eat in or get takeout. It offers good Asian fusion cuisine drawing on local ingredients and features soups, entree salads, curries, and pork, beef, and chicken. Try the local flank steak and kale salad, if you get a chance. Lunch specials offered until 3 p.m. are a really good deal. Open Mon through Thurs 3 to 9 p.m., Fri, Sat noon to 10 p.m., and Sun noon to 7 p.m. $–$$.

Pacific Grill. 800 N. Date St.; (575) 894-7687. The fish dishes at this popular restaurant are top-notch and very fresh tasting, considering the distance from the ocean. Both the salmon and the halibut are good, and salads are made with local farmers' market produce. Save room for their fresh key lime pie and a margarita. Open for lunch Tues through Fri 11 a.m. to 2 p.m.; dinner Tues, Thurs, Fri, and Sat 5 to 8 p.m. $–$$.

Passion Pie Cafe. 406 Main St.; (575) 894-0008. This delightful cafe near the Geronimo Springs Museum offers delicious breakfasts and lunches. Choose from fresh homemade breakfast and lunch croissant sandwiches, soups, salads, quiche, and pizza, as well as specials like the hummus plate, ceviche, and elk shepherd's pie. Naturally, it's the baked goods that earn the raves, from sinfully rich scones and cupcakes to, of course, really good pie. They have gluten-free items, and the coffee is locally roasted. Open 7 a.m. to 3 p.m. daily. $.

The Restaurant at Sierra Grande. 501 McAdoo St.; (877) 2TURNER; tedturnerreserves .com/sierra-grande. Under the ownership of Ted Turner, the fine-dining restaurant at the Sierra Grande Lodge has reopened and now offers upscale modern Western seasonal cuisine, focusing on game such as bison, antelope, and steelhead trout; locally sourced produce; and innovative Southwest dishes like pecan-crusted chile rellenos. For breakfast, the dining room serves a hot breakfast menu to overnight guests; other breakfast specials include Southwest eggs Benedict, fresh-griddle burritos, and the Hatch Dream omelette with cheese and chiles. Open for breakfast Sun through Fri 7 to 11 a.m. and Sat 7 a.m. to noon; Sunday brunch 11 a.m. to 2 p.m.; dinner nightly 5 to 9 pm. $–$$$.

where to stay

Sierra Grande Lodge and Spa. 501 McAdoo St.; (877) 2TURNER; tedturnerreserves.com/sierra-grande. The historic 1929 Sierra Grande Lodge roared back to life under the watchful eye of French-born New York restaurateur Serge Raoul in 1991, who found personal healing in the mineral waters and enduring friendships with the town's two famous artists, Delmas Howe and the late Joe Waldrum, and moved here. He and his brother remodeled the hotel to European standards, creating 17 beautifully appointed king and queen guest rooms and suites and a garden casita, a spa offering massage and other body treatments using local products, and an enclosed hot spring with tile mural (30-minute soaks are complimentary with your room, along with a substantial hot breakfast). Now part of environmentalist and entrepreneur Ted Turner's portfolio, the hotel serves as a base for guests taking tours of his nearby Ladder and Armendaris game ranches, but is open to all and still a great place for a romantic getaway and meal. $$–$$$$.

day trip 02

south

> **mining ghosts, mogollon ruins, mountain air, and desert parks:**
> hillsboro, kingston, mimbres river valley, deming, las cruces, organ mountains–desert peaks national monument

This drive takes in parts of the Geronimo Trail, Lake Valley, and Trail of the Mountain Spirits Scenic Byways and offers an interesting juxtaposition of ancient and modern, mountain and desert, wilderness and city, and a pleasingly rugged beauty. The first part of the tour winds through quiet ghost towns over high passes and narrow back roads, and the second part covers a lot of desert terrain, so you'll want to allow time to explore. Leaving I-25 just south of Truth or Consequences, SR 152 heads west for a slow 75 miles to Silver City, over the Black Range, taking in the tiny former mining towns of Hillsboro, Lake Valley, and Kingston; Emory Pass; Gila National Forest; and Gila Cliff Dwellings National Monument, via the Mimbres Valley, on SR 35 and SR 15. From here, you can either break your journey in Silver City (see Southwest Day Trip 01) or head directly south on US 180 to Deming, visiting City of Rocks State Park on the way. From Deming, it's a speedy drive east on I-10 to Las Cruces, New Mexico's second-largest city, to visit museums, Old Mesilla, the Oñate Trail in Mesilla Valley, and expansive Organ Mountains–Desert Peaks National Monument, one of the state's newest national monuments. With more time, on the return north on I-25, visit the ruins at Fort Selden Historic Site and the chile capital of Hatch during the late summer chile season.

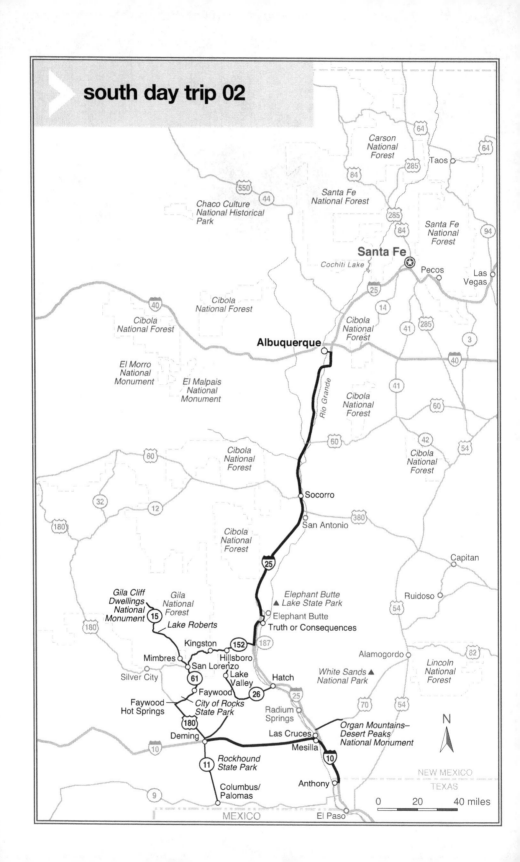

hillsboro

Founded in 1877 as the result of a gold discovery in the hills surrounding Percha Creek, Hillsboro is about 12 miles west of I-25 on SR 152 via Lake Valley Scenic Byway. More of a sleepy little village than a destination, you'll find a small farm stand on the way into town, a winery tasting room, a cafe in an old mercantile, a quaint historic bed-and-breakfast inn, and a little town museum.

where to go

Black Range Museum. Main Street (SR 152); (575) 895-5233; hillsboronmhistory.info/main-street-hillsboro-nm-88042. Housed in a former hotel and brothel across from a public picnic area on the east side of the village, this little museum is run by the local historical society and filled with artifacts from the mining era. Open Fri through Sun 11 a.m. to 4 p.m. Free.

Black Range Vineyards Tasting Room. Main Street (SR 152); (575) 895-3334; blackrangevineyards.com. Founded in 2007 by Nicki and Brian O'Dell, this small winery is an unexpected find in this tiny village. It grows Pinot Noir and Cabernet Sauvignon grapes in a nearby canyon in the foothills of the Black Range and specializes in dry red vintage wines. Their tasting room and patio are in an attractive 1890s adobe building and in addition to wine tastings also serve tapas. Open Thurs through Sun noon to 6 p.m.

Lake Valley Historic Townsite. SR 27, 17 miles south of Hillsboro; (575) 525-4300; blm.gov/visit/lake-valley-historic-townsite. The mining town of Lake Valley, south of Hillsboro, was founded in 1878 following the discovery of silver and almost overnight grew into a major settlement with a population of 4,000 people. It moved twice, finally settling on this location when the Bridal Chamber Mine was found in 1882, which yielded 2.5 million ounces of silver so pure it was shipped to the US Mint unsmelted. Lake Valley became a stage stop and railhead and had stores, newspapers, saloons, hotels, churches, and a school. It was wiped out during the Silver Panic of 1893, and a fire destroyed Main Street in 1895. Today, all that remains is a dusty ghost town, but its last residents actually left quite recently, in 1994, and moved to Deming (SR 26 continues south to Deming and I-10, but this drive returns you to SR 152). The site is managed by the Las Cruces District of the BLM, which has now restored the chapel and schoolhouse and stabilized the other buildings and the hundreds of others in Lake Valley. The restored schoolhouse offers a look at what schooling in a rural area was like in the early 1900s. A self-guided walking tour brochure can be picked up at the site. Note: Buildings are closed to entry. Open year-round Thurs through Mon 9 a.m. to 4 p.m. Toilet and water available. Free.

where to eat

Hillsboro General Store Cafe. 100 Main St.; (575) 895-5306; hillsborogeneralstore.com. Continuously in operation since 1876, this tiny cafe in a former general store has seen both boom and bust while variously serving as a post office, stage stop, telegraph office, soda fountain, and phone company. It phased out its "general store" function in the late 1990s and now concentrates on serving up hearty breakfasts and lunches five days a week (and dinners on some Saturday evenings and for special occasions), featuring soups, sandwiches, burgers, and a few New Mexican selections. Though the store no longer stocks the necessities of a rural household, it has adopted a gift-shop function, and the ambiance of the old general store remains in the period decor and glass display cases. Open Fri through Tues 8 a.m. to 3 p.m., dinner some Sats and special occasions until 7 p.m. $

where to stay

Enchanted Villa Bed & Breakfast. 10682 SR 152; (575) 895-5686; enchanted-villanm .com. Run by innkeeper Maree Westland, this lovely whitewashed historic home was designed by Maree's great-aunt in 1941 as a romantic retreat for a member of Burmese royalty called Sir Victor Sassoon, a multinational entrepreneur. The inn's 3 large guest rooms are fresh and inviting and have well-positioned windows for maximum light, king and queen beds, and en suite bathrooms. Reasonable rates include full breakfast. The inn has a large library and Wi-Fi. $.

kingston

Kingston was once a bustling Wild West town of 7,000 that entertained the likes of Butch Cassidy and the Sundance Kid and Black Jack Ketchum after silver was discovered in the Solitaire Mine in 1882. The town had 23 saloons (some of which served oysters), 14 grocery and general stores, a brewery, three newspapers, and an opera house. You would never know it now, as Kingston has become so sleepy that you could easily blink and miss the village, set off to the right, as you round a bend on SR 152. That would be a shame, because a walk in the historic cemetery is quite educational, there are museums in the former schoolhouse and bank building, and you can spend the night in an atmospheric rambling bed-and-breakfast, the Black Range Lodge, that was built from the ruins of Pretty Sam's Casino and the Monarch Saloon. Both Hillsboro and Kingston have attracted artists and artisans to live there, and Kingston offers occasional straw-bale workshops, art exhibits, and events, but again . . . blink and you will miss them, so call ahead.

where to go

Kingston School House Museum. Water Street; (575) 895-5501. The little town museum is in an 1880s building and houses lots of artifacts and archives from the town's mining history. It is run by a nonprofit organization, the delightfully named Spit and Whittle Club in Kingston, one of the oldest social clubs in the West. Open first and third Sat of the month 11 a.m. to 4 p.m.; call for private tour other times. Free.

Percha Bank Museum. 46 Main St.; (575) 895-5652. The only fully intact historic building left in Kingston, the Percha Bank stands out even today as being quite grand. It has exhibits on the town's history and also hosts special art exhibits. Open by appointment. Free.

where to stay

Black Range Lodge. 119 Main St.; (575) 895-5652, (800) 676-5622; blackrangelodge .com. Run by Hollywood escapee and filmmaker/innkeeper Catherine Wanek and her husband, Pete Fust, this two-story rock-and-timber lodge has the feel of an Old West boardinghouse. It's group- and family-friendly, with separate buildings that can sleep multiple guests, and pet-friendly. There are 7 rooms in the lodge and a large common area on the lodge's second floor, with a piano, CD player, TV, and video games, as well as Wi-Fi access. A popular straw-bale guesthouse sleeps 4 and has a fully equipped kitchen, Jacuzzi, and satellite dish. It is uphill from the lodge and has breathtaking views of the mountains of the Black Range. A studio apartment sleeps 2 adults and 2 children, and the family-oriented Percha Creek House sleeps 14. The lodge offers workshops and retreats in addition to overnight lodging. Bocce ball court. Check their website for details. $–$$.

mimbres river valley

After leaving Kingston, the road climbs and winds steeply through the fragrant pine forests of the Gila National Forest, gaining nearly 3,000 feet in 9 miles, before reaching 8,200-foot Emory Pass, a great spot to park and take in fabulous views looking back east across the Black Range. At mile marker 22.5, at the Kneeling Nun Vista, views to the west are equally spectacular of the Kneeling Nun rock formation, a landmark for Apaches, early explorers, and settlers. From this point on, SR 152 descends into shady canyons with pretty riverside Forest Service campgrounds, such as the nicely developed Gallinas Campground, and steep cliffs clad in juniper and scrub oak. Eventually, the road levels out in the Mimbres River valley at San Lorenzo, where the Geronimo Trail National Scenic Byway ends and the Trail of the Mountain Spirits National Scenic Byway loop north on SR 35/15 to Gila Cliff Dwellings National Monument begins.

where to go

City of Rocks State Park. Faywood, off SR 61; (575) 536-2800; emnrd.state.nm.us/spd/ cityofrocksstatepark.html. Take SR 61 south at San Lorenzo to to reach City of Rocks State Park in Faywood. This relatively flat park is filled with vertical rock formations averaging 40 feet high that resemble the monoliths at Britain's Stonehenge. The rocks are the result of erosion on the remains of volcanic eruptions that occurred 34.9 million years ago. Because you can climb on the rocks, as well as hide behind them, this park is a natural playground for kids of all ages. The botanical garden here has examples of desert flora. The attractive new visitor center offers information. Camping in primitive sites and developed sites is available. Note: This location is at 5,200 feet elevation and very exposed and hot in summer. Open daily 7 a.m. to 9 p.m. Admission fee.

Faywood Hot Springs. 165 SR 61; (575) 536-9663; faywoodhotsprings.com. This rustic hot springs resort sits on natural geothermal springs in the desert adjoining City of Rocks State Park and offers private and public bathing, primitive camping, and cabins. A little funky and probably best enjoyed during cooler weather in the desert. Bring a flashlight to find your way around at night. Admission fee.

Gila Cliff Dwellings National Monument. (575) 536-9461; nps.gov/gicl. Tucked into natural caves under a canyon ledge, you'll find the remains of 40 pueblo-type cliff dwellings, granaries, and kivas, constructed by the Mogollon people and occupied for about 60 years starting in AD 1270 (for more on the Mogollon, see Southwest Day Trip 01). Guided ranger hikes to the cliff dwellings take place on the hour, and there is a small visitor center with exhibits and a bookstore. You'll find hot springs in the backcountry and numerous places to hike and camp in the Gila Wilderness, the country's oldest wilderness, a portion of which is named for naturalist Aldo Leopold. Outside the cliff dwellings and wilderness, you'll find developed campgrounds in the national forest, along with basic food, gas, and supplies and a couple of lodgings and restaurants. Note: There are two routes up to Gila Cliff Dwellings, which can be done as a loop: SR 15 from Silver City to the ruins, a trip of 44 miles, or this more easterly route on SR 35, via the Mimbres River valley, which is gentler and joins SR 15 beyond Lake Roberts. Allow plenty of time to visit the ruins, and don't forget to build in some downtime to relax. Gila Cliff Dwellings is open daily 9 a.m. to 4 p.m.; extended summer hours. Admission fee.

Mimbres Culture Heritage Site. 12 Sage Dr., Mimbres; MM 4 on SR 35; (575) 536-3333; mimbrescultureheritagesite.com. This privately run archeological site preserves an early pit house and a later pueblo that once housed up to 200 people belonging to the Mimbres branch of the Mogollon culture, early Puebloans who lived in this region 1,000 years ago. The Mattocks Ruin, named for the family who owned the site when it was first excavated in the 1920s, yielded some of the finest examples of Mimbres black-on-white pottery ever excavated and has long attracted archeologists. You can walk around the 19th-century farmstead, whose Gooch House is one of the only Territorial adobe homes left standing and contains exhibits on the Mimbres and pioneers in the valley and a gift shop. The best time to visit is the end of July, when the property holds a two-day Hummingbird Festival, celebrating the return of the tiny migrant birds from Mexico, which flock to over 20 feeders here. You can watch volunteers banding hummingbirds, learn about hummingbird life cycles from speakers, and enjoy music and food. Birding is a popular activity in the Mimbres and Gila

River valleys and Gila National Forest near Silver City, with some 140-plus species of birds recorded, including 7 species of hummingbirds. Open daily 11 a.m. to 3 p.m. Apr through Oct; Fri through Sun 11 a.m. to 3 p.m. Nov through Mar. Admission fee.

where to stay

Lake Roberts Cabins & General Store. 869 SR 35; (575) 536-9929; lakeroberts.com. If you don't feel like camping, these charming rustic cabins on Lake Roberts may be just the ticket. Groceries and other supplies can be purchased in the general store. Two-night minimum. Located 21 miles northwest of Mimbres, just before SR 35 joins SR 15 to Gila Cliff Dwellings. $.

Mesa Campground, Lake Roberts, Gila National Forest. SR 35; (575) 536-2250; fs .usda.gov/recarea/gila/recreation. I enjoy spending the night in the Mesa Campground overlooking Lake Roberts, relaxing with a book and enjoying the cool mountain air, visiting Gila Cliff Dwellings, then getting something nice to eat in Silver City. If you like, you can also fish for your dinner, as the lake is well-stocked with rainbow trout and catfish. There are 24 first-come, first-served sites available, and half have hookups. Fishing, boating, and hiking on a trail around the lake; flush toilets and water. If this one is full, Upper Campground is nearby, which has 12 sites. Located 21 miles northwest of Mimbres, just before SR 35 joins SR 15 to Gila Cliff Dwellings. $.

deming

US 180 meets I-10 at Deming, a rather homely city but one with a big heart that has offered much-needed shelter, medical attention, and supplies for Central American asylum seekers leaving detention centers en route to family sponsors. The main visitor attractions here, besides gas stations, diners, and chain motels, are a nice little hometown museum displaying Mimbres pottery and an odd but surprisingly well-attended event in late August called the Great American Duck Race, which brings thousands to New Mexico's border country. For an interesting detour, history buffs should drive south on SR 9 for 32 miles to the US-Mexico border to visit Columbus, famed as the location of Pancho Villa's attack on a military camp there in 1916.

where to go

Great American Duck Race. McKinley Duck Downs, Courthouse Park, Deming; (575) 546-2674; demingduckrace.com. This unique event is held annually on the fourth weekend in August. Dreamed up over 20 years ago in a bar (of course) as a way to create more interest in the area, it has put Deming on the map internationally. In addition to actually racing ducks, there's a parade, a golf tournament, a chile cook-off, a hot-air balloon rally, several sporting tournaments, and even a "Duck Queen" contest.

Luna Mimbres Museum. 301 S. Silver, Deming; (575) 546-2382; lunacountyhistorical society.com. Located in the 1916 three-story, redbrick National Guard Armory building, this museum is run by the Luna County Historical Society and has a variety of themed rooms, including the Military Room, Quilt Room, Doll Room, and Tack Room. The museum also depicts life in the Southwest, focusing on ranching, railroading, and mining. The Mimbres Room showcases examples of centuries-old Mimbres Indian pottery (see Southwest Day Trip 01) decorated with distinctive black-on-white geometric designs that feature animals and spiritual motifs. Open Mon through Sat 9 a.m. to 4 p.m. Free.

Pancho Villa State Park. 400 SR 9, Columbus; (575) 531-2711; emnrd.state.nm.us/spd/panchovillastatepark.html. About 32 miles south of Deming, the border town of Columbus makes an interesting detour (and also offers the chance to cross the border into Mexico for a visit or to get medical care). Columbus is best known for having been invaded during the 1916 Mexican Revolution by insurgent leader General Francisco "Pancho" Villa and 1,000 of his men in a ferocious battle that left 160 Americans and Mexicans dead. For 11 months, General "Black Jack" Pershing, who later commanded Allied forces during World War I, and 10,000 soldiers pursued Pancho Villa 400 miles into Mexico without capturing him. Several buildings dating from the time of Villa's raid still stand in Columbus, and the US Customs House, built in 1902, serves as the visitor center. The 60-acre state park displays army vehicles used by Pershing in the US retaliation for Villa's raid, the first foreign attack since the War of 1812 and the last on US soil. It has picnic facilities and a large RV campground. Open 24 hours. Admission fee.

Rockhound State Park. 9880 Stirrup Rd. SE, off SR 11, Deming; (575) 546-6182; emnrd .state.nm.us/spd/rockhoundstatepark.html. Located on the west side of the Little Florida Mountains, this state park is a mecca for anyone who loves gems and precious stones because you can, in fact, go rockhounding here, as the name implies, and gather up to 15 pounds of rocks per visit, including a variety of quartz crystals, agates, and opals. Open Wed through Sun 7 a.m. until sunset. Primitive and developed camping is available. Admission fee.

where to eat

Adobe Deli. 3970 Lewis Flats Rd. SE, Deming; (575) 546-0361; adobedeli.com. This Western-style steakhouse is known for its huge juicy steaks and French onion soup. It also has a saloon, cigar and oxygen bars, and a deli serving Boar's Head meats that will set you up with picnic fare. Open Mon through Sat 11 a.m. to 10 p.m., Sun 11 a.m. to 9 p.m. $–$$.

Elisa's House of Pies. 208 1/2 S. Silver Ave., Deming; (575) 494-4639. This tiny eatery is a little tricky to find—it's down an alley and a bit out of the way—but is the place if you have a hankering for Southern fried chicken and barbecue ribs with corn bread, collard greens, and all the fixings, not to mention homemade pie. There are four choices each day from a huge roster; the pineapple coconut chess, key lime, and buttermilk pies have their own fan club. $.

Irma's. 123 S. Silver Ave., Deming; (575) 544-4580; irmasrestaurant.four-food.com. Homemade authentic Mexican food, from the fresh frijoles to the guacamole, keeps them coming. This is where the locals eat. Open 7 a.m. to 8 p.m. daily. $.

Patio Cafe. 23 Broadway, Columbus; (575) 531-2495; patiocafedeming.bestcafes.online. This cafe in sleepy Columbus specializes in fresh juicy burgers made with a variety of fixings. You will also find a selection of salads and sandwiches and a kid-friendly menu. Open Mon through Fri 9 a.m. to 3 p.m.; closed weekends. $.

where to stay

La Quinta Inn and Suites. 4300 E. Pine St., Deming; (575) 546-0600; wyndhamhotels .com/laquinta/deming-new-mexico. Always a solid choice and very budget-friendly, La Quinta, located a mile from the Deming Airport, has spacious rooms, comfy beds, flat-screen TVs, and sitting areas and offers free hot breakfast and Wi-Fi. Pool, hot tub, workout room, business center, and vending machines. Pet-friendly. $.

Los Milagros Hotel. 204 W. Lima, Columbus; (575) 531-2467; losmilagroshotel.com. This attractive family-run hotel in the downtown historic district is a welcoming place for travelers, some of whom use it as home away from home while driving over the border to Mexico for medical and dental treatment, doing trainings in the area, or hiking/bicycling the Divide Trail. There are 5 large upstairs rooms and a large room downstairs; a room with two beds, a bathroom, and kitchen facilities is available through Airbnb; and there is also an RV campground. Nightly and weekly rates available. Continental breakfast included. $.

las cruces and environs

New Mexico's second-largest and fastest-growing city sprawls between the Rio Grande and Organ Mountains in the Mesilla Valley, close to the border with Mexico. Named for the crosses that early Spanish travelers noted on the hills, Las Cruces has grown from a traditional farming community to embrace the modern era. It is home to the second-largest university in New Mexico, several museums, and a visitor center for nearby Spaceport America, but much of its ranching and agricultural background remains. There is a historic downtown, but many attractions lie on the periphery, including Old Mesilla and the nearby Oñate Trail's wineries and nut farms down SR 28, a highly recommended detour to the south. New Mexico's newest national monument, Organ Mountains–Desert Peaks National Monument, surrounds the town, and although undeveloped, has brought increased tourism, particularly in the cool months, when temperatures are comfortable enough to camp, hike, and enjoy the rugged natural beauty of the Organ Mountains.

where to go

New Mexico Farm and Heritage Museum. 4100 Dripping Springs Rd. (1.5 miles east of NMSU Golf Course); (575) 522-4100; nmfarmandranchumuseum.org. Located between the lush, irrigated farmlands of the lower Rio Grande valley and the cattle ranches on the slopes of the dramatic Organ Mountains, the 47-acre museum complex has a Mogollon pit house and a replica of a grain storage room from Chaco Canyon, as well as horse-drawn plows and early mechanized farm equipment, but also showcases the modern, scientific agricultural era. Outdoor exhibits include an adobe blacksmith shop, a relocated log cabin, and a windmill. Regular demonstrations include blacksmithing, weaving, quilting, and butter churning; the milking demonstration in the dairy barn is the most popular with old and young alike. There are also classes on adobe making, gardening, roping and other cowboy skills, photography, and wool spinning. Besides dairy cows, animals on the grounds include Belgian draft horses, longhorn cattle, Jerusalem donkeys, and Churro sheep and goats. The museum hosts La Fiesta de San Ysidro (the patron saint of agriculture) each May. To reach the museum, take exit 1 off I-25 (University Boulevard, which turns into Dripping Springs Road). A visit to the museum pairs well with a visit to the Dripping Springs Area of Organ Mountains–Desert Peaks National Monument, which is farther down the road and dead-ends at the Organ Mountains. Open Mon through Sat 9 a.m. to 5 p.m. and Sun noon to 5 p.m. Admission fee; discounts for seniors and young people ages 5 to 17; free for kids under 5, museum members, and military veterans.

Old Mesilla. oldmesilla.org. Old Mesilla, 5 miles south of Las Cruces on SR 28 (Avenida de Mesilla), is famous as the place where the Gadsden Purchase was signed in 1853, fixing the boundary between the US and Mexico and ceding vast areas of the Southwest to the US that had once been Mexican territory. Unlike Las Cruces, it retains the ambiance of Old Mexico in its compact downtown plaza and is a delightful destination for lunch or dinner and to wander around. On the plaza are La Posta, the old Butterworth Overland Mail stage station; the Billy the Kid Gift Shop, on the site of the courthouse where the Kid was sentenced to hang in 1881; and San Albino Church, built in 1906 to replace the 1856 adobe church. There's a farmers' market on Thurs and Sun.

Oñate Trail. SR 28 south of Mesilla. Named for Spanish explorer Don Juan de Oñate, often cited as the founder of New Mexico, the roadway traces part of the route that Oñate took into New Mexico more than 400 years ago. Roughly parallel to both the Rio Grande and I-25, this more leisurely route through the Mesilla Valley connects rural communities southwest of Las Cruces, which are home to several interesting places to stop and shop. **Stahmann Farms** (22505 SR 28, La Mesa; 575-526-2453; stahmannpecan.com) began in 1932 and now boasts 168,000 pecan trees on 3,200 acres (1,295 hectares), making it one of the world's largest pecan groves. About 17 miles farther south, **La Viña Winery** (575-882-7632; lavinawinery.com) is New Mexico's oldest winery. Founded in 1977, it offers tastings and hosts a Harvest Festival in Oct, a Fourth of July Picnic, and a Spring Festival at the end of Apr. Winery open Thurs through Tues noon to 5 p.m.; tours daily by appointment at 11:30 a.m.

where to eat

Chope's Bar and Grill. 16145 S. SR 28, La Mesa; (575) 233-3420; facebook.com/chopes bar. People make a special trip down the Oñate Trail from Las Cruces for inexpensive, authentic New Mexican and Mexican food at this century-old family-run restaurant originally started in a home. They are known for their chile rellenos. Open daily 11:30 a.m. to 1:30 p.m. for lunch and 5 to 8:30 p.m. for dinner. $.

Double Eagle Restaurant. Old Mesilla Plaza; (575) 523-6700; doubleeagleonline.com. This high-end restaurant in a restored 1849 adobe mansion is famous for its aged steaks and unique atmosphere, where you dine beneath gold-leaf ceilings, crystal chandeliers, antique furnishings, and 19th-century paintings. There are even ghosts! Open Mon through Sat 11 a.m. to 10 p.m.; Sunday brunch seatings at 11 a.m. and 1:30 p.m.; takeout service Sun noon to 5 p.m. $$–$$$.

La Posta de Mesilla. 2410 Calle de San Albino, Mesilla; (575) 524-3524; laposta-de -mesilla.com. This historic family-run eatery on the Mesilla Plaza is in an 18th-century stagecoach station and has been serving good, inexpensive New Mexican and Mexican food and steaks since 1939. There's also a tequileria, a gift shop, an aviary, and oddly enough, a piranha tank. $–$$.

where to stay

Hotel Encanto de Las Cruces. 705 S. Telshor Blvd., Las Cruces; (866) 383-0443; hotel encanto.com. This resort hotel in downtown Las Cruces is a former Hilton hotel but has a lot of Southwest charm. Comfortable and good value for your money, it offers soothing dark-wood Mission-style furnishings, Wi-Fi, microwaves and fridges in the rooms and suites (on request), an on-site bar, and a Garduños restaurant serving good New Mexican food. It's managed by Heritage Hotels and Resorts, which also runs the distinctive Chimayo de Santa Fe and Lodge at Santa Fe hotels in Santa Fe, two good bets for boutique hotels in the "City Different." The hotel has been designated a Doña Ana County Virgin Galactic Preferred Hotel for astronauts and their families taking part in the upcoming Spaceport America commercial flights. Located in the historic downtown. Pool and fitness room. Dog-friendly. $$.

Lundeen Inn of the Arts. 618 S. Alameda, Las Cruces; (575) 526-3326, (888) 526-3326; innofthearts.com. Located just 5 minutes from Mesilla and run by Linda and Jerry Lundeen, this bed-and-breakfast consists of 2 adobe homes and adjoins Linda's art gallery and Jerry's architectural office. Works by Southwestern artists are everywhere, including the guest rooms, and most of the 300-plus pieces are for sale. Each of the 7 oversize guest rooms is unique in both configuration and decor and named after an American artist, such as Georgia

O'Keeffe and Navajo artist R. C. Gorman. All rooms have queen-size beds and private baths, and some even have fireplaces and kitchenettes. The inn offers weeklong architecture and arts classes, including silversmithing and pottery making; Jerry is a lay minister who performs wedding ceremonies at the inn. Weekly and monthly rates are available. Pets are welcome for an extra fee. $–$$.

organ mountains–desert peaks national monument

New Mexico's newest national monument was set aside by President Obama in May 2014 to protect significant historic, prehistoric, geologic, and biologic resources. Managed by the Las Cruces office of the BLM, the 496,330-acre national monument is divided into three main sections surrounding the city: the spectacular 9,000-foot-high Organ Mountains, east of Las Cruces; the Desert Peaks, which comprise the Robledo Mountains, Sierra de las Uvas, and the Doña Ana Mountains, northwest of Las Cruces, adjoining Prehistoric Track-way National Monument; and the Potrillo Mountains, southwest of Las Cruces, which contain volcanic features, including Kilbourne Hole Volcanic Crater National Historic Landmark, an 80,000-year-old volcanic maar crater used as a training ground by Apollo astronauts. This is a large, wild, remote, and exposed national monument and requires time and planning to visit. Dripping Springs Natural Area, just east of Las Cruces but on the west side of the scenic Organ Mountains, is the main visitor-friendly section.

where to go

Dripping Springs Natural Area. 15000 Dripping Springs Rd., Las Cruces; (575) 522-1219; blm.gov/visit/dripping-springs-natural-area. Dripping Springs is your best bet for a look at the national monument. It has a visitor center with exhibits and information, 12 picnic tables, restrooms, water, and 4 miles of trails. One of the trails leads past La Cueva Rock Shelter, which dates from the Desert Archaic period, 5000 BC, to the historic period, when it was occupied by Apaches and later by an eccentric recluse named Giovanni Maria Agotino, known locally as "the Hermit." In the mid-1970s approximately 100,000 artifacts were recovered from here by the University of Texas at El Paso. Another trail leads to the ruins of Dripping Springs Resort, built in 1873 by Colonel Eugene Patten and in 1917 converted to a sanitarium. Note: Camping is not allowed at this location. Dripping Springs Natural Area is located 10 miles east of Las Cruces, on the west side of the Organ Mountains. From exit 1 on I-25, take University Avenue/Dripping Springs Road east to the end. Open daily except for holidays; gates open 7 a.m. to sunset Apr through Sept, 8 a.m. to sunset Oct through Mar; visitor center open 8 a.m. to 5 p.m. Admission fee.

where to stay

Aguirre Spring Campground. Aguirre Spring Road (1.1 miles after San Augustine Pass on US 70), Las Cruces; (575) 525-4300; blm.gov/visit/aguirre-spring-campground. The views of White Sands and the Tularosa Basin are absolutely spectacular from this developed campground east of and directly below the soaring Organ Mountains, south of US 70 before you get to Holloman Air Force Base. The main campground for the national monument, Aguirre Spring has 55 campsites, available on a first-come, first-served basis, and 2 group campsites that may be reserved. All are nicely screened by piñon and juniper, and have tent pads, metal shelters and tables, and fire rings. Pit toilets; water is only available from the camp host, who may not be there, so bring everything you need. The Baylor and Pine Tree Trails leave from this campground. After leaving the interstate, the road up to the campground is 6 miles and becomes one way. Some important notes if you plan on camping here (the only campground in the Las Cruces area): (1) it is exposed and scorching hot in summer, so it's best to come off-season and be sure to carry water, food, and all you need, as there are no stores anywhere nearby; (2) after leaving the highway, the road up to the campground is a narrow and winding 6 miles and becomes one way, and it is not recommended for RVs; and (3) the entry gate is locked early each evening at 6 p.m., so plan accordingly and be sure you don't get locked out, or locked in if you need to be somewhere. $.

with more time

Fifteen miles north of Las Cruces, on I-25, you'll find **Fort Selden State Historic Site** (1280 Fort Selden Rd.; 575-526-8911; nmhistoricsites.org/fort-selden), the ruins of the adobe military fort built in the mid-1800s to protect Las Cruces settlers and travelers from Apache attacks. It was the boyhood home of General Douglas MacArthur from 1884 to 1886, when his father was the post commander; the acclaimed Buffalo Soldiers, a regiment of black soldiers honored for their success in subduing the Plains Indians, were also stationed here. A visitor center explains the history of the fort and displays articles of interest found here. Trails wind around the ruins, with interpretive signs showing old photos of the fort as it was in the 1800s. To get there, take the Radium Springs exit and head west a couple of miles. Open Wed through Mon 8:30 a.m. to 5 p.m. Admission fee.

In northwestern Doña Ana County is the community of **Hatch,** renowned as the "Chile Capital of the World." It produces some of the highest quality, as well as largest quantities, of New Mexico's lucrative chile pepper crop. The **Hatch Valley Chile Festival** (575-267-1095; hatchchilefest.com) takes place over Labor Day weekend and includes a chile cook-off and *ristra* (strings of red chiles) arrangement competition, among other events. Hatch is on SR 26, 2 miles southwest of I-25 (exit 41) on the Rio Grande. This road is called the Deming Cutoff because it offers a quicker route to I-10 and Deming, avoiding Las Cruces.

While in Hatch, check out **Sparky's** (115 Franklin St.; 575-267-4222; sparkysburgers.com), a retro cafe famous for its juicy green chile cheeseburgers and barbecue served up in a fun fair-like vintage atmosphere. A Tucson writer friend likes to make a special detour off I-10 on the Deming Cutoff when headed east just to eat a burger at Sparky's. It's brightly painted— you can't miss it. Open Thurs through Sun 10:30 a.m. to 7 p.m.

southwest

day trip 01

southwest

>>> landscape art, telescopes, and
very good pie:
magdalena, datil, pie town, quemado,
reserve, glenwood, silver city

US 60 takes you across some beautiful, moody country along New Mexico's volcanic western edge. As a former northern Arizona resident, I enjoy driving this quiet route into Arizona via the Mogollon Rim and White Mountains rather than busy I-40. This long day trip explores western New Mexico, starting in Magdalena and going as far as Quemado, before dropping down for a spectacular drive on the other side of the Mogollon Mountains along US 180 to Silver City. Not only is the scenery entrancing, but you'll also meet a wonderful variety of folks, from ranchers, artists, and independent pioneer types to the best pie bakers around. The highlights of the journey are the Very Large Array, an important cluster of 27 large radio telescopes on the Plains of San Agustin; tasty home cooking in Pie Town on the Continental Divide; Walter de Maria's Lightning Field installation near Quemado; Mogollon ghost town; Gila National Forest; and old mining towns, including one that is now a delightful artist mecca: Silver City.

magdalena

To begin this day trip, drive south on I-25 to Socorro and head west on US 60 to Magdalena, the first community you will visit. In the 1800s Magdalena was the main railhead for shipping livestock to market. There are scant reminders of the importance of this blink-and-you-miss-it town now, save for a few notable downtown structures that you can view on

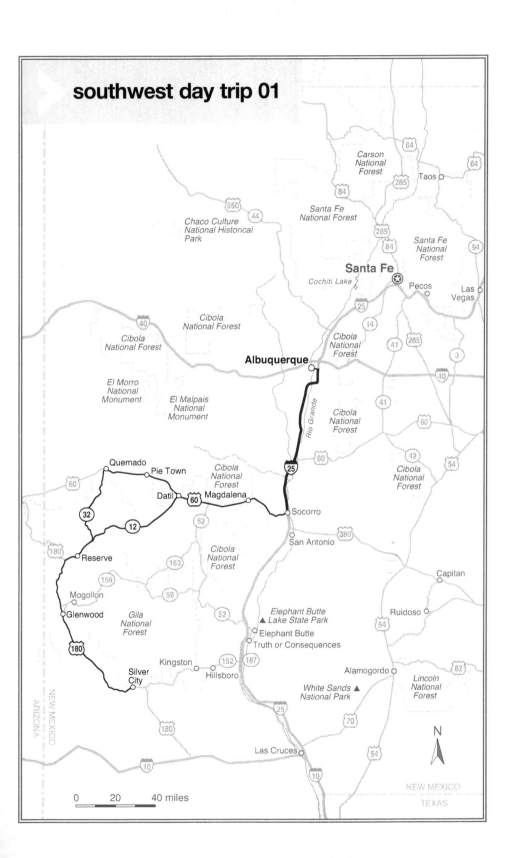

southwest day trip 01

a self-guided historic walk. Antiquated buildings are slowly being remodeled for other uses by new residents drawn by the quiet open spaces, inexpensive land, and good highway access. One historically interesting building, an authentic maternity hospital from the 1920s, now houses a motel. Several writers, artists, and craftspeople live in the area, and Magdalena is reinventing itself as an art town with numerous galleries and studios in the village. Magdalena was named by a fanciful local cowboy in the 1880s who thought a geological landmark near town looked like Mary Magdalene.

where to go

The Very Large Array. Off US 60; (575) 835-7410; public.nrao.edu/very-large-array. They come into view like a surreal sci-fi Western hallucination on the Plains of San Agustin, 25 miles west of Magdalena. If the 27 radio telescopes pointed at the sky in search of signs of life in deep space seem familiar, it's because they have been featured in *Contact*, the film based on Carl Sagan's futuristic book starring Jodie Foster. Each dish antenna is 82 feet wide and mounted on a rail that allows reconfiguration. A small visitor center has exhibits and a gift shop. A 9-minute film narrated by Jodie Foster explains radio astronomy, interferometry, and the VLA itself; other slide shows and films offer information on the Very Large Baseline Array and doing a self-guided tour, which takes you out the back to the base of a 230-ton antenna and up to an observation platform. Guided tours are offered by New Mexico Tech, the administrator, on the first and third Sat of the month at 11 a.m., 1 p.m., and 3 p.m. While visiting the VLA, photography is okay, but turn off electronic devices like cell phones, as they interfere with the radio signals. Visitor center open daily 8:30 a.m. to dusk. Free.

where to shop

Evett's Café and Gallery. 504 1st St.; (575) 517-7489; facebook.com/MagHighDesert. Opened in 2018, this art gallery and coffeehouse is in the historic Magdalena Bank building and owned by a Socorro children's author and artist and her son. It displays paintings, ceramics, photographs, fine woodwork, and weavings by local artists. The gallery is part of a burgeoning art scene in Magdalena, which now has several galleries and hosts an annual Gallery and Studio Tour in May featuring 16 venues. Open Wed through Sun 9 a.m. to 5 p.m.

where to eat

Kelly's Place Café. 404 2nd St.; (575) 517-0250; facebook.com/KellysPlaceCafe. This little cafe in the lobby of the restored Magdalena Hall Hotel is a real find, both for quality and price. It offers an eclectic menu of home-cooked New Mexican food with fresh red and green chile, homemade soups and cakes, and daily sandwich options and specials such as meat loaf, steak, and trout. Kelly, the chef-owner, is a big-city dropout and works the magic in the kitchen. The menu is posted on the cafe's Facebook page daily. Open Wed noon to 7 p.m., Thurs through Sat 11 a.m. to 7 p.m., and Sun 9 a.m. to noon. $

where to stay

Magdalena Hall Hotel. 404 2nd St.; (575) 854-2040; magdalenahallhotel.com. This three-story former cowboy hotel was built in 1917, and after a sensitive historic renovation by local owners, it reopened in 2019 as a charming boutique hotel with 3 comfortable rooms—a double, a queen, and a suite—all of which have kitchenettes, attractive modern Western furnishings, pine floors, quilts, and amenities such as Los Poblanos lavender toiletries. The friendly service, excellent on-site cafe, and reasonable room rate make this a winner. $.

The Western Motel and RV Park. 404 1st St.; (575) 418-7278; thewesternmotel.com. Located in the former Mrs. Butterfield's Lying-In Hospital, actually an adobe home in a residential neighborhood, this quaint place has been a motel since the late 1990s, after the owners bought the property from Magdalena's mayor and his wife. It offers 6 small Western-cabin-style rooms, with knotty-pine walls, quilts, and ranch knickknacks. Large indoor hot tub, landscaped grounds, gazebo, and adjoining 17-site RV park. A good budget option. $.

datil

Beyond the Very Large Array, you enter the wild, unspoiled ranch country of Catron County. Seismic movements along the Mogollon-Datil volcanic field have thrown up craggy mountain ranges and in between are vast prairies still used for cattle, sheep, and goat grazing. The main community gathering place in Datil is the 1920s-era Eagle Guest Ranch. It was built and run by the sister of early settler Agnes Morley Cleaveland, whose book *No Life for a Lady* described 1880s pioneer ranching in the area. You can get a bed for the night, a cooked meal, gas, and supplies here, but the best food in the area is in Pie Town, 22 miles ahead, where you can join local ranchers for a proper home-cooked meal and a slice of pie at one of several good cafes there.

Note: Datil is located at the junction of US 60 and SR 12, which leads south to US 180 and Silver City, where this day trip will end up. If you visit Pie Town and Quemado, you can take SR 32 over the Gallo Mountains for a scenic drive to pick up US 180 near Reserve.

where to go

Datil Well Recreation Area. US 60; (575) 835-0412; blm.gov/visit/datil-well-recreatio -area-campground. There are 3 miles of hiking trails among piñon-juniper vegetation at this historic location along the 19th-century cattle trail to Magdalena. It's a good place for a quiet backcountry walk and scenic views of the Plains of San Agustin and the mountains. The 22 primitive campsites have picnic tables and fire pits, and there are restrooms and water. No day-use fee; $5 overnight fee.

pie town

Pie Town sits astride the 8,000-foot-high Continental Divide pretty much in the middle of nowhere. Considering the "town" consists of a handful of businesses strung along US 60, it's remarkable how famous this remote settlement has become. It grew up in ad hoc fashion in the 1920s, when local rancher Ed Jones began walking 7 miles from his ranch to sell homemade pies to Dust Bowl refugees heading west on the dirt track that preceded US 60. Soon Jones and other entrepreneurs had a popular business supplying travelers, and Pie Town was born. Modern travelers are still grateful to stop for good food and supplies at this windswept spot today, whether motoring US 60 or hiking, riding, or biking the portion of the 3,100-mile Continental Divide Trail that passes through New Mexico near here (continentaldividetrail.org), which attracts cyclists from around the world. If you call any of the three cafes ahead of your visit, they'll usually make your favorite pie. Pie aficionados will want to time their visit to coincide with the annual Pie Festival in September, when there are pie-eating contests, hot-air ballooning, fiddle music, and square dancing.

where to eat

Daily Pie Cafe. 5596 US 60; (575) 772-2700; dailypie.com. This cafe is popular with local ranch families for burgers, barbecue, sandwiches, and, of course, its daily pies, which are listed on what else but a "pie chart." A big thumbs-up on the Cherry Bomb and Smithsonian apple pies, but they change daily. Open Fri through Tues 9 a.m. to 5 p.m. $–$$.

The Gatherin' Place. 5693 US 60; (575) 772-2909; thegatherinplace.wordpress.com. This cafe offers breakfast, lunch, and dinner and is the most likely of the three cafes to be open when you pass through, no matter what time of year. Try the huevos rancheros for breakfast and their award-winning barbecue pork for lunch or dinner, and don't forget the pecan-custard pie for dessert! Gift shop. Open 7:30 a.m. to 6 p.m. daily. $–$$.

Pie-O-Neer Cafe. 5613 US 60; (575) 772-2711; pieoneer.com. The pie cafes here all have their fans, but I think the Pie-O-Neer has the edge for hospitality, atmosphere, and pies that are not only tasty but beautiful. Illinois native Kathy Knapp has been baking her "very good pies" in the kitchen here since 1995, when she and her mother bought the old Pie-O-Neer as a family concern. Kathy now runs the cafe with partner Stan King, owner of the Silver Creek Inn in Mogollon, and they focus on pie. Kathy is famous for her oatmeal-pecan and cookie pies, as well as delicately beautiful berry pies with heart-shaped pastry decorations and a rather extraordinary red chile–chocolate chess pie; personally, I don't think you can beat the strawberry-rhubarb pie, a classic. All are now served from a handsome and inviting Pie Bar and tend to go fast. A feast for the eye as well as the tum! Kathy greets everyone as a friend when they walk through the door, making the long drive to get here well worth it, and many people do in fact make the long drive or bike ride specifically to eat here, so you will always meet someone interesting. On chilly days, there's a big woodstove putting out heat

images of the great depression

Moving black-and-white photographs of the poverty and living conditions of Pie Town ranchers during the Great Depression were taken by Texas documentarian Russell Lee for the Farm Security Administration in the 1930s. Like the iconic images of migratory workers made famous by Dorothea Lange, these photos capture the strength and will to overcome that often arises in the human spirit during difficult times. Lee's Pie Town photos are included in the 2004 anthology Bound for Glory: America in Color 1939–43.

to warm you up and usually some green chile stew in the pot. There is also an art gallery and gift shop, and Stan and Kathy sometimes play live music. Note: This cafe is only open Thurs through Sat 11:30 a.m. to 4 p.m., or until the pies are gone, from Pi Day (March 14) to Thanksgiving, so plan ahead; I highly recommend that you call Kathy ahead of time and ask her to bake your favorite pie and save you a slice or the whole thing to purchase. $–$$.

quemado

Quemado ("burned" in Spanish) is 22 miles west of Pie Town on US 60. It was named by settler José Antonio Padilla in 1880, when he discovered brush burned by local Indians. The town offers a few visitor services and is the field office for visits to The Lightning Field.

where to go

The Lightning Field. PO Box 2993, Corrales; diaart.org/visit/visit/walter-de-maria-the-lightning-field; reservations@ lightningfield.org. An interesting counterpoint to the Very Large Array, this large-scale earth art is composed of 400 stainless steel poles spaced 220 feet apart in a rectangular grid measuring 1 mile by 1 kilometer in an isolated prairie about an hour's drive north of Quemado. To view it, you must make reservations by email no earlier than February 1 for the year you wish to visit, as space is very limited. Guests are driven from Quemado to The Lightning Field and stay overnight in a simple three-bedroom cabin; meals are basic. It's best to form your own group if you wish to avoid sharing with strangers (two bedrooms have twin beds and one has a queen). Open May through Oct only. Admission fee.

Quemado Lake Recreation Area. 16 miles south of Quemado, via SR 32 and 103; (575) 388-8201; fs.usda.gov/recarea/gila. This 131-acre man-made lake in the Gila National Forest, 20 miles south of Quemado, is stocked with trout and is popular with anglers. It has 7 miles of hiking trails and 3 campgrounds. Admission fee.

reserve

This cute ranch town, formerly known as Lower San Francisco Plaza, has a couple of cafes and antiques stores. Its plaza was famous as the spot, in 1884, where lawyer, politician, and self-appointed lawman Elfego Baca holed up and refused to come in for questioning for the murder of a ranch foreman killed during an incident in which Baca was trying to apprehend and punish a drunken cowboy. During the Frisco Shootout, as it became known, Baca killed 4 of the 80 cowboys deputized to bring him in and wounded 8 more. Over the next 33 hours, more than 4,000 shots were allegedly fired into the home, but none killed Baca. He finally was persuaded to surrender and was charged, tried, and acquitted after his defense produced the door of the home, which was peppered with 400 bullets. In 1958 Baca's colorful life was immortalized in Walt Disney's television miniseries *The Nine Lives of Elfego Baca* starring Robert Loggia. From Quemado, travel south on SR 32 and then south on SR 12. Or, from Datil, take SR 12 south into Reserve.

where to eat

Ella's Cafe. 96 Main St.; (575) 533-6111; facebook.com/EllasCafe. The sign on its door, "If you don't climb the mountain, you can't see the view," announces that this cafe believes in aspiration. Obviously, they are doing something right. This popular little hometown diner in ranch country is on New Mexico Tourism's Green Chile Cheeseburger Trail, so, in a state where green chile cheeseburgers abound, that's quite a recommendation. Ella's also serves sandwiches and American diner favorites, such as omelets, chicken-fried steak, and homemade pies, as well as Mexican food. The cafe is right on Main Street, a good place to walk off that huge burger. Open for breakfast, lunch, and dinner 7 a.m. to 8 p.m. Tues through Sun. $.

the great green chile cheeseburger trail

Along with the Owl Bar and Cafe and Buckhorn Tavern in San Antonio, Blake's Lotaburger in Socorro, and Santa Fe Bite in Santa Fe, Ella's Cafe is part of the state's recently inaugurated Great Green Chile Cheeseburger Trail (there's a map at newmexico.org). New Mexico invented the green chile cheeseburger, and we take them very seriously here. When Buckhorn Tavern recently won with its green chile cheeseburger on Food Network's Throwdown With Bobby Flay, *Governor Bill Richardson honored the restaurant with a statewide Buckhorn Tavern Day.*

glenwood

From Reserve, pick up US 180 via SR 12 South. US 180 South passes the 10,000-foot Mogollon Mountains and pierces the spectacular 3.3-million-acre Gila National Forest, which contains three wilderness areas, including the nation's first — the Gila Wilderness, designated in 1924 at the urging of celebrated forester and conservationist Aldo Leopold. Stop at the Glenwood Ranger District station on US 180 near the Catwalk for more information on activities in the national forest and area attractions. Open Mon through Fri 8 a.m. to 4:30 p.m.

where to go

Catwalk Recreation Area. SR 174, off US 180; (575) 539-2481; fs.usda.gov/recarea/gila. The 0.5-mile Catwalk, located off US 180, 30 miles south of Reserve and 11 miles north of Glenwood near mile marker 41, is a wooden boardwalk trail suspended above a rushing creek in narrow Whitewater Canyon. It was built by the Civilian Conservation Corps (CCC) in 1935 and follows the route of a water pipeline built in 1893 to bring water to Graham, a silver-mining camp in the canyon. The CCC also built a pleasant US Forest Service campground in nearby Pueblo Park, atop an old pueblo, that is one of my favorite camping spots. Whitewater Canyon was a hideout of Butch Cassidy, who frequented nearby WS Ranch. Open daily from dawn to dusk. Note: Trail No. 207 is accessible for its first 0.5 mile, then continues from the Catwalk into the Gila National Forest for longer hikes and backpacking trips. Admission fee.

Mogollon Ghost Town. SR 159, off US 180. The 9-mile single-lane road to the old mining town of Mogollon (pop. 15) is not for the faint of heart. The narrow, winding road, which was built by convict labor in 1897, twists and turns alarmingly above a vertiginous drop to reach Whitewater Mesa and clings to the western slope of the Mogollon Mountains. It offers dramatic views of old mines such as the Little Fannie Mine before descending 600 feet. It requires a steady hand on the wheel and eyes glued to the road but is well worth the drive. At its terminus in Silver Creek Canyon, you'll find the charming ghost town of Mogollon on the edge of the national forest, where the air is fresh and cool and all is silent except for the roar of Silver Creek pouring off the mountain. A small museum has exhibits about the town, which produced about $5 million of gold and silver around 1915 and had a whopping 1,500 residents, 5 saloons, 4 general stores, a theater, a hospital, and 2 red-light districts. Just beyond the ghost town, there are several nice hiking trails into the national forest.

where to stay

Silver Creek Inn Bed and Breakfast. Located right at the entrance to Mogollon, opposite the little town museum; (866) 276-4882; silvercreekinn.com. You can enjoy yet more of Pie-O-Neer Cafe owner Kathy Knapp's memorable pies if you decide to spend a romantic weekend at this restored 1885 adobe, which she runs with partner Stan King. It was once

gila national forest and the mogollon people

US 180 winds through forested peak-and-canyon country along the Arizona–New Mexico border that begs exploration. This daunting terrain was home to the ancient Pueblo people who lived in the Mogollon region of southwest New Mexico. They were long known as the Mogollon culture, but archeologists now call them Ancestral Puebloan, in recognition of the cultural florescence that started in southwestern New Mexico and spread north. Several branches of the culture inhabited the region. The best known were the Mimbres, who lived in the Mimbres River drainage—talented artisans who developed magnificent black-on-white pottery. Another branch of the Mogollon lived north of Alamogordo, at what is now the Three Rivers Petroglyph site. In the early Christian era, the Mogollon enjoyed a remote existence in these resource-rich mountains, where they were expert hunter-gatherers who lived in extended family units in scattered pit-house villages. Contact with travelers from Mesoamerica around 2,000 years ago led them to develop pottery very early on, beginning with a lovely basic reddish ware and ending up with the refined Mimbres ceramics. These were recognizably related to Pueblo pottery manufactured in Chaco and Mesa Verde and became important trade items in the prehistoric Southwest. Gila Cliff Dwellings, a Mogollon village in the cliffs here, was built in AD 1280 in five caves that had been used for centuries by early hunters. The Gila is best known today for its recreational opportunities, wildlife watching, and former mining towns, several of which have been revived. For more information, visit fs.usda.gov/gila.

a barber shop and general store. Open May through Oct for stays in one of 4 lovely period rooms, with bathrooms; there are no TVs or phones. The fully equipped kitchen is available to guests to cook their meals (for a small fee, to cover assistance and cleanup). No dogs and no one under 21. Check-in time is 4 p.m. The main door is locked at 10 p.m., so call if you are going to be late. $$.

where to eat

Purple Onion Cafe. Located in the old 1900 post office; (575) 539-2710; facebook.com/purpleonionnm. This little cafe is pretty much your only dining option in Mogollon, and then only on weekends—another reason to come prepared with your own food. It is known for its hearty breakfasts, excellent green chile cheeseburgers, barbecue, and homemade pies (whole pies are available for purchase). Open weekends May through Oct 9 a.m. to 5 p.m. $.

silver city

From Glenwood, it's another 60 miles along US 180 to Silver City, which sprang up next to the Legal Tender silver mine in the 1870s. It's infamous as the teenage home of Billy the Kid, who was first jailed here in 1875 for stealing clothes from a Chinese laundry. In 1895 a flood tore through Main Street, gouging out a 30-foot-deep gully; the Big Ditch, as it's known, is now a municipal park. Copper and silver are still mined at the nearby Santa Rita Mine, but today Silver City is a liberal oasis: It's home to Western New Mexico University and a slew of enjoyable art galleries, coffeehouses, restaurants, historic inns, artists, writers, and alternative healers. It's a good base for visiting nearby Gila Cliff Dwellings, birding, soaking in natural hot springs, and other outdoor activities in the national forest, before enjoying a great dinner back in town in the evening.

where to go

Gila Riparian Preserve. (505) 988-3867; nature.org/en-us/get-involved/how-to-help/places -we-protect/the-gila-riparian-preserve. The Nature Conservancy owns this important 120,000-acre riparian preserve encompassing 5 miles of the Gila River, northwest of Silver City near the village of Cliff. It is part of more than 250,000 acres of Gila River habitat collaboratively managed by the Nature Conservancy, landowners, state and federal land managers, and local organizations. Three hundred bird species have been recorded in the cottonwood bosque along the riverbanks, including 250 pairs of endangered Southwest willow flycatchers, western yellow-billed cuckoos, Gila woodpeckers, and rarely seen common black hawks. A flock of 200 greater sandhill cranes winters here. To reach the preserve, drive 28 miles north of Silver City on US 180, turn right on NM 211, and bear left on NM 293 after 1.5 miles. After 7 miles the road dead-ends at a Gila National Forest campground. The preserve is north of the green fence. Open daily. Free.

Pinos Altos Historical Museum. Main Street, Pinos Altos, off SR 15; (575) 388-1882. Housed in a log cabin built in the 1860s after gold was discovered on nearby Bear Creek, this hole-in-the-wall museum in tiny Pinos Altos, 7 miles north of Silver City, has lots of mining and frontier artifacts. Open daily 10 a.m. to 5 p.m. Free.

Western New Mexico University Museum. 10th Street, Silver City; (575) 538-6386. The university museum, which recently reopened after a $3.2 million remodel to historic Fleming Hall, holds the world's largest collection of prehistoric Mimbres black-on-white pottery, all excavated from a single site. Made around AD 1000, these priceless treasures depict mythical beasts, parrots, and all kinds of other stylized wildlife and speak volumes about the worldview of these remarkable people. The pottery is an important link with the gateway pueblo of Casas Grandes, south of the border in Chihuahua, Mexico, which traded pottery with Chaco Canyon via the Mimbres/Mogollon region. Unmissable. Open Mon through Fri 9:30 a.m. to 4:30 p.m. and Sat and Sun 10 a.m. to 4 p.m. Free.

where to eat

Buckhorn Saloon and Opera House. 32 Main St., Pinos Altos, off SR 15; (575) 538-9911; buckhornsalonandoperahouse.com. This 1863 saloon in Pinos Altos, just north of Silver City, underwent a remodel under new chef-owner Thomas Bock in 2010 but remains an atmospheric place for a cozy dinner in a dining room with white tablecloths and candlelight. You're in cattle country—try the prime rib or the very good bison burger; Bock's homemade ice cream and other desserts offer the perfect end to the meal. You can also dine at the Western bar out front and enjoy live blues and folk music, although it's a bit dark and noisy (in fact, the light in this place is so "atmospheric," you can hardly read the menu). It has a niche supposedly used as a hiding place by Billy the Kid. The adjoining Opera House, which was used to stage popular melodramas in the summer for many years, now holds concerts by some of the Southwest's best musicians. There is live music 4 nights a week, as well as an open mic night. Open Mon through Sat from 3 p.m., with food served in the saloon at 4 p.m. and in the dining room from 5 to 10 p.m.; reservations recommended for dining room. $$.

Diane's Restaurant and Bakery. 510 N. Bullard St., Silver City; (575) 538-8722; dianes restaurant.com. This family-owned restaurant is my favorite spot to eat fresh, delicious, glob-ally inspired food in Silver City. It's a treat to dine in the old-fashioned storefront room, with its hardwood floors, lace curtains, and friendly hometown feeling. The eclectic menu includes weekend brunch dishes such as a green chile Hatch Benedict and a veggie scramble served with a mimosa. For lunch, try their always good sandwiches, quiche, spanakopita, or a main course salad. For dinner, you can't go wrong with the hand-cut rib eye steak or one of the pasta dishes made from family recipes. The newer Parlor wine bar offers tapas and pizzas for small appetites and budgets. Open Tues through Sun 11 a.m. to 2 p.m. for lunch; Tues through Sat 5 to 9 p.m. for dinner; Sat and Sun brunch 9 a.m. to 2 p.m. Parlor open Tues through Sat 11 a.m. to 9 p.m. and Sun 11 a.m. to 2 p.m. $–$$$.

Javalina Coffee House. 117 W. Market St., Silver City; (575) 388-1350; javalinacoffee house.com. Wake up to a cup of organic morning joe at this tiny corner coffeehouse, the oldest in Silver City, where you'll find a nice patio and sofas inside to hang out on, art on the walls, and locally baked bagels, pastries, and cookies. Free Wi-Fi. Open 6 a.m. to 6 p.m. daily. $.

Tapas Tree Grill. 619 N. Bullard St., Silver City; (575) 597-8272; tapastreegrill.com. This casual lunch spot serves "Globally Inspired Street Food" featuring crepes, tapas, noodle dishes, burgers, lamb kofta with tzadziki, salads, and sandwiches. Open Tues through Thurs 11 a.m. to 3 p.m., Fri 11 a.m. to 7 p.m., and Sat 11 a.m. to 4 p.m. Dog-friendly, including complimentary "pooch patties" for your little guy. $–$$.

where to stay

Bear Mountain Lodge. 60 Bear Mountain Ranch Rd., Silver City; (575) 538-2538; bear mountainlodge.com. This luxurious bed-and-breakfast is located on 178 acres bordering the Gila National Forest and offers a comfortable base for explorations of the Silver City area. The 1928 lodge was a school, a country club, and a dude ranch before being purchased by birder and conservationist Myra McCormick, who ran it as a rustic lodge for 41 years. She willed the property to The Nature Conservancy on her death, which transformed it into a terrific eco-lodging. It was sold to the owners of the Blue Dome Gallery in Silver City in 2009, and they have kept up much of what the Conservancy started, including excellent birding, eco day trips, and delicious, hearty gourmet breakfasts, while expanding its arts focus and cafe offerings. For an extra charge, you can now eat dinner here (6 to 7 p.m.) as well as purchase a packed lunch, and popular weekend brunches (11 a.m. to 3 p.m.) and holiday meals are open to nonguests by reservation. There are 11 beautiful guest rooms with baths, local artisan touches, and views—6 in the lodge, 4 in Myra's Retreat, and 1 in the private Wren's Nest—as well as a suite downtown next to the Blue Dome Gallery (2-night minimum). $$–$$$.

Palace Hotel. 106 W. Broadway, Silver City; (575) 388-1811; silvercitypalacehotel.com. The historic Palace Hotel is well situated in the heart of downtown Silver City. It opened in 1900 in an 1882 bank building, and at the time was considered a modern showplace, but faded over the years. Now restored to its former elegance, it offers an attractive but budget-friendly option, especially for history buffs, who love its ambiance. It has 17 antique-filled guest rooms and suites and offers a complimentary continental breakfast served in the skylit garden room upstairs. $.

west

day trip 01

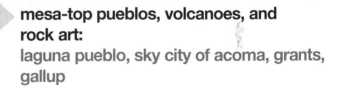

mesa-top pueblos, volcanoes, and rock art:
laguna pueblo, sky city of acoma, grants, gallup

An easy drive west on I-40 leads directly to the Indian pueblos of Laguna, Acoma, and Zuni, with stops in between to view lava flows and rock art at two national park units, ending up at the Route 66 town of Gallup, adjoining the Navajo Nation. A highlight of this day trip is a visit to the ancient Sky City of Acoma Pueblo and a chance to drive the scenic back road of SR 53 through a hypnotic landscape of mountains, mesas, and badlands. Best done as an overnight or weekend trip.

laguna pueblo

Laguna was established in the late 17th century by Keresan-speaking refugees forced by the Spanish to move from their farming villages along the Rio Grande. Today, the pueblo has 7,700 tribal residents and is the largest Keresan-speaking pueblo in New Mexico. Residents live in six small villages and the old pueblo. The tribe operates two casinos right along I-40: Route 66 Hotel/Casino and Dancing Eagle Casino. Buffalo, Corn, and Eagle Dances are performed at the pueblo on the Feast of Saint Joseph in March and September.

where to go

San José de Laguna Mission Church, Old Laguna. 1 Friar Rd.; (505) 552-9330; nps .gov/nr/travel/route66/pueblo_laguna.html. A National Historic Landmark built by Pueblo

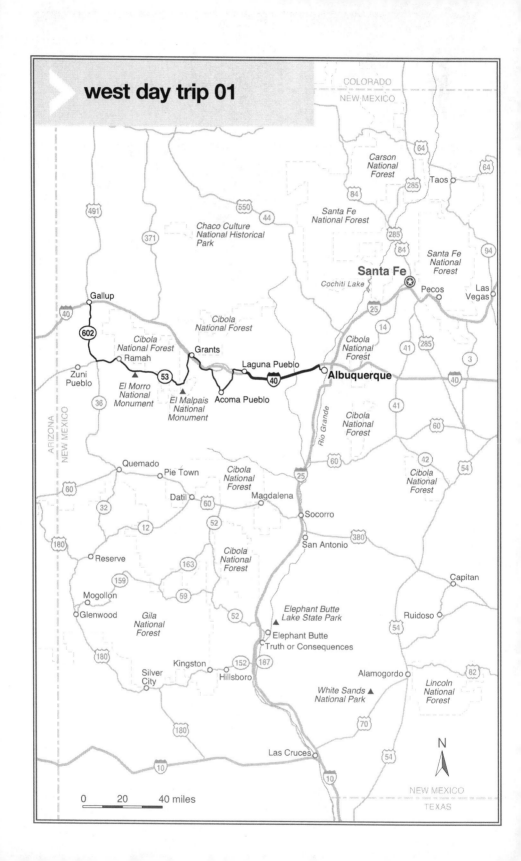

west day trip 01

people after the Pueblo Revolt, in 1699, San José de Laguna Mission Church sits on a hill surrounded by adobe homes in the picturesque old pueblo of Laguna, directly off I-40. If you don't have time to visit the village, a pullout on I-40 offers good views of Old Laguna. You will find vendors in the Old Pueblo selling beautiful black-on-white Laguna pottery and other arts and crafts. The best time to visit is during the feast days and dances, when the pueblo is bustling with activity. The historic church is open Mon through Fri 10 a.m. to 2 p.m., Sat 11 a.m. to 3 p.m., and Sun 2 to 5 p.m.

To'hajiilee Indian Reservation. Formerly known as the Canoncito Indian Reservation, this is a small noncontiguous part of the Navajo Nation, surrounded by the Laguna Indian Reservation, just north of I-40. Some 1,600 Navajo live here. Services are few; nearby Apache Canyon Ranch serves as an ad hoc information center and hosts art shows and other gatherings. To'hajiilee (meaning "dipping water") lies on the Rio Puerco, an important drainage that was heavily used by Chacoan refugees in the 1100s and has many backcountry archeological sites. Its volcanic landmarks, including the distinctive Cabezon Peak, appear in Navajo origin stories (see Northwest Day Trip 06).

where to eat

Bibo Bar and Grille. 1175 SR 279 (exit 114 from I-40, 11 miles north on SR 279), Seboyeta; (505) 552-9428; bibobar.com. This remodeled roadhouse in a former 1913 reservation trading post is a rather remarkable find in the little-traveled Cubero/Seboyeta area of the Laguna reservation. The bar is run by a Lebanese family—the grandson of the original trading post owner, in fact, who built this spot at the tender age of 22 and served the local Native population. Today's iteration has pool tables and jukeboxes and makes a mean full half-pound green chile burger, which has the New Mexico Green Chile Cheeseburger Trail stamp of approval. This is a popular destination for motorcyclists and car clubs on weekends. Bar open Mon through Thurs 11 a.m. to midnight, Fri and Sat 11 a.m. to 2 a.m., and Sun noon to 7 p.m.; grill open Mon through Sat 11 a.m. to 8 p.m. and Sun noon to 7 p.m. $.

where to stay

Apache Canyon Ranch Bed and Breakfast Country Inn. 4 Canyon Dr., Laguna; (505) 377-7925; facebook.com/apachecanyonranch. This modern adobe B&B is run with true Southern hospitality by innkeeper Ava Marie Bowers, who moved here 25 years ago with her husband TC to build their dream home and a purpose-built B&B. The two suites in the main house have lovely Southwest furnishings and Jacuzzi tubs; a casita has a kitchen, kiva fireplace, and canopy bed. Nature trail, sauna, and exercise room. Rates include breakfast and can include dinner. Just sit back, relax, and let Ava take care of you. Gluten-free available; holiday meals open to nonguests. The inn is 2.9 miles north of I-40, exit 131. $–$$$.

Route 66 Casino/Hotel. I-40, exit 140; (505) 352-7866, (866) 352-RT66; rt66casino.com. The Laguna tribe opened this Route 66–themed casino, 10 minutes west of Albuquerque, in

2003. It riffs on the neon and nostalgia of Route 66, with Mother Road memorabilia and raz-zamatazz. The Legends Theatre has arena-style seating for 3,000 and hosts touring national acts. The hotel opened in 2008 and has 154 contemporary rooms with large flat-screen TVs. Dining in Thunder Roads Steakhouse & Cantina. $$.

sky city of acoma

A visit to Acoma via a 16-mile road south of I-40 is the highlight of this day trip. Perched atop a mesa 367 feet above the canyon floor, Sky City, founded in AD 1150, is one of the oldest continually inhabited villages in the country. Spiritual leaders still live on the mesa today, while the other 4,800 tribal members live scattered around the reservation. In 2006, after years of operating out of a sad-looking trailer, the tribe proudly opened a handsome cultural center at the foot of the mesa containing a museum, gallery exhibits, restaurant, shop, and embarkation area for shuttle tours to the mesa pueblo.

Acoma is famous for its beautiful polychrome pottery. It is the "fine bone china" of Pueblo pottery, with thin walls smoothed and shaped using a gourd and polishing stone, then painted with natural dyes using a fine yucca brush. Potters sell from their homes in the old pueblo. Look for pieces that have a pinkish-cream base color, indicating that they are made from local clay; super-white pieces, while lovely in their own right and certainly authentic, are made from store-bought clay and do not feel the same to the touch as those made from rough local clay.

where to go

Sky City Cultural Center and Haak'u Museum. (800) 747-0181; acomaskycity.org. The desert-hued modern cultural center is in a sustainable building with clean lines that blends organically with its iconic surroundings. Its museum and gallery have white walls that set off exceptional pottery and black-and-white historic photos, and a good restaurant serves Pueblo-inspired food and Starbucks coffee. Tours of the old pueblo are offered on the half hour from the center and last 1.5 hours. Buses provide transportation to the top of the mesa, where an Acoma guide points out various elements of the pueblo and Acoma's long and colorful history. Note: The mesa-top pueblo provides stunning views of the surrounding area, including spectacular 400-foot-high **Enchanted Mesa,** said to be the home of the ancestral Acomas.

The most impressive structure in the old pueblo is **Mission San Esteban Del Rey,** a church completed in 1640 after 11 years of intense labor by Acoma residents. The massive roof beams were carried from the forests of Mount Taylor, 40 miles away, without ever touching the logs to the ground, according to legend. The church, whose adobe walls are 7 to 9 feet thick, has no windows, because it was used as a fortress. The cultural center and museum are open daily from early Mar through Oct, with tours from 9:30 a.m. to 3:30 p.m.; Nov through early Mar the cultural center and museum are only open Fri through Sun 9 a.m.

a legacy of sorrow

*Acoma's tragic encounters with conquistadors in the early Spanish Colonial period
are central to understanding the fierce pride this pueblo feels in its enduring legacy.
Like other Pueblos, Acomas were required to pay tribute to their new Spanish mas-
ters, providing trade goods in return for "protection" from settlers who had been
"granted" large tracts of former Pueblo lands. Outraged, Acomas killed a party of
Spanish tribute collectors in 1598, including one of Governor Juan de Oñate's own
nephews. Soldiers stormed the pueblo, killing hundreds of residents and dragging
the survivors to Santo Domingo Pueblo (now called Kewa Pueblo), where Oñate
personally ordered the amputation of one foot and 20 years of slavery; Acoma
women and children were condemned to 20 years of servitude. Oñate also ordered
two Hopi men captured at Acoma to have their right hands cut off, then set them
free to "convey the news of this punishment" as a warning to other rebellious Indians. This goes a long way toward explaining Oñate's poor reputation in New Mexico, where at least two statues of him were vandalized in the 2000s.*

to 4 p.m., with tours 9:30 a.m. to 2:30 p.m. Tours cease during Easter weekend, June 24
and 29, July 10 to 13, July 25, either the first or second weekend in Oct (it varies), and the
first Sat in Dec. The pueblo may be closed to the public during other times of the year without advance notice, so be sure to call before you come. Admission fee for 1.5-hour guided
tours; cultural center is free.

where to go

Sky City Casino. (877) 552-6123; skycity.com. For my money, this is one of the most
attractive Indian casinos in New Mexico, with its beautiful Acoma pottery sitting in niches in
natural rock walls. The casino has 800 slot machines, game tables, and bingo, and there's
a coffee shop, snack bar, and restaurant serving buffet items and New Mexico favorites like
posole and steaks. The adjoining hotel has 131 elegant rooms and suites. Spa, fitness room,
Wi-Fi, and free shuttle to Sky City. The travel center offers gas and a large convenience
store.

grants

This homely ranch town boomed briefly during the uranium rush of the 1950s and '60s but
has seen better days. Located on I-40, its main attractions are its small mining museum
and its proximity to Mount Taylor, one of the four sacred peaks of the Navajo, to the north

and to El Malpais and El Morro National Monuments and Zuni Pueblo along the quiet and beautiful scenic byway of SR 53 to the south, which offers an unmissable backcountry drive linking Grants and Gallup. The Cibola Arts Council works to promote the increasing number of artists moving to the area, attracted by the beautiful scenery and low cost of living. The Northwest New Mexico Visitor Center is a one-stop shop for visiting the area. Rangers can help you plan your visit to local attractions, and there's a bookstore and a wonderful view through huge windows of 115,000-year-old El Calderon lava flow.

where to go

El Malpais National Monument. SR 53; (505) 876-2783; nps.gov/elma. This hypnotically beautiful wilderness preserves lava flows, cinder cones, lava tubes, ice caves, geological windows, and other volcanic features that resulted when Mount Taylor erupted two to four million years ago. It also protects one of the state's longest natural sandstone arches, historic ranches and homesteads, and the historic Zuni-Acoma Trail. The Malpais ("badlands") repelled Spaniards crossing on foot but now draws more than 100,000 visitors a year to drive the scenic highways and hike and bike. Picnicking and primitive camping only are available. The monument is open 24 hours. For information, stop at El Malpais National Monument Visitor Center in Grants; the NPS-run Malpais Information Center on SR 53 is now closed due to staffing issues. The small Malpais Ranger Station (505-761-8993) run by the BLM is located east of the monument on SR 117, 9 miles south of exit 89 on I-40, and remains open Thurs through Mon 8:30 a.m. to 4:30 p.m. Admission fee.

El Malpais National Monument Visitor Center. 1900 E. Santa Fe Ave., Grants; (505) 876-2783; nps.gov/elma/planyourvisit/mac1.htm. This attractive visitor center at the top of scenic SR 53, exit 85 on I-40, is the main visitor center for El Malpais now (it was once a multiagency center but now run by the NPS). It has terrific views through soaring windows, and is a good first stop so that rangers can help with trip planning. An award-winning film on the area is shown regularly in the theater, and there is a nice well-stocked bookstore. Open daily 9 a.m. to 5 p.m.; closed holidays.

El Morro National Monument. SR 53; (505) 783-4226, ext. 801; nps.gov/elmo. The sandstone bluff and pool of water at its base protected in this small park were used for 700 years by travelers on the high desert as a campsite and watering hole. Pueblos built 875-room Atsinna Pueblo atop the sandstone bluff in AD 1275. Their descendants, at nearby Zuni Pueblo, were the first inhabitants encountered by Spanish conquistadors, governors, soldiers, and missionaries who passed through in the Spanish Colonial era. After Mexico ceded the region to the US, army surveyors, camel expeditions, emigrant wagon trains, and railroad crews stopped here too. We know this because, while they were resting up at this important oasis, travelers inscribed their names on the base of the sandstone rock. An easy 0.5-mile trail leads past the inscriptions; the 2-mile Headland Trail to Atsinna Pueblo climbs 250 feet and is slightly more strenuous, but the views of the Zuni Mountains on top are well worth the effort. I'll tell you one of my little secrets: There is a lovely little 9-site campground here, with roomy campsites, picnic tables, grills, tent pads, and shade under the piñon-juniper woodland. It has good vault toilets but no water in winter and no hookups; get here early to get a spot. Visitor center open daily 8 a.m. to 7 p.m. June to Sept, 9 a.m. to 5 p.m. the rest of the year; trails close 1 hour before the visitor center; closed holidays. Free.

New Mexico Mining Museum. 100 Iron Ave., Grants; (505) 287-4802; grants.org/Mining-Museum/tabid/220/Default.aspx. This small, free museum has exhibits on mining technology, gems and minerals, and local history; there's a re-created mineshaft that visitors can explore for a small fee. Open Mon through Sat 9 a.m. to 4 p.m.

Ramah. Founded in 1874 by Mormon farmers, who dammed Cebolla Creek to create Ramah Lake, this small village along SR 53 remains an attractive oasis but has no visitor services.

Ramah Navajo Reservation. PO Box 308, Ramah; (505) 775-7140; ramahnavajo.org. Part of the Checkerboard area, a patchwork of lands in private and public ownership south of I-40 containing noncontiguous Navajo reservations apart from the "Big Rez" (the term Navajos themselves, with typical Indian humor, use for the main reservation, or Big Reservation), Ramah has 3,000 residents, most of them young people in their 20s. Among the activities here are youth leatherworking training, rug weaving by men as well as women, and rearing historic Churro sheep for their wool. Because it is small, there are no formal visitor activities here; however, Indian reservations are fascinating places to go in order to visit with the people themselves, if you get the opportunity. Stop at the Ramah Chapter House and have a chat. Chances are good that someone will offer to take you around the village and introduce you to rug makers and artists. If that happens, be sure to offer payment to your guide (this is often left up to you). Ramah rugs are very attractive, and you may get a bargain here.

Zuni Pueblo. PO Box 339, Zuni; (505) 782-7238 (visitor center); zunitourism.com. Continue on SR 53 to reach Zuni Pueblo. Descendants of El Morro's Atsinna Pueblo—the Zuni—settled villages to the west, including Hawikuh, where conquistadors first made contact with Pueblos in 1540. Zuni Pueblo is now the largest of the New Mexico pueblos, with residents living in Black Rock, a modern subdivision, and old Zuni Pueblo, occupied for over 700 years and known as Halona Idiwan'a, the "Middle Place of the World." Zuni artisans make gorgeous channel inlaid silver-and-turquoise jewelry, bolo ties, and fetishes. You can buy arts and crafts from their arts cooperative and tribal store and on the Zuni Pueblo ArtWalk-Studio Tour, held the first Sat of each month. **A:shiwi A:wan Museum and Heritage Center** (505-782-4403; ashiwi-museum.org) is open Mon through Fri 8 a.m. to 5 p.m. and has interesting programs and exhibits on Zuni culture. **Our Lady of Guadalupe Mission** is famous for its historic church and restored murals of ceremonial figures. Ask at the Zuni Visitor and Arts Center (1239 SR 53) about tours of the Old Pueblo if you wish to view them.

where to shop

Double Six Gallery. 1001 W. Santa Fe Ave.; (505) 287-7311; cibolaartscouncil.com. This 5,000-square-foot space in central Grants, run by the Cibola Arts Council, occupies a large warehouse-like building and displays work by 50 local artists. Over the years, the Cibola Arts Council has done an excellent job of promoting the work of the many artists who have been attracted to live in these quiet, beautiful open lands. It is the unexpected places that so often attract creative people, and the growth of the artist community in Grants has been one of its most positive developments in the last decade. Open Tues through Sat 1 to 5 p.m.

Inscription Rock Trading and Coffee Company. SR 53, MM 46; (505) 783-4706; inscriptionrocktrading.com. Located next to El Morro National Monument, this is an attractive trading post with a typical smorgasbord of items for sale. There are snacks and coffee, but you'll need to head next door to Ancient Way Cafe to get real food or keep moseying west toward Zuni. Open Tues through Sat 9 a.m. to 5 p.m. and Sun 10 a.m. to 5 p.m.

Pueblo of Zuni Arts and Crafts. 1222 SR 53; (505) 782-5531. This tribally owned arts-and-crafts cooperative is the most popular destination for visitors to Zuni. It sells the locally made finely worked silver jewelry for which Zuni is famous, inlaid with designs in turquoise and other precious stones; carved stone fetishes of bears and other sacred animals; beautifully crafted polychrome ceramic *ollas* (water jugs), seed pots, bowls, and other pottery; contemporary paintings; and other arts and crafts. Buyer beware: In recent times, the market has been flooded with inexpensive foreign-made jewelry that looks Indian made. Try to buy directly from the artist, from a tribal arts cooperative like this one, or from a reputable trading post or gallery, such as Keshi—the word is a traditional Zuni greeting—in Santa Fe, which sells authentic Zuni-made items. If you buy from a store, there should be a certificate of authenticity, stating that the item is Indian made, with the artist's name and other details. Open Mon through Fri 9 a.m. to 6 p.m. and Sat 9 a.m. to 5 p.m.

where to eat

Ancient Way Cafe. SR 53; (505) 783-4612; elmorro-nm.com/ancient-way-cafe. This backcountry diner in a small log cabin is part of a rustic RV/cabin resort like no other, and take it from me, it's the best place to eat in these parts by a country mile. Everything is cleanly sourced and often organic, from on-site free-range eggs to hormone-free house-smoked brisket from Colorado, and everything is homemade, including the bread and desserts. Located just east of El Morro National Monument, the cafe is not much to look at, but inside it is cozy and friendly. They also rent out RV campsites with showers and tiny log cabins, a boon if you get caught in a snowstorm here, as I have done in the past. The cafe is open for hearty breakfasts and lunches and also serves espresso and really good baked goods, such as butterscotch, toffee, or pecan scones; pies and cookies; and dessert specials. A prix fixe gourmet dinner menu is served Fri and Sat by reservation; the menu is posted on the website listed above ahead of time; a harpist entertains guests. On those nights, the resort offers cabin rental with dinner for two for just $125 per night, a popular deal, so make reservations early. Open year-round Sun through Tues and Thurs 9 a.m. to 5 p.m. and Fri and Sat 9 a.m. to 8 p.m.; dinner starts at 5 p.m. $.

where to stay

Cimarron Rose Bed and Breakfast. 689 Oso Ridge Rd.; (800) 856-5776; cimarronrose .com. Former NPS park ranger Sheri McWethy and her partner Tom Kennedy, director of tourism for the Zuni tribe, run this backcountry eco-inn right off SR 53 in the forested Zuni Mountains, and you could not get a lovelier setting and more informed and interesting hosts on this area and its people. They rent 3 adorable Western-style suites with knotty-pine walls, wood and tile floors, beamed ceilings, and kitchens. One suite has a wood-burning stove; another has a lovely private patio. Gourmet breakfasts include omelets, quiche, breakfast burritos, homemade granola, oatmeal, fruit salad, and tea and coffee and are personally delivered to each suite daily. Library/art gallery on-site. Discount for longer stays. $$–$$$.

Inn at Halona Bed and Breakfast. 23B Pia Mesa Rd.; (505) 782-4547, (800) 752-3278; halona.com. The only lodging at Zuni, this idiosyncratic 23-room family-run inn opened in 1998 and is an eclectic place, chockablock with local art. The front desk can arrange tours for guests. Room rate includes a cooked country breakfast, or continental breakfast for early risers. $–$$.

gallup

Gallup bills itself as the "Indian Capital of the World" and one of the best places to buy arts and crafts in the area. That's true, but there's nothing artsy-craftsy about this rough-hewn former mining town. Most of the art venues here are spit-and-sawdust trading posts and atmospheric old pawn shops that function, as they always have, as places where local Navajo artisans congregate, share news, buy raw materials, sell their finished goods, and pawn items for ready cash. The town is strung out for miles along the railroad, I-40, and Route 66. Visitor attractions are concentrated downtown between Route 66, Coal Avenue, and 1st and 4th Streets. There are a vast number of vintage Route 66 motels north of there, including an authentic fading "grande dame": the El Rancho Hotel, a 1937 historic landmark that served as a base for famous movie actors filming Westerns in the area. Do check out its wonderful lobby, which is lined with signed headshots of actors like John Wayne and Ronald Reagan, but the cramped rooms are hot and bereft of modern comforts, so you may prefer to stay in a chain motel, of which there are many. I can recommend La Quinta Inn and Suites.

where to go

Gallup Cultural Center. 201 E. US 66; (505) 863-4131; southwestindian.com. The Southwest Indian Foundation (SIF) operates this cultural center in the renovated 1923 Santa Fe Depot building as a sort of town square. In the museum, you'll find exhibits on the city's history and galleries dedicated to Native American arts. Outlets sell local arts and crafts, regional books, music, gifts, and skateboards. **Angela's Café** (505-722-7526) sells coffee drinks and daily soups, sandwiches, salads, and desserts; open Mon through Fri 8 a.m. to 4 p.m. Sunset Indian dances every night in summer between 7 and 9 p.m. SIF runs programs that benefit local Native people by donating such items as stoves to needy families. The center is open Mon through Fri 9 a.m. to 5 p.m. and Sat 8 a.m. to 5 p.m.; outlet hours vary. Free.

Red Rock Park. 825 Outlaw Rd., Churchrock; (505) 722-3829; gallupnm.gov/207/Red-Rock-Park-and-Museum. This park, a few miles east of Gallup, is famous for its Gallup Inter-Tribal Indian Ceremonial, held every August. It brings together 30 tribes and 50,000 spectators over 5 days for dances, rodeo, art shows, parades, and educational programs. Red Rock Museum has year-round exhibits on Southwest Indian arts. The developed campground (with showers) is very pleasant and has trails and lots of sites among the beautiful red Zuni sandstone. Admission fee.

Rex Museum. 300 W. US 66; (505) 863-1363; gallupnm.gov/208/Rex-Museum. The former Rex Hotel, built in 1900 and once known for its "ladies of the night," now serves as the town museum. It is a typical hometown museum with all kinds of historic "Grandma's attic" doodads, from pioneer tools to items from the town's coal-mining and railroad days. Open Mon through Fri 9 a.m. to 5 p.m. Free.

where to shop

Richardson's Trading Company. 223 W. Historic Route 66; (505) 722-4762. Open since 1913 and the head honcho of trading posts, you'll find a large selection of authentic Indian-made jewelry at Richardson's. Look particularly for "old pawn." These are unique Indian family heirlooms, such as heavy Navajo squash blossom necklaces, that are usually only brought out for special occasions and have been pawned by their owners for ready cash and redeemed. Since historic times, trading posts such as Richardson's and those on the Navajo reservation have functioned as a sort of bank for Navajos, and this is a business deal like any other for Native people who are well known as traders themselves. Since old pawn jewelry is synonymous with quality and historic value, anyone buying it should also view it as an investment. The prices aren't necessarily cheap, so do your homework about quality, price, and investment potential, then only buy something that you truly love. Open Mon through Sat 9 a.m. to 6 p.m.

where to eat

Badlands Grill. 2201 W. US 66; (505) 236-4875; badlandsgrill.com. This historic family-owned supper club is a good place for fine dining in Gallup. You'll find enormous servings of steak, lamb, chicken, pork, game meats, and burgers, as well as seafood such as salmon; they also have main course salads and vegetarian options such as pasta. Special senior menu offers discounted dishes. Open Mon through Sat 4:30 to 9:30 p.m. $$–$$$$.

Fratelli's Pizza Bistro and Ice Creamery. 1209 N. US 491 (in the Plaza del Norte); (505) 863-9201; fratellisbistro.com. For casual dining or good homemade gelato to cool down on a hot day, you can't beat Fratelli's, an Italian eatery conveniently located in the main shopping area north of I-40. The menu is light, fresh, and tasty, and in addition to pizza includes soups, substantial salads, sub sandwiches, and pasta. Pet-friendly. Open Mon through Sat 11 a.m. to 9 p.m. $–$$.

Gallup Coffee Company. 203 W. Coal Ave.; (505) 410-2505; facebook.com/GallupCoffee Company. A relief from all the truck-stop fare along I-40, this little coffeehouse is a popular local hangout in a historic building next to the old El Morro Theater in downtown Gallup. The main draw here is the excellent coffee, roasted in-house and available in coffee drinks or as beans for sale. Never fear, good tea is also available, from black to honeybush! They also bake a variety of fresh, delicious bagels (great with cream cheese at any time of day), muffins, scones, and other sweet and savory pastries. Look for the neon sign. Open Mon through Sat 7 a.m. to 9 p.m. (6 a.m. to 6 p.m. in winter) and Sun 9 a.m. to 3 p.m. Wi-Fi. $.

where to stay

El Rancho Hotel. 1000 E. US 66; (505) 722-2285; elranchohotelgallup.com. Originally built in 1937 by the brother of movie mogul D. W. Griffith, El Rancho became a Hollywood hideaway in the 1940s and 1950s after scores of actors were drawn to Gallup by the many films (mostly Westerns) made in the area. Spencer Tracy, Katharine Hepburn, Humphrey Bogart, Rita Hayworth, and Ronald Reagan all stayed at the hotel; the two-story lobby is lined with autographed photos of Hollywood stars of the era. Be aware: Rooms are small and antiquated. $.

La Quinta Inn and Suites. 3880 E. US 66; (505) 722-2233; wyndham.hotels/laquinta/gallup-new-mexico. This popular chain motel is newly built and has modern, spacious rooms with fridges, microwaves, sitting areas, comfy king beds, safes, and flat-screen TVs. Free hot breakfast, pool, and Wi-Fi. Pet-friendly. $.

northwest

day trip 01

northwest

>>> **ranches and wineries in albuquerque's rural north valley:**
los ranchos de albuquerque, corrales, bernalillo

This relaxing day trip follows Rio Grande Boulevard, just east of the Rio Grande, through traditional agricultural villages that feel like they're a hundred miles from Albuquerque. The purple-hued Sandia Mountains loom over horse paddocks, fields, and city-designated Open Space areas along the river that provide much-needed breathing space from the dense downtown. Highlights include wetlands, wineries, farmers' markets, a lavender farm, art galleries, a historic Spanish Colonial plaza, a contemporary pueblo, the remains of an ancient pueblo that hosted Coronado in 1540, and the Indian Pueblo Cultural Center, which interprets all 19 New Mexico pueblos. The Rail Runner train between Albuquerque and Santa Fe stops in Los Ranchos and Bernalillo.

los ranchos de albuquerque

The fertile soil of Los Ranchos de Albuquerque and its northern neighbor Corrales has been worked for centuries—the remains of several Ancestral Puebloan farming and ranching villages lie beneath *estancias* (family ranch estates) and *ranchos* (large land-grant ranches) created by settlers from Puebla, Mexico, in the 1700s and in cultivation ever since. Farm stores abound, and there are four wineries (only two open to the public). Open Space trails begin at Rio Grande State Park and follow tree-shaded irrigation ditches that parallel the river. They are popular with Albuquerque residents for outdoor recreation, from walking and jogging to

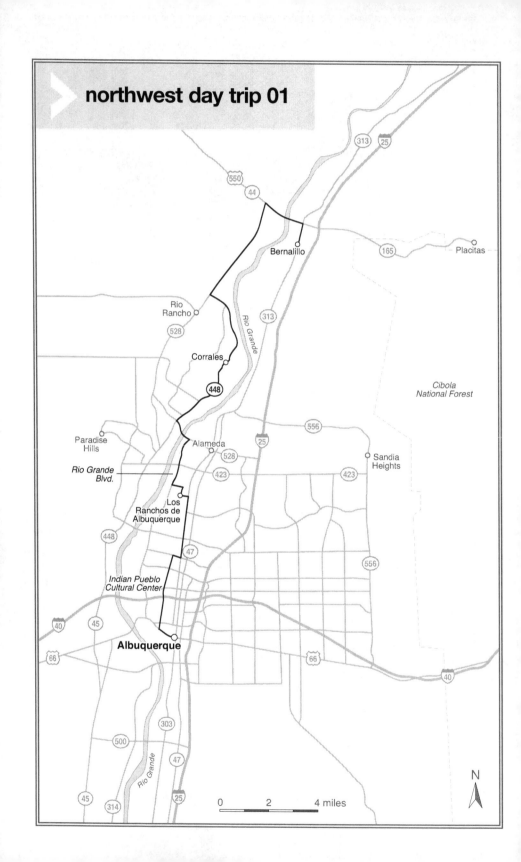

bicycling and horseback riding, but the trails also offer quiet spots to hang out, relax, and watch wildlife. A lavender festival takes place on the Fourth of July at Los Poblanos, a beautiful and significant historic property that includes a modern country inn, a restaurant and bar, an organic farm and shop, and a historic cultural center. Not technically in Los Ranchos de Albuquerque, the Indian Pueblo Cultural Center is a popular destination northwest of downtown Albuquerque's main museums and well worth visiting on this day trip.

where to go

Indian Pueblo Cultural Center. 2401 12th St. NW; (505) 843-7270, (800) 766-4405; indianpueblo.org. If you don't have time to go to the pueblos, this Indian-owned cultural center is the next best thing, especially if you have kids. A 10,000-square-foot museum traces the beginning of the Pueblo Indians through modern times, focusing on New Mexico's 19 pueblos. Particularly interesting is the Indians' own version of the Spanish Conquest and Pueblo Revolt. Indian dances are held on Sat and Sun between 11 a.m. and 4 p.m. The gift shops sells jewelry, pottery, rugs, and other items made by Native artisans. Top-rated **Pueblo Harvest Cafe** (505-724-3510; puebloharvestcafe.com) serves authentic American Indian and Southwest dishes such as buffalo tenderloin and bread baked in a traditional outside oven known as an *horno*, or beehive oven. Cultural center open daily 9 a.m. to 5 p.m. Cafe open Mon through Sat 7 a.m. to 9 p.m. and Sun 7 a.m. to 4 p.m. Admission fee; free for kids under 4 years of age.

Rio Grande Nature Center State Park. 2901 Candelaria Rd. NW; (505) 344-7240; emnrd .state.nm.us/SPD/riograndnaturecenterstatepark.html. This 270-acre preserve has three ponds, nature trails, an outdoor classroom, a rehabilitation center for injured birds, and a native plant garden. A concrete visitor center has exhibits and a huge picture window in the library overlooking wetlands. Microphones allow you to hear the sounds of red-winged blackbirds, geese, ducks, and other pond life, a meditation in themselves. On-site nature store. Park open daily 8 a.m. to 5 p.m.; visitor center open 10 a.m. to 5 p.m. Admission fee.

Unser Racing Museum. 1776 Montaño Rd. NW; (505) 341-1776; unserracingmuseum .com. This steering-wheel-shaped museum celebrates the accomplishments of several generations of motor racing's Unser family. Exhibits include historic photos, shiny racing cars used by family members, and other memorabilia. Open daily 10 a.m. to 4 p.m. Admission fee; 16 and under free; senior and military discount.

where to shop

Bookworks. 4022 Rio Grande Blvd. NW; (505) 344-8139; bkwrks.com. Arguably Albuquerque's best independent bookstore, Bookworks has a great staff, an intelligent and varied selection of books, and a cozy fireplace area for winter browsing. The store hosts regular readings and signings by nationally known authors. Open daily 9 a.m. to 6 p.m.

Casa Rondeña Winery. 733 Chavez Rd. NW; (505) 344-5911, (800) 706-1699; casa rondena.com. One of four family-run vineyards in Los Ranchos (only two are open to the public), this attractive estate winery is an enjoyable place to sample award-winning hand-crafted wines. Offerings include a Viognier; a blended Merlot, Cabernet Franc, and Cabernet Sauvignon; a Founder's Reserve Cabernet Sauvignon; and a blended Riesling and Gewürtz-traminer. Open daily noon to 7 p.m.

Los Poblanos Farm Shop. 4803 Rio Grande Blvd. NW; (505) 344-9297; farmshop.los poblanos.com. Located in the original Creamland Dairy building on the 26-acre estate sur-rounding Los Poblanos Historic Inn and Cultural Center (see Where to Stay below), this wonderful farm shop sells a variety of homemade and beautifully packaged gifts, including numerous items made with lavender, from toiletries and jam to cookies, as well as cook-books, gourmet foods, delicious sourdough bread, and seasonal items such as authentic hot crossed buns. You can get something to eat here, too, as well as in the main adjoining restaurant, Campo Bar and Grill.

Los Ranchos Growers' Market. 6718 Rio Grande Blvd. NW; (505) 344-6582; losranchos nm.gov/growers-market. This year-round farmers' market sells local organic produce. Among the vendors here is Los Poblanos Organic Farm, which grows more than 75 variet-ies of fruit, veggies, herbs, and flowers on 16 acres of the estate surrounding Los Poblanos Historic Inn and Cultural Center (see Where to Stay below). The market sells homemade posole, burritos, pastries, coffee, and other refreshments, and local artists have booths. Live music. Dog-friendly. Open every Sat 8 a.m. to noon from May to mid-Nov; every other Sat 10 a.m. to noon in winter and spring.

where to eat

Flying Star Cafe. 4026 Rio Grande Blvd. NW; (505) 344-6714; flyingstarcafe.com. A North Valley branch of the popular Albuquerque cafe serving reliably good New Mexican and American comfort food and extraordinary desserts made from locally sourced and organic produce. A big selling point is that it's next to Bookworks (see Where to Shop) in a small, attractive retail plaza with great views and good parking. Open Mon through Thurs 6:30 a.m. to 10 p.m., Fri and Sat 6:30 a.m. to 10:30 p.m., and Sun 7 a.m. to 9:30 p.m. Other branches on Central (Nob Hill), Menaul, Corrales, Juan Tabo, and Paseo del Norte. $–$$

where to stay

Los Poblanos Historic Inn and Cultural Center. 4803 Rio Grande Blvd. NW; (505) 344-9297; lospoblanos.com. Consider spending the night just to experience this stunningly beautiful 26-acre estate. It was developed by congresswoman Ruth Hanna McCormick and her husband in 1934 when they remodeled the 19th-century Armijo homestead with the help of Santa Fe style architect John Gaw Meem. Among the many highlights are 6 acres of formal English garden laid out by famed landscape artist Rose Greeley, which is dotted with whimsical rock paths created by Mountainair folk artist Pop Shaffer (see Southeast Day Trip 01). The property is now owned by Armin and Penny Rembe and their son Matthew, who took the reins in 2004. The Rembes' collection of *santos* decorates the historic *hacienda*, and the adjoining La Quinta Cultural Center has a mural by artist Peter Hurd and unusual doors carved by printmaker Gustave Baumann. After a sensitive and successful expansion, the inn now offers 20 light and bright rooms and suites in the *hacienda*, casita, and reno- vated dairy buildings near the farm shop and restaurant/bar. The new Farm and Field rooms and suites have fresh white walls, modern four-poster beds, hardwood floors, and patios, while the Meem rooms and suites in the *hacienda* are traditional with vigas, fireplaces, four- poster beds, and New Mexico art on the walls. All rooms are allergen-free, beds have high- end organic linens, and, of course, bathrooms have Los Poblanos's own lavender toiletries. Delicious breakfasts and dinners are served in Campo, the on-site farm-to-fork restaurant; light meals, coffee, and tea are available in the Farm Shop (see Where to Shop). Guests receive a complimentary drink in Bar Campo on arrival and have the use of a saltwater pool, fitness room, and cruiser bicycles. Wi-Fi. Tours available to nonguests for a fee. $$–$$$$.

corrales

The heart of historic Corrales is its photogenic 19th-century church named after San Ysidro, patron saint of farmers, and nearby Casa San Ysidro, an 18th-century adobe *hacienda* for- merly owned by descendants of Don Felipe Gutierrez, recipient of the Bernalillo land grant in 1704. The village oozes with charm and is the happy home to a large number of unusual pets, including llamas and potbellied pigs. The Old Town has art galleries, boutiques, New Age spas, bistros, and bed-and-breakfasts. Corrales celebrates its agricultural roots year- round, but May is the biggest month, when festivities include the Feast of San Ysidro and a tour of 70 to 80 artists' studios (corralessocietyofartists.org).

where to go

Casa San Ysidro. 973 Old Church Rd.; (505) 898-3915; cabq.gov/culturalservices/ albuquerque-museum/casa-san-ysidro. This 19th-century land-grant property was bought, restored, and expanded into a Spanish Territorial *rancho* by Shirley and Ward Alan Minge in the 1950s to house their collection of traditional artifacts. The Albuquerque Museum acquired the Minge Collection in 1997, and the couple donated the home and land. Heritage Day, on May 15, features living-history demonstrations, food, and music. Open for guided tours June through Aug, Tues through Sat at 10:30 a.m., noon, and 1:30 p.m.; Sept through Nov and Feb through May, Tues through Fri at 9:30 a.m. and 1:30 p.m. and Sat at 10:30 a.m., noon, and 1:30 p.m. Admission fee.

Old San Ysidro Church. 966 Old Church Rd.; (505) 897-1513; corraleshistory.org/html/ the_old_church.html. This lovely old Spanish Colonial church was built in 1868, after a flood destroyed the previous church. It has been deconsecrated and now serves as a community center for the village of Corrales, hosting a variety of meetings, lectures, and cultural activities. One of the big events of the year is San Ysidro Feast Day celebrations in late May. A 10 a.m. mass is held at the church, then the statue of San Ysidro is paraded along Old Church Road to the new church. The Winter Craft Show and Festival of the Nativities, displaying crèches from around the world, are held in Dec. The church is run by the Corrales Historical Society and open to the public for guided tours Sat (call for hours and details) Apr to Oct. Free.

where to shop

Corrales Bosque Gallery. 4685 Corrales Rd.; (505) 898-7203; corralesbosquegallery .com. This diverse and interesting artists' cooperative gallery offers work in mixed media, photography, jewelry, and one-of-a-kind gift items. It was established in 1994 by local artists and serves as a focal point of the artist community in the old village of Corrales. Holiday shows, fund-raisers for community nonprofit organizations, and special guest artist shows are held throughout the year. Open daily 10 a.m. to 5 p.m.

Corrales Winery. 6275 Corrales Rd.; (505) 898-1819; corraleswinery.com. This family-run winery creates small quantities of fruity, award-winning Cabernet Sauvignons, Francs, and Rieslings from New Mexico grapes. The Silverstones grow muscat grapes in an adjoining vineyard for their popular Muscat Canelli dessert wine. Open Wed through Sun noon to 5 p.m.

Hanselmann Pottery. 4908 Corrales Rd.; (505) 510-2019; hanselmannpottery.com. Purchase rustic handmade stoneware in lovely desert hues at this local pottery. The studio is owned by Fritz Allen, who also owns the Corrales Bistro Brewery next door (see entry below). Both are located in the Corrales Artisan Building. I love the idea that I can purchase a beautiful, handmade gift and refuel in one location. Open daily 11 a.m. to 10 p.m.; the studio operates on an honor system, so you can self-checkout purchases if no one is available.

where to eat

Corrales Bistro Brewery. 4908 Corrales Rd.; (505) 897-1036; cbbistro.com. This local rendezvous serves home brews and an eclectic, globally inspired pub-grub menu that ranges from big, juicy burgers and main-course salads to hot and cold sandwiches, interesting wraps, and Mexican food. Most items on the menu are $12 and under, and there are some nice foodie flourishes, such as white and sweet potato fries to accompany burgers. The brewery always has 12 beers from local brewers on tap, including its own Belgian ale, as well as a selection of quality wines from small vineyards. You can order a sample of the 12 beers with your meal. Beer is also served in a custom stoneware stein created by Hanselmann Pottery; if you become a member of the brewery, you get your own personalized mug refilled at low cost and 10 percent off food and wine. Live music by local musicians most nights. Open daily 11 a.m. to 10 p.m. $.

Hannah & Nate's. 4512 Corrales Rd.; (505) 898-2370; hannahandnates.com. This second location of the family-run restaurant is a reliable standby for set-you-up breakfasts of steak and eggs and hearty sandwiches and freshly made salads at lunch. Try the chile-sparked Rio Grande Club on sourdough or Tuscan meat loaf on a baguette. Patio. Open daily 8 a.m. to 2 p.m. $.

Indigo Crow Cafe. 4515 Corrales Rd.; (505) 898-7000; indigocrowcafe.net. This locally owned bistro occupies a nice old building and is consistently praised for its elegant seafood dishes. Try the seared ahi tuna, served as an entree or sandwich, or steak frites at lunch. Open for lunch and dinner Tues through Sat 11:30 a.m. to 9 p.m. and Sun 10 a.m. to 9 p.m. (brunch 10 a.m. to 3 p.m. on Sun). Happy hour daily 3 to 5 p.m. $–$$$.

where to stay

Sandhill Crane Bed and Breakfast. 389 Camino Hermosa; (505) 898-2445, (800) 375-2445; sandhillcranebandb.com. This perennially popular, cozy, family-operated *hacienda* sits on 2 acres adjoining Corrales Bosque Preserve. The 3 guest rooms display work by local artists on the walls and have queen-size beds, private baths, Wi-Fi, TVs, and robes; one room is a suite with kitchenette and one is pet-friendly. A hot, multicourse gourmet breakfast is served. A variety of cooking classes are offered here, and if you're visiting a Corrales resident, you receive a 10 percent discount. $$.

bernalillo

Bernalillo was founded by Don Diego de Vargas in 1695 and grew from a series of family *placitas* (adobe family homes built around small plazas) into a commercial center on the Rio Grande. It now sits near the busy intersection of I-25 and US 550. Several large prehistoric and historic pueblos were located here, including Kuaua, a pueblo that hosted conquistador Don Francisco Vasquez de Coronado and his expeditionary force their first winter in New Mexico. Bernalillo itself is a bit lacking in charm; pueblo history is the main draw. Coronado Historic Site preserves the remains of Kuaua and intriguing murals displaying images of kachina cult dancers taken from the great kiva.

where to go

Coronado Historic Site. US 550; (505) 867-5351; nmhistoricsites.org/coronado. A mile-long trail goes through what's left of Kuaua, the once-mighty Tiwa-speaking pueblo on the Rio Grande built in AD 1300 and commandeered by Coronado in 1540. Museum exhibits in the visitor center (designed by famed architect John Gaw Meem) help you visualize what the pueblo might have looked like. A separate room houses the famous kachina murals taken from the great kiva by the Civilian Conservation Corps, which excavated the pueblo in 1940 during the 400th anniversary of Coronado's *entrada*. Open Wed through Mon 8:30 a.m. to 5 p.m. Admission fee.

where to eat

Range Café. 925 S. Camino del Pueblo; (505) 867-1700; rangecafe.com. The original location of the popular Range Café features excellent modern home-style cooking in a fun, kitschy, Western-themed room on the main drag in Bernalillo. Open for breakfast, lunch, and dinner daily from 7:30 a.m. to 9 p.m. (For more, see Plaza Hotel, Las Vegas, in Northeast Day Trip 02). $–$$.

day trip 02

northwest

>>>

rock art and balloons:
petroglyph national monument, balloon
fiesta park, rio rancho, santa ana pueblo

Two of Albuquerque's top attractions are the highlights of this day trip to the Albuquerque Westside. Petroglyph National Monument, a unit of the National Park System within city limits, interprets Albuquerque's interesting volcanic history and preserves 25,000 prehistoric and historic petroglyphs carved into the lava escarpment of West Mesa. October's famous hot-air balloon extravaganza, the largest in the world, takes place each year at Balloon Fiesta Field and is worth planning a special trip around. Any other time of the year, visit the Anderson-Abruzzo Albuquerque International Balloon Museum, which celebrates ballooning history and has lots of kid-friendly exhibits. Both attractions adjoin the sprawling city of Rio Rancho, New Mexico's fastest-growing new community, and Santa Ana Pueblo, whose spectacular Hyatt Regency Tamaya Resort is among Albuquerque's top places to spend the night. Start your day trip at Petroglyph National Monument, reached by driving west on I-40 to Unser Boulevard (exit 154) and heading north. Units of the park are strung along Unser, Paseo de Volcan, and Montaño roads. You will intersect Alameda Boulevard to reach Balloon Fiesta Park. Santa Ana Pueblo adjoins US 550 and Rio Rancho.

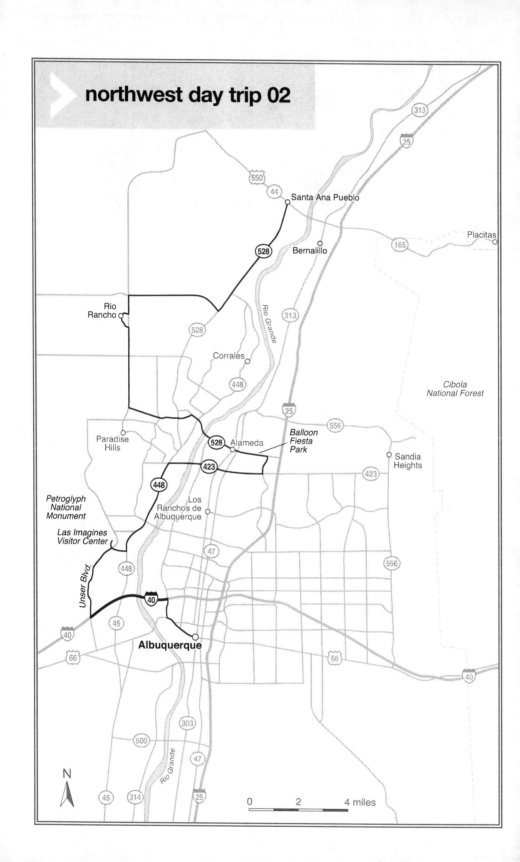

northwest day trip 02

petroglyph national monument

This 11-square-mile national monument preserves one of the most impressive collections of Indian and Hispanic rock inscriptions in the world, as well as more than 350 archeological sites and a variety of volcanic features associated with the Rio Grande rift zone. The monument has three units managed by the National Park Service—Boca Negra Canyon, Rinconada Canyon, and Volcanoes Day Use Area—and one unit managed by the City of Albuquerque Open Space Division: Piedras Marcadas. The park is located on the west side of Albuquerque. To reach it from I-40, take the Unser Boulevard exit (exit 154) and drive north 3 miles to Western Trail. Turn left, or west, onto Western Trail and follow the road to the Las Imagines Visitor Center. From I-25, take the Paseo del Norte exit (exit 232) and drive west to Coors Road, south exit. Drive south on Coors Road to Western Trail. Turn right, or west, onto Western Trail and follow the road to the visitor center.

Petroglyphs at the monument include a remarkable array of symbols and images. Look for the familiar humpbacked flute player Kokopelli, reptiles, birds, insects, four-legged animals, anthropomorphs, geometric designs, mysterious masked serpents, and what look like unearthly star beings. The oldest of the petroglyphs may be up to 3,000 years old, dating to the earliest Basketmaker period, when people still lived in pit houses. About 90 percent are in the Rio Grande style, carved by Ancestral Pueblo people between AD 1300 and 1650. This was a period when the Rio Grande region saw a massive influx of refugees from the drought-ridden Four Corners area, and contact with Europeans marked the transition from prehistoric to historic times. The petroglyphs were probably used in ceremonies and are still used for ritual purposes by modern Pueblos today. As well as Indian petroglyphs, there are a number of Hispanic inscriptions and carvings made by Anglo ranchers in the 1800s.

where to go

Las Imagines Visitor Center. 6001 Unser Blvd. NW; (505) 899-0205, ext. 33; nps.gov/petr. Housed in the former 1948 adobe home of one of Albuquerque's most important archeologists, Dr. Sophie Aberle, the visitor center is located 3 miles north of I-40, adjoining Boca Negra Canyon. This should be your first stop for an orientation and information about visiting the four units of the park; the sites themselves do not have phones, and you should get a park map to help you get around. The visitor center offers a 22-minute film on the national monument and a small display about park geology, rock art, and archeology. Western National Parks Association runs a bookstore that sells many books on the area. Note: There are no trails with petroglyphs at this location. Open 8:30 a.m. to 4:30 p.m. daily, except Thanksgiving, Christmas, and New Year's Day.

Boca Negra Canyon Unit. Unser Boulevard NW, 0.25 mile north of Montaño Boulevard; nps.gov/petr. Formerly Indian Petroglyph State Park, 70-acre Boca Negra Canyon is the most developed and heavily visited unit of the park. It was set aside in 1973 to protect a fraction of the petroglyphs from vandalism and has water, toilets, picnic tables, and 3 partially paved trails that lead to about 100 petroglyphs. A fourth unpaved trail (Canyon Trail) offers more secluded hiking. No dogs allowed at Boca Negra, but they are allowed on a leash at the other undeveloped units. Parking fee. Open daily 8:30 a.m. to 4:30 p.m.

Piedras Marcadas Unit. Off Golf Course Road, at northern end of Unser Boulevard NW; nps.gov/petr. This undeveloped unit on the northern end of the monument is owned and managed by the City of Albuquerque Open Space Division. It preserves a huge unexcavated multilevel pueblo, one of many built to accommodate an influx of new residents from drought-stricken areas of northern New Mexico around AD 1300. The ground floor alone has 1,000 rooms, which gives you some idea of the original size of this agricultural pueblo. At the base of the escarpment are the remains of field houses and water control features made of basalt used in cultivating seasonal crops. The undeveloped trail leads to 300 to 500 petroglyphs and is 1.5 miles round-trip. No water, restrooms, or shade, and parking is tight here. Open daily 8:30 a.m. to 4:30 p.m.

Rinconada Canyon Unit. 1 mile south of Las Imagines Visitor Center on Unser Boulevard NW; nps.gov/petr. The closest unit to the park visitor center, this unit has a 2.2-mile round-trip unpaved trail that leads through sand dunes into a narrow valley for a quiet hike along the northern escarpment. There is a wide variety of petroglyphs pecked into the 150,000-year-old basaltic rocks, about 200 to 300 petroglyphs in all. Vault toilet but no water; bring plenty of water, wear good shoes and sun protection, and watch for millipedes and rattlesnakes, both prevalent at the monument. Open daily 8 a.m. to 5 p.m.

Volcanoes Day Use Area. Located off Atrisco Vista Boulevard, exit 149, approx. 4 miles north of I-40; nps.gov/petr. Albuquerque's five cinder cones—hills formed from volcanic debris—are one of its most distinctive features, especially late in the day when they are silhouetted against the setting sun. They last erupted 150,000 years ago, creating the lava escarpment where petroglyphs are carved. You can explore the volcanoes and other features, such as "geological windows" (from a German reference for eroded holes in the overhanging rock in a volcanic thrust zone) by driving out to this day-use area. JA Volcano is a good place to start. An easy 1-mile round-trip trail leads to a scenic viewpoint with great vistas of Albuquerque, the Rio Grande valley, and the Sandia Mountains. A moderate 0.8-mile loop leads to Black Volcano; if you wish to go farther, continue on the moderately strenuous 2-mile Vulcan Volcano loop to visit another cinder cone. Open daily 9 a.m. to 5 p.m.

balloon fiesta park

Located between Alameda and Tramway Northeast, west of I-25, this park is home to the Albuquerque International Balloon Fiesta, the world's largest ballooning event, held the first two weeks of October.

where to go

Albuquerque International Balloon Fiesta. 4401 Alameda Blvd. NE; (505) 821-1000; balloonfiesta.com. As many as 800,000 people attend this annual 9-day event, when more than 500 hot-air balloons from around the world rise in mass ascensions that fill the sky with balloons of every shape, size, and color. Particularly popular are the special-shape balloon ascensions, when balloons that look like dinosaurs, flying shoes, bottles, fantasy castles, and other whimsies take to the skies. The ascensions begin at dawn and are worth getting up early to see, but if you're not an early riser, try attending one of the balloon glows: against a dark sky, the enormous, colorful balloons lit by the flame from their propane burners resemble oversize lightbulbs lined up on the launch field—a beautiful and eerie sight. In addition to balloons there are food vendors selling coffee, hot chocolate, breakfast burritos, and other goodies; clothing concessions; and live music. Admission fee, but children under 13 get in free.

Anderson-Abruzzo Albuquerque International Balloon Museum. 9201 Balloon Museum Dr. NE; (505) 768-6020; balloonmuseum.com. Opened in 2005, the Balloon Museum is named for two pioneers of ballooning—Ben Abruzzo and Maxie Anderson—and co-managed by the City of Albuquerque. It occupies a beautiful facility that was purpose-built to celebrate all aspects of ballooning, from scientific experiments and space exploration to spying and adventure. Exhibits trace the development of ballooning from 1783 to the present day, using films, hands-on scientific experiments, and the Soukup and Thomas International Balloon and Airship Collection. There are 50 historic balloon gondolas, a number of which were involved in record-setting flights, such as the *Kitty Hawk* in which Maxie Anderson and his son Kristian crossed North America in 1980. There are lots of hands-on exhibits for kids; storytelling for the very young is free on Wed mornings. Open year-round Tues through Sun 9 a.m. to 5 p.m. Admission fee, but kids under 3 years of age are free.

rio rancho

With its new cookie-cutter tract homes, bland apartment complexes, ubiquitous chain businesses, and windswept dusty location on the edge of town, sprawling Rio Rancho feels rather soulless and conservative, but it is close to good eateries and lodgings in Corrales and Santa Ana Pueblo. Rio Rancho holds an annual barbecue contest called Pork and Brew in the 160-acre Santa Ana Star Center (505-891-7300), an event center that is a co-venture of nearby Santa Ana Pueblo and the City of Rio Rancho and includes a stadium and food outlets. The Convention and Visitors Bureau inside will help arrange balloon rides, but other than that, most attractions lie on the periphery.

where to go

Balloon Rides. 3200 Civic Center Circle NE, Rio Rancho; (505) 891-7258; visitriorancho .org. The Rio Rancho Convention and Visitors Bureau maintains a list of 9 companies with FAA-certified pilots offering balloon rides to visitors. Contact them at the number above for listings. Rides usually take place early morning or evening and last about 2 to 3 hours.

santa ana pueblo

Santa Ana Pueblo operates high-visibility businesses along US 550, including Santa Ana Star Casino Hotel and Santa Ana Golf Club, which offers on-site gourmet dining at Prairie Star Restaurant and Wine Bar. The pueblo's star attraction, however, is Hyatt Regency Tamaya Resort, a luxury resort on 500 acres of hauntingly beautiful ancestral lands, which offers cultural tours, guided outdoor activities such as horseback riding and nature walks, and fine dining at the Corn Maiden Restaurant. Santa Ana artisans are known for their crosses of inlaid straw and polished polychrome pottery, skills that have been revived to great acclaim. The Ancestral pueblo of Tamaya, 9 miles away, is closed to visitors except on feast days. A nice little museum at the entrance to the resort interprets tribal history.

where to go

Santa Ana Golf Club. 288 Prairie Star Rd.; (505) 867-9464; mynewmexicogolf.com. "One of America's three best true links-style golf courses," according to the *New York Times,* this 27-hole golf course follows in the tradition of golf's first links-style courses and is highly rated by both *Golf Week* and *Golf Digest.* Amenities include a 22,000-square-foot clubhouse, containing the award-winning four-star fine-dining restaurant Prairie Star and a casual grill; eight lakes; a full-service pro shop; practice facilities; and hospitality quarters. One fee for all-day play. The sister course **Twin Warriors Golf Course** (1301 Tuyuna Trail; 505-771-6155) is nearby and adjoins Tamaya Resort.

Santa Ana Star Casino Hotel. 54 Jemez Canyon Dam Rd.; (505) 867-1234, (844) 4NMB-EST; santaanastar.com. The tribe's casino was the first tribal enterprise to be built along US 550. Its success, in large part, is what has allowed the tribe to go on and build its beautiful Hyatt Regency Tamaya Resort on tribal lands just west of the casino. It has now added a hotel to the casino, which offers 204 nonsmoking rooms and suites, a pool, hot tub, and fitness center. The casino is a gaming mecca, with blackjack, craps, poker, roulette, and over 1,600 slots. The five on-site restaurants have food at different price points: there's mainstream buffet dining at the Feast Buffet; New Mexican food and cocktails at Cantina Rio; a casual bar at Lounge 54; sandwiches, burgers, and desserts at Mesa Grille; pizza, hot dogs, burgers, and New Mexican food at the Starlight Bar and Grill adjoining the bowling alley; and steak and seafood at the Juniper fine-dining restaurant. The Stage at Santa Ana Casino offers live entertainment nightly, and there's family bowling at the 36-lane Starlight Bowling Center.

where to eat

Corn Maiden Restaurant. 1300 Tuyuna Trail; (505) 772-6060; hyatt.com/en-US/hotel/new-mexico/hyatt-regency-tamaya-resort-and-spa/tamay/dining. Hyatt Regency Tamaya Resort's elegant dinner restaurant offers upscale dining in a softly lit room with picture windows framing the Rio Grande and the Sandia Mountains. Try the delicious native sweet corn bisque with crema followed by the restaurant's signature rotisserie meats; one plate features native beef strip loin, buffalo sausage, and chicken breast and another features duck breast, seared tuna, and jumbo prawn. There are vegetarian options at this meat-heavy restaurant, so don't let that stop you from enjoying a special dinner. Be sure to save room for a seasonal crème brûlée or green chile apple pie with caramel sauce for dessert. Open Thurs through Sat 5:30 to 9 p.m. $$–$$$$.

Prairie Star Restaurant and Wine Bar. 288 Prairie Star Rd. (US 550 and SR 528); (505) 867-3327; mynewmexicogolf.com/prairiestar. Santa Ana Pueblo's original fine-dining restaurant is tucked away in an old adobe mansion on the Santa Ana Golf Club, just under 2 miles from the tribe's main Tamaya Resort. Its unusual location at a golf club hasn't stopped Prairie Star from gaining a loyal local following of diners who come to savor superb New American cuisine from a creative young chef whose cuisine leans heavily on local organic produce. Small plates may include rabbit and foie gras sausage rillettes and cornmeal-crusted calamari. For an entree, try bacon-wrapped pheasant, braised lamb shank, or perhaps the pan-seared Idaho white trout. Prices are very reasonable here for the quality and creativity of the menu. The extensive award-winning wine list has over 500 selections, more than 40 by the glass, available at the wine bar from 5 p.m. Open Tues through Sat 5:30 to 8 p.m. $$–$$$.

where to stay

Hyatt Regency Tamaya Resort. 1300 Tuyuna Trail; (505) 867-1234; hyatt.com/en-US/hotel/new-mexico/hyatt-regency-tamaya-resort-and-spa/tamay. Laid out in a style reminiscent of Chaco Canyon, this large, art-filled resort has extensive attractive grounds landscaped with native plants and cascading water in a large swimming pool. Among the guest amenities are the Tamaya Mist Spa and Salon, which offers not only the usual soothing massages and pampering body treatments but energy work like Reiki and craniosacral therapy, as well as acupressure-point shiatsu and reflexology. Activities include the nationally known Twin Warriors Golf Course, tennis, horseback riding, nature trails through the Rio Grande bosque, fine dining, a cultural museum, and gift store. The 350 rooms and suites have restful decor and offer all amenities. Ask for a Mountain Vista room with balcony for awesome views of the Sandia Mountains and Rio Grande. $$–$$$.

day trip 03

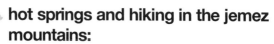
northwest

>>> **hot springs and hiking in the jemez mountains:**
jemez pueblo, jemez springs, la cueva, bandelier national monument

The Jemez Mountain Trail offers a wonderful drive into the Jemez Mountains northwest of Albuquerque. It starts out in Bernalillo on busy US 550, the main route to the Four Corners, then turns right at San Ysidro to follow narrow, winding SR 4 north through red-rock canyons, pueblo lands, quaint villages, hot springs, high-country forests, lakes, and federally managed parks and preserves. Funky but fun Jemez Springs, nestled in the heart of San Diego Canyon, is a good place to break this 100-mile trip, which is best done as a weekend getaway. You'll find unique lodgings and restaurants, a state historic site preserving a pueblo and mission, and several places to enjoy hot springs. After resting up here, plan on outdoor activities the next day. In spring, summer, and fall, you can fish, hunt, and camp in the national forest and hike in Valles Caldera National Preserve—the collapsed caldera of the Jemez volcano—and popular Bandelier National Monument, which protects unusual cave dwellings and a large pueblo in Frijoles Canyon. The relative flatness of the crater in between Valles Caldera and Bandelier makes this a popular cross-country ski area in winter; there's a small downhill ski area, Pajarito, outside Los Alamos. From here, you can loop back to Santa Fe, via Los Alamos, reversing North Day Trip 05, or continue into the Española Valley, Georgia O'Keeffe Country, and Indian Country (Northwest Day Trips 04, 05, and 06).

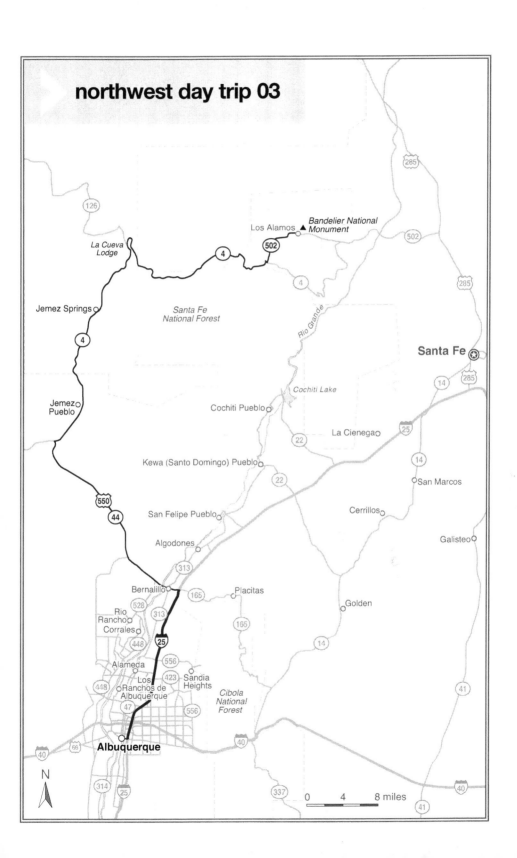

northwest day trip 03

285

126

La Cueva
Lodge

Los Alamos ▲ Bandelier National
Monument

502

502

4

285

Jemez Springs

4

Santa Fe
National Forest

Rio Grande

Santa Fe ⊛

4

285

14

Cochiti Lake

Jemez
Pueblo

Cochiti Pueblo

La Cienega

25

22

14

Kewa (Santo Domingo) Pueblo

San Marcos

550

44

San Felipe Pueblo

22

Cerrillos

Galisteo

Algodones

313

Bernalillo

313

165

Placitas

Golden

528

Rio
Rancho

313

165

Corrales

14

448

25

Alameda

556

Los
Ranchos de
Albuquerque

423

Sandia
Heights

Cibola
National
Forest

41

448

47

556

40

Albuquerque

40

66

N

314

25

337

41

0   4   8 miles

40

41

jemez pueblo

The ancestors of the Jemez people migrated into the Jemez Springs area from Mesa Verde in the 1100s, after a long drought emptied out the Four Corners. They built multistory pueblos on the mesa tops of San Diego Canyon and farmed and hunted in this well-watered area. By the early 1600s, they were facing new enemies as European diseases and warfare decimated the population. The Jemez coalesced into two large pueblos: Giusewa in Jemez Springs and Walatowa a few miles to the south. Giusewa—a reference to the hot springs now protected as Jemez Historic Site—was missionized by the Spanish in 1621 but abandoned by 1640. In 1706 the remaining population moved to Walatowa (meaning "This Is the Place"), where 3,400 descendants now live on 89,000 acres of beautiful forested mountain country.

Towa-speaking Jemez Pueblo has a strong arts tradition. Among its best-known contemporary artists and writers are N. Scott Momaday, author of the Pulitzer Prize–winning *House Made of Dawn*, and sculptor Cliff Fragua, whose marble statue of Pueblo Revolt leader Popé (traditionally spelled Po'pay) is one of two statues representing New Mexico in the US Capitol. (The selection of a sculpture of a Pueblo Revolt hero by a Jemez artist speaks volumes.) Jemez women originally produced black-on-white ceramics but abandoned this style to protest the 1692 Spanish reconquest. Contemporary Jemez pottery is black-on-red and black-on-tan in style, similar to that of neighboring Zia Pueblo. Jemez is only open on the November 12 feast day of San Diego; information, exhibits, and tours are available at the tribe's attractive modern Walatowa Visitor Center among the red rocks on SR 4, about 50 miles northwest of Albuquerque. The tribe's annual Walatowa Arts and Crafts Show is one of its most popular events.

where to go

Gilman Tunnels. Just north of Walatowa Visitor Center, turn left on SR 485 and cross the Jemez River for an interesting side trip following the Rio Guadalupe to the village of Gilman. SR 485 climbs through a series of narrow tunnels blasted through the volcanic tuff of the Jemez Mountains by logging companies in the 1920s. There are great views of some of the oldest rocks in the 1.1-million-year-old Jemez Mountains, including Virgin Mesa. Just past the tunnels, the pavement ends. Stay on FR 376 and drive east on paved SR 126 to La Cueva and Fenton Lake and pick up SR 4. You can loop back to Jemez Springs if you wish. The whole 43-mile loop is a popular mountain-bike outing.

Walatowa Visitor Center. SR 4; (575) 834-7235; jemezpueblo.com. This small modern facility has exhibits on the area's natural and cultural history and geology, a cultural museum, reconstructed field house, and pottery displays. The tribe shares space with the US Forest Service, which offers information on hiking, camping, fishing, hunting, and other recreation on Forest Service lands. There are amazing views of the red rocks from the courtyard and on guided hikes of the easy 1.5-mile Red Rock Canyon Trail. Ask about special guided cultural tours for groups that include bread making and a visit to an artisan, among other things. Visitor center open daily 8 a.m. to 5 p.m., 10 a.m. to 4 p.m. in winter. Guided hikes at 10 a.m. and 1 p.m. daily. There is a fee for guided hikes and other trips.

where to shop

Singing Stone Studio. 1050 Day School Rd.; (575) 252-8870; singingstonestudio.com. Cliff Fragua's sculpture studio is open to visitors. To reach it, take SR 4 to mile marker 4 and turn left on Broken Arrow Road; go to the end of Broken Arrow and make a left on Day School Road; then go to the first building on the left, building #1050. Call ahead to make sure Cliff is available. Small and monumental bronze, marble, and other pieces are for sale. Among Fragua's themes are the heroes of the Indian past: people such as Popé, the leader of the 1680 Pueblo Revolt, whose likeness Fragua sculpted in marble for installation in the US Capitol.

jemez springs

This rustic hot springs resort community, about an hour's drive from Albuquerque via US 550 and SR 4, is in the heart of scenic San Diego Canyon, a few miles north of Jemez Pueblo. It has a number of ways to rest and recharge: charming bed-and-breakfast inns, vacation rentals, and retreats; several riverside restaurants; massage therapy; and your choice of developed hot springs at the 1870 town bathhouse or a private day spa, as well as clothing-optional Spence Hot Springs, an undeveloped spring along a nearby forest trail. Jemez Historic Site, which preserves the ruins of Giusewa and a Spanish mission, is at the north end of the village. Park and walk around; everything is close together here.

where to go

Jemez Historic Site. SR 4; (575) 829-3530; nmhistoricalsites.org/Jemez. It's hard to imagine now that Giusewa was once a large pueblo that sprawled all the way to the river—the Spanish mission and large church of San José de los Jemez built on top of the ancestral Jemez pueblo completely dominate this 7-acre site. The pueblo is protected under a series of hummocks, but you can see a restored kiva. A small museum has exhibits including rare examples of prehistoric Jemez Pueblo black-on-white pottery. Kids will enjoy touching sheepskins, grinding corn, and other hands-on exhibits. Open Wed through Sun 8:30 a.m. to 5 p.m. Admission fee; free to NM residents first Sun of the month.

Jemez Springs Bath House. Jemez Springs Plaza; (575) 829-3303; jemezspringsbath house.com. This quaint 1870 bathhouse is run by the City of Jemez. It offers mineral soaks in 8 private tubs; herbal wraps and therapeutic massage using locally made products are available in treatment rooms. The naturally occurring minerals in the Jemez hot springs are acid carbonate, aluminum, calcium, chloride, iron, magnesium, potassium, silicate, sodium, and sulphate. Temperatures are 154 to 186 degrees Fahrenheit. Discounts for seniors and military; packages. Open Sun through Tues 10 a.m. to 5 p.m. and Thurs through Sat 10 a.m. to 6 p.m. Admission fee.

where to shop

Jemez Fine Art Gallery. 17346 SR 4; (575) 829-3340; jemezfineart.com. Thirteen local artists working in a variety of media sell their work at this artists' cooperative. The work is of a high caliber and includes landscapes in pastel, watercolor, and oil, as well as sculpture, abstracts, and fiber arts by artists from Jemez Pueblo and throughout the valley. Open Thurs through Tues 11 a.m. to 5 p.m.

where to eat

Highway 4 Coffee. 17502 SR 4; (575) 829-4655; hwy4coffee.com. Adjoining the Lizard Inn, this little cafe is now run separately and is a good spot to stop for coffee and get a bite to eat. You'll find pastries and pies in the case and a variety of breakfast burritos and breakfast dishes, with burgers, fish-and-chips, panini, pizza, and quiche at lunchtime. Open Mon and Tues 8 a.m. to 3 p.m., Wed 8 to 11 a.m., Thurs 8 a.m. to 3 p.m., Fri 8 a.m. to 4 p.m., Sat 8 a.m. to 7 p.m., and Sun 8 a.m. to 4 p.m. $.

Los Ojos Restaurant and Saloon. SR 4; (575) 829-3547. American food in a smoky roadhouse atmosphere for when you have a yen for a bunkhouse breakfast, greasy burger and fries, a big steak, and live honky-tonk music. Breakfast on weekends only. Open Mon through Fri 11 a.m. to midnight and Sat and Sun 8 a.m. to midnight. $–$$.

where to stay

Cañon del Rio Retreat and Spa. 16445 SR 4; (575) 829-4377; canondelrio.com. This peaceful retreat center on 3 riverside acres feels perfectly attuned to its surroundings with its rustic elegance, warm desert hues, Native-inspired rooms, on-site art gallery, day spa, ponds, nature trails, and workshops geared toward personal growth. There are 6 guest rooms with clean lines and lovely furnishings. Wi-Fi. A sumptuous gourmet breakfast is served family style in the great room. Popular for yoga retreats. $$.

Casa Blanca Guest House and Garden Cottage. 17521 SR 4; (575) 829-3579. Located next to Jemez Springs Pottery, this riverside property offers an adobe guesthouse with kitchen, living room with vigas and kiva fireplace, and two bedrooms (queen-size bed in one room, single bed and rollaway bed in the other). The garden cottage across the courtyard has wood-paneled walls, an open sleeping area with queen-size bed, sitting room with woodstove, kitchenette, and gas grill; it sleeps 2. $–$$.

Laughing Lizard Inn. 17526 SR 4; (575) 829-3108; thelaughinglizard.com. Located in the village, this hometown favorite across from the river is a good budget option. It has 4 newly renovated rooms and 1 suite with a kitchen. $.

la cueva

North of Jemez Springs, SR 4 follows the river through the canyon. There are numerous recreation opportunities, including hiking, fishing, camping, and hike-in hot springs along the Jemez River. La Cueva is at the junction of SR 4 and SR 126. East of the junction are five cross-country ski areas adjoining Valles Caldera National Preserve and Bandelier National Monument. The US Forest Service at Walatowa Visitor Center has information.

where to go

Battleship Rock. 5 miles north of Jemez Springs on SR 4. Made of volcanic tuff and strewn with bits of sharp volcanic glass, or obsidian, collected by early prehistoric hunters, this distinctive 200-foot rock next to SR 4 is a dramatic landmark. You can try climbing it if you're feeling energetic. The Las Conchas Trail is a good outing for families.

Fenton Lake State Park. 455 Fenton Lake Rd.; (575) 829-3630; emnrd.state.nm.us/SPD/fentonlakestatepark.html. A trout-fishing haven, this 37-acre high-country lake is also a good place to canoe. The lake is a rest-and-nest stopover for migratory waterfowl and is also used by wild turkeys, elk, bobcats, and mule deer. The campground has a handful of campsites, 5 with water and electric, and vault toilets but no showers. Open 24 hours. Admission fee.

McCauley Warm Springs. This undeveloped hot springs can be reached from either Battleship Rock or Jemez Falls Campground (14 miles north of Jemez Springs). Park at either location for the 2.5-mile hike in to the springs. Day-use only, sunrise to sunset. No overnight camping.

San Antonio Hot Springs. These hot springs are 9 miles north of Jemez Springs. To reach them, turn west at La Cueva onto SR 120. Go approximately 3 miles to FR 376 and drive 5 miles north. Note: FR 376 is typically closed in winter due to snow. Day-use only, sunrise to sunset. No overnight camping.

Spence Hot Springs. These undeveloped hot springs are 7 miles north of Jemez Springs and the most popular backcountry hot springs in the area. Park in the gravel parking lot, and walk down the short trail to the Jemez River and up the other side to the springs. Day-use only, sunrise to sunset. No overnight camping.

Valles Caldera National Preserve. SR 4, MM 39.2, PO Box 379, Jemez Springs; (505) 829-4100; nps.gov/vall. The spectacular collapsed caldera at the heart of the Jemez Mountains, long a private ranch used for grazing and logging, has been in public ownership since

2000 and is the nation's newest national preserve. Initially run by a board of trustees, the preserve was recently transferred to the National Park Service, which now manages the preserve for scientific research, limited grazing and logging, hiking, wildlife watching, cross-country skiing, snowshoeing, fishing, hunting, and horseback riding. Stop at the Valles Caldera Entrance Station, 2 miles from MM 39.2 on SR 4, to pay the entrance fee and get a park map and information on front-country trails suitable for your fitness level. The La Jara and History Grove Loops are popular; another trail visits a movie-set cabin. You can park your car at the entrance station and walk the trails; restrooms are available. To enter the backcountry, you must purchase a day-use backcountry access permit for your vehicle. Only 35 permits are available daily to protect the resource and backcountry experience, on a first-come, first-served basis. There is no on-site camping, but campgrounds are available nearby. You can get a sense of the preserve by driving SR 4 around Valle Grande, as it is known locally, in itself a scenic drive. The caldera is only one of many studded with meadows and eruption domes, including 11,274-foot Redondo Peak, sacred to local Indians for its obsidian. Entrance station open daily 8 a.m. to 6 p.m. May 15 to Oct 31, 9 a.m. to 5 p.m. Nov 1 to May 14.

bandelier national monument

Located among the volcanic cliffs and canyons of the Pajarito Plateau near Los Alamos, Bandelier National Monument is one of New Mexico's must-experience parks. It was set aside to protect the almost 3,000 archeological sites in and around Frijoles Canyon that were inhabited between the 12th and 16th centuries by ancestors of people from modern Cochiti, Santa Clara, San Ildefonso, San Felipe, and Kewa (Santo Domingo) Pueblos. The highlights of the park are a late 13th-century pueblo on the canyon floor and unusual 12th-century cave-type cliff dwellings carved out of soft volcanic tuff. A separate unit of the park, Tsankawi, protects a pueblo near Los Alamos. Some 70 percent of the park is wilderness, making this a superb place for backcountry hiking and camping. The monument is named for Adolph Bandelier, the 19th-century archeologist who first visited it. It was excavated in the early 1900s by archeologist Edgar Lee Hewett, founder of the School of American Research in Santa Fe. Hewett, who helped write the 1906 Antiquities Act and get it signed into law, was instrumental in having Bandelier set aside as a national monument in 1916.

where to go

Alcove House Trail. Formerly called Ceremonial Cave, this small cave pueblo is located 140 feet above the canyon floor and is reached via a half-mile spur from the main loop. You must climb four steep ladders to reach the alcove and ceremonial cave (kiva), making it unsuitable for kids and those afraid of heights.

Bandelier National Monument Frijoles Visitor Center and National Historical District. 15 Entrance Rd., Los Alamos (off SR 4); (575) 672-3861; nps.gov/band. The visitor center is in a historic 1930s stone building built by the CCC. With its dark vigas, adobe walls, tinwork, and other notable features, it is interesting and enjoyable to visit in itself. This is the place to pay admission, get information from rangers on visiting the park, pick up a permit for backcountry hiking and camping, and look at interpretive exhibits in the small museum. There's an interesting selection of books in the bookstore run by the nonprofit Western National Parks Association. A well-produced 10-minute film about Bandelier plays in the auditorium. Frijoles Canyon and Tsankawi are both open from dawn to dusk year-round. The visitor center at Frijoles Canyon is open daily 8 a.m. to 6 p.m. spring/summer, 9 a.m. to 5:30 p.m. fall, and 9 a.m. to 5 p.m. winter. Closed Christmas week. Admission fee.

Note: Due to parking problems in Frijoles Canyon between the hours of 9 a.m. and 3 p.m. during peak season, May 16 to Oct 16, visitors are required to take a free shuttle bus from the White Rock Visitor Center (off SR 4 in White Rock) to the main visitor areas in Frijoles Canyon, including the visitor center, Main Loop Trail, and Falls Trail. Shuttles run every 30 minutes on weekdays and every 20 minutes on weekends. The only exemptions are those arriving by bicycle, outside the hours listed, staying in the campground, displaying

artistry at bandelier national monument

The Bandelier visitor complex includes several historic adobe structures and roads built by the Civilian Conservation Corps (CCC) as part of FDR's New Deal in the 1930s. The CCC arrived in 1933 to build an entrance road and new stone park buildings. Frijoles Canyon Lodge (now the gift shop, snack bar, and administrative buildings) was built in 1939–40. Evelyn Frey, who had come to Frijoles Canyon with her husband George and son Richard to manage a guest ranch there, stayed on to run the lodge until her retirement in 1978. The old ranch buildings were pulled down around 1940. Bandelier protects the largest concentration of CCC structures, furnishings, and tinwork and some of the best WPA art in the National Park System. Among the pieces of art created by local artists as part of the WPA program are bright pastels of Bandelier by German immigrant artist Helmut Naumer. In the 1930s, Naumer was friends with Santa Fe's famous Cinco Pintores ("Five Painters"), particularly Fremont Ellis, who gave Naumer 6 acres of land southeast of Santa Fe (Ellis Ranch, behind Cafe Fina) to construct a large adobe ranch home. Between 2006 and 2008 I was fortunate to have the chance to live in the converted workshop section of the Naumer home, built around an old shepherd's cabin, and to experience firsthand Naumer's unique creative spirit.

a disability sticker, and traveling with pets (however, pets are not allowed on trails, so you are advised to leave Fido at home).

Falls Trail. This enjoyable 2.5-mile trail descends 700 feet to two waterfalls above the Rio Grande and offers a look into the volcanic history of the monument.

Frey Trail. This 1.5-mile trail was the main route into the canyon before the highway was built by the CCC. It provides access to the canyon from Juniper Campground on the mesa above and descends 550 feet.

Main Loop Trail. The easy 1.2-mile Main Loop begins behind the visitor center and meanders along the bottom of Frijoles Canyon. It takes you past Big Kiva; Tyuonyi Pueblo, which has all the hallmarks of a Chaco Canyon great house; Talus House; Long House; and a number of *cavates* (cliff dwellings) excavated from volcanic tuff and reached via ladders.

Tsankawi. Tsankawi is a separate unit 12 miles from the main park atop a mesa top with an eastern exposure. A 1.5-mile trail leads to petroglyphs, *cavates*, and the Ancestral Pueblo of Tsankawi. To reach the unit, take SR 4 from Bandelier and turn right at the third stop light. Watch for a gravel parking lot on the right.

where to stay

Juniper Campground. This is the main campground at Bandelier for groups of 10 or less. There are 3 loops. Campsites are well-screened with piñon and juniper, and each has a picnic table and grill. Running water, toilets, trash pickup. Nearby Ponderosa Campground is a group campground. You may also camp in the backcountry with a permit. Open year-round. $.

day trip 04

northwest

>>> cliff dwellings, canyons, and ancient springs in the española valley:
santa clara pueblo, el rito, ojo caliente

From Los Alamos, pick up SR 30 north along the west bank of the Rio Grande, the back route to Española. The scenic road beneath Pajarito Plateau has fabulous views of sacred Black Mesa and the braided rivers and badlands of Las Barrancas in the Española Valley. The highlight of the day trip is a visit to Santa Clara Pueblo, famous for its polished black pottery and Puye Cliff Dwellings, the tribe's ancestral home in the Pajarito Plateau, which offers guided tours daily. Santa Clara is about a mile south of Española. Head north into the scenic Chama River valley on US 285 and then west on SR 554 to visit the traditional Hispanic wood-carving village of El Rito. Nearby is Ojo Caliente, famous for its hot springs resort. It's the perfect place to end your day, relaxing with a soak in outdoor mineral springs and enjoying a massage. You can spend the night there or at a local bed-and-breakfast.

I have set up this day trip as a continuation of North Day Trip 03; however, you could simply do it as a continuation of Northwest Day Trip 03, if you prefer. if you plan on driving up directly from Albuquerque, take I-25 north, then get on NM 599 to bypass Santa Fe and pick up US 285/84 North. Continue to Española, then take SR 30 south to Santa Clara Pueblo to start the day trip.

santa clara pueblo

With an estimated 1,009 tribal members and 47,000 acres, Tewa-speaking Santa Clara Pueblo, or Kha' p'oo Owinge ("Valley of the Wild Roses"), is the second largest of the Eight

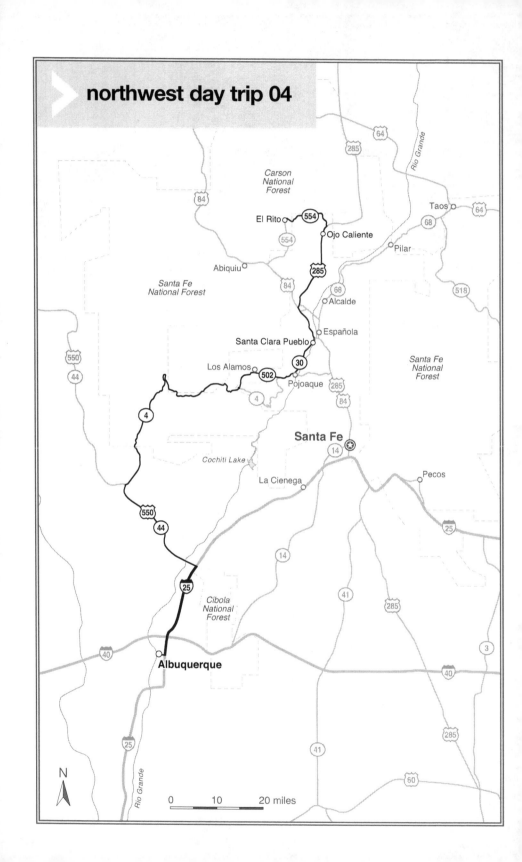

northwest day trip 04

Northern Pueblos in landmass. Santa Clara people trace their ancestry to Tewa-speaking forebears who moved to the Pajarito Plateau between AD 900 and 1300, with many fleeing drought in the Four Corners in the 12th century. Santa Clara is unusual for its proximity to the tribe's ancestral pueblo, Puye, a series of cliff and mesa-top dwellings occupied between the 900s and 1580, similar to those seen at Bandelier National Monument. Other pueblo attractions include Santa Clara Canyon, a nearby recreation area, and Black Mesa Golf Club, a top-ranked course in La Mesilla. The main village is a good place to visit artisans making Santa Clara's famous polished black pottery and redware. Among Santa Clara's best-known contemporary potters is Roxanne Swentzell, whose monumental clay sculptures of Pueblo women are instantly recognizable. Swentzell is a member of the famous Santa Clara Naranjo family of artists, known for their pottery and activism. The Comanche Dance is performed on June 13, the tribe's feast day. In August, Harvest and Corn Dances are performed to honor Saint Clare. The tribe opened its Santa Claran Hotel Casino, an expanded resort on the site of its former Big Rock Casino in downtown Española, in January 2010. Please check in at the tribal headquarters upon arrival at the pueblo. Guided tours are available; inquire at Puye Cliff Dwellings Welcome Center.

where to go

Black Mesa Golf Club. 115 SR 399, La Mesilla; (505) 747-8946; blackmesagolfclub.com. Designed by architect Baxter Spann, this scenic course, named for nearby Black Mesa, has a wild Irish links appeal. Its Black Mesa Grill serves basic breakfasts of eggs and burritos and lunches of burgers, hot dogs, and tacos. Open dawn to dusk. Greens fee.

Puye Cliff Dwellings National Historic Landmark. Santa Clara Road; (505) 917-6650, (888) 320-5008 (tours); puyecliffdwellings.com. A drought in 1580 forced the 1,500 residents of Puye to abandon their carved cave-like "apartments" in the compacted volcanic ash, or tuff, of Pajarito Plateau and move closer to the Rio Grande. The mile-long ruins are open daily for guided tours. Purchase tickets at Puye Cliffs Welcome Center at the Valero gas station on SR 30. Basic entrance admits you to the Harvey House, a late 19th-century bed-and-breakfast built by the famous railroad entrepreneur Fred Harvey at the foot of the cliffs; it is the only one built on an Indian reservation and now serves as an interpretive center and museum and offers photo opportunities of the cliff dwellings from below. Four different guided tours of the mile-long ruins are offered. In addition to the Harvey House tour, there are separate tours of the cliff face and the mesa top, and one combined tour of all locations. Visitors on the mesa-top tour are driven to the top; cliff-face tours require hiking along a paved trail in the cliffs. The site is quite exposed and rugged. Wear good footwear, a hat, and sun protection, and bring food and water. No reservation required; however, if your group has fewer than 8 people, you will be asked to join another group. Open daily summer 8 a.m. to 6 p.m., winter 8 a.m. to 4 p.m. Summer tours begin at 9 a.m. and end at 4 p.m.; winter 9 a.m. to 2 p.m. Admission fee.

Santa Clara Canyon. Santa Clara Road; (505) 753-7326. This deep, tree-lined canyon near Puye Cliff Dwellings offers trout fishing and camping in developed sites. Contact the tribe for a use permit. Open Apr through Oct. Admission fee.

el rito

The tiny one-horse town of El Rito is famous for its traditional Spanish Colonial wood carving, Rio Grande–style weaving (a distinctive style of Hispanic blanket weaving, influenced by Mexican Saltillo rugs, that uses rougher wool, colored bands, diamonds, and sometimes a tapestry effect), tinsmithing, *santo* making, Spanish-language immersion programs, and folk music. These are the focus of unique offerings at the El Rito campus of Northern New Mexico College, an important center of traditional arts during the New Deal era, when local artisans received government support to keep regional folk arts such as these alive. Campaigns for Latino rights during the 1960s and 1970s benefited northern New Mexico communities like El Rito, which has a community clinic and a small hometown library that functions as a community center. Not all the arts are traditional. Contemporary artist Nicholas Herrera makes remarkable *retablos* (altar backdrops) and *santos*, which adorn lowrider cars as well as other media. Herrera and roughly 135 artists participate in the annual El Rito Studio Tour in early October (elritoartassociation.com/studio-tour).

where to go

El Rito Library. 182 Placitas Rd.; (575) 581-4608; elritolibrary.org. This excellent little library is much beloved as a community meeting place and a good place to enjoy occasional poetry readings and find out about community events. To get there, go through El Rito and turn right on SR 215 to reach Placitas Road. Open Tues through Fri noon to 5 p.m. and Sat 9 a.m. to 2 p.m.

Northern New Mexico College, El Rito Campus. (575) 581-4115; nnmc.edu. Opened in 1909 as the Spanish American Normal School, a teacher-training college, this campus has become an important center of vocational arts, where four-year degrees are offered and students apprentice with master craftspeople. It's a pleasant historic campus to walk around, and there's an on-site cafeteria. Open to visitors 7 a.m. to 10 p.m.

where to eat

El Farolito. 1212 SR 554 (Main Street); (575) 581-9509; facebook.com/MarisolTrujilloPerry. This funky hole-in-the-wall on the main drag will appeal to fans of quaint roadside diners in out-of-the-way places. The menu features American standards and an array of chile-drenched northern New Mexico favorites—from green chile stew and green chile burgers to chile rellenos and Frito pies. Food is eaten at picnic tables. Open Tues through Sun 11:30 a.m. to 8 p.m. $.

ojo caliente

The hot springs here have been used since prehistoric times and remain popular with New Mexico residents. Like most hot springs resort villages in rural settings, the community that grew up here is free-form and funky. This used to be Ojo's greatest appeal, but sadly some of that has gone now. Following a fire, new owners upgraded the venerable old Ojo Caliente Hot Springs into a destination resort complete with amenities designed to appeal to high-end travelers. While you should on no account pass up the unique experience of the pools and body treatments at Ojo, or a nice healthy meal in the Artesian restaurant on-site, be aware that lodging at this destination resort is now a little on the pricey side, although perfect for a special getaway. The best all-around value for food and nice casita lodging in the area, for my money, is the Abiquiu Inn on US 84. The inn is conveniently located right next door to the starting point for tours of the Georgia O'Keeffe Home in Abiquiu (see Northwest Day Trip 05) and not far from Ojo Caliente, which allows you the best of both worlds and a head start exploring Georgia O'Keeffe Country.

where to go

Ojo Caliente Mineral Springs Resort and Spa. 50 Los Baños Dr.; (888) 939-0007; ojo-spa.com. The mineral waters at Ojo Caliente were named by 16th-century explorer Cabeza de Vaca but had long been considered sacred by local Tewa Indians who built a pueblo adjoining the hot springs. The attractively landscaped spa resort that is there today is spread out over 1,100 hilly acres along the river. Most people come to enjoy the communal outdoor pools (bring your own swimsuit and towel or rent them at the desk). Some 100,000 gallons of hot mineral water, at temperatures between 80 and 109 degrees Fahrenheit, emerge from the pale volcanic rocks along the river. Choose from 10 pools containing a unique combination of mineral waters long said to have curative properties: arsenic for arthritis, stomach ulcers, and skin conditions; lithia for depression; soda for digestion; and iron for the blood. The Mud Pool is a fun place to cover yourself in therapeutic mud and sunbathe as it dries on you. I highly recommend the original Milagro Wrap, in which guests soak in the mineral waters and then are swaddled in heavy woolen blankets to accelerate the release of toxins from the body and placed in a restful room. It's a good deal for the overly busy and stressed that has stood the test of time. Other spa offerings include facials, therapeutic massage, hot stone massage, relaxing Indian head massage, and other relaxing treatments. Note: Sunrise Springs, southwest of Santa Fe, is under the same ownership. Ojo Caliente is open year-round. Mineral pools are open 9:30 a.m. to 10 p.m. daily for day guests, 7:30 a.m. to 10 p.m. for overnight guests. No children under 13 in the springs. Admission fee, with sunset rates after 6 p.m. A variety of good winter specials are available.

where to eat

Artesian Restaurant at Ojo Caliente Mineral Springs Resort and Spa. Adjoining the historic hotel, this lovely restaurant serves breakfast, lunch, and dinner. There are many light, healthful dishes among the globally inspired menu items drawing on produce from the resort's own organic Ojo Farm. Try the chile relleno made with buffalo sausage or the Ojo Breakfast Bowl with quinoa, beans, radishes, salsa, and poached eggs for breakfast; the fish tacos or chicken potpie for lunch; or wild Scottish salmon or grilled trout for dinner. There is even a Farm Menu, featuring special salads made from Ojo produce. Open daily for breakfast 7:30 to 11 a.m.; lunch 11:30 a.m. to 2:30 p.m.; and dinner 5 to 9 p.m. (Sun through Thurs) and 5:00 to 9:30 p.m. (Fri and Sat). From Nov 3 through May, the restaurant closes one-half hour earlier. On-site wine bar. Coffee and tea service from 6 to 8 a.m. in the hotel lobby features Ojo's own roasted coffee blend from Iconik Coffee in Santa Fe and beautiful loose teas from Tea-o-Graphy in Taos. $–$$$.

where to stay

Ojo Caliente Mineral Springs Resort and Spa. The resort now offers a number of lodging options. The quaint old adobe hotel captures the European spa feel with its wooden floors, old-fashioned fixtures, and white linens. If you're a light sleeper, note that the walls are quite thin and there are only half-baths; guests shower at the public bathhouse. The 8 historic North Cottages and 11 Plaza Suites have half-baths with showers and kitchenettes. New Mexico–style Posi, Pueblo, and Cliffside Suites have all amenities, including kiva fireplaces and your own hot tub on a private patio. You can also now rent one of the 4 beautifully modernized vintage Airstream trailers for the night. Larger parties can rent one of the 2 fully furnished private historic homes with 3 or 4 bedrooms in Ojo Caliente. There is also an RV campground, a good budget option that offers early entry to the springs and a 15 percent discount. $$–$$$$.

day trip 05

northwest

>>> **georgia o'keeffe country:**
abiquiu, ghost ranch, tierra amarilla,
chama

This day trip takes you on a pilgrimage into the landscape painted by famed American artist Georgia O'Keeffe (1887–1986), known for her bold, sensuous depictions of flowers, bones, adobe buildings, and the colorful volcanic badlands of the Chama River valley. O'Keeffe first visited as a guest of Taos socialite Mabel Dodge Luhan in 1929; for the next 30 years she returned every summer to paint. Initially, O'Keeffe stayed at Ghost Ranch, a dude ranch owned by publisher Arthur Pack, who first loaned, then sold, her an adobe home on the ranch (not open to visitors). In 1949, after a 15-year campaign to buy it from the Catholic Church, O'Keeffe bought a ruined 18th-century *hacienda* in Abiquiu. Local writer Marie Chabot oversaw the extensive renovations, and O'Keeffe moved into the house following the death of her husband, photographer Alfred Stieglitz, in New York. Although strangely frozen in museum perfection now, the walled property, with its gardens and traditional feel, is worth visiting to experience how midwesterner O'Keeffe applied her spare aesthetic to a living space. The sweeping views of the river valley from the large glass windows in her bedroom and studio tell you all you need to know about what was truly important to her. Other highlights of this tour are Ghost Ranch, now a retreat center; Poshouingue, a nearby pueblo ruin; the traditional Hispanic weaving village of Tierra Amarilla; the historic narrow-gauge railway at Chama; and outdoor activities on and around the Chama River.

I have set up this day trip as a continuation of another day trip, Northwest Day Trip 04; however, if you are coming from Albuquerque, drive north on I-25, avoid Santa Fe by taking the SR 599 bypass, pick up US 285/84 north to Española, then take US 84 northwest to Abiquiu.

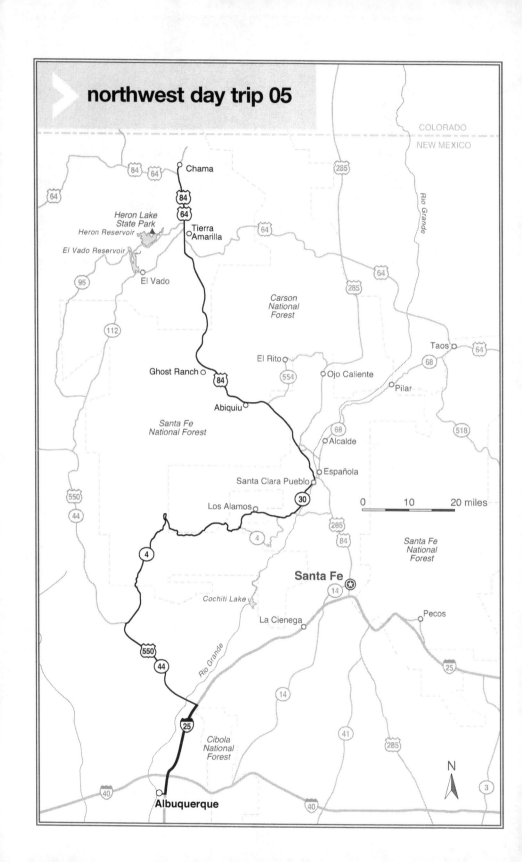

northwest day trip 05

abiquiu

Abiquiu is on US 84. It is a popular stop but so sleepy today, it's hard to grasp its earlier importance as a culturally mixed frontier trading center that by 1793 had a population of 1,363 and by the mid-1800s rivaled Taos for business. It was founded in 1754 by *genizaros*, Hispanicized former Indian captives of low status who were given land in return for establishing villages on the frontier as a buffer between Spaniards and Indians. Plains Indians arrived every fall to trade deerskins for Spanish horses, corn, and slaves. The 1,200-mile Spanish Trail, blazed by Antonio Armijo from Abiquiu to the Pacific Coast in 1829, sealed its importance as a place for traders to outfit themselves for the trip to the West Coast. During the American period, the US Army used Abiquiu as a headquarters for monitoring Navajo, Ute, and Jicarilla Apache activities, and it served as a Ute Indian agency and trading post from 1852 to 1873. Its main attraction today is the Georgia O'Keeffe home, a 1940s church designed by John Gaw Meem, and Penitente *moradas* (chapels) and crosses. The latter hints at the struggle between Archbishop Lamy and the Penitente folk religion, a particularly fervent underground version of Catholicism that took hold during the Mexican period when priests left New Mexico, leaving the faithful in each village to carry out their own religious observances and care for one another. It was driven underground, where it remains today, after the US took control of New Mexico, but it is still an important force in remote northern New Mexican villages.

where to go

Abiquiu Artists Studio Tour. (505) 257-0866; abiquiustudiotour.org. Thirty local artisans, making everything from raku pottery and fiber art to paintings, sculptures, and organic herbal lotions, take part in this popular studio tour every Oct. Reserve lodging well in advance.

Abiquiu Dam and Lake Recreation Area. 4731 SR 96; (505) 685-4371; spa.usace.army .mil/Missions/Civil-Works/Recreation/Abiquiu-Lake. This popular boating and fishing spot is just north of Abiquiu at the turnoff for SR 96, which links US 84 with US 550, the main route to the Four Corners. The lake is a reservoir created by the second of three dams on the Rio Chama built by the US Army Corps of Engineers. Views of iconic Cerro Pedernal are available from the lake, which is known as one of the top fishing spots in northern New Mexico. The Riana Campground on a 154-foot-high bluff overlooking the lake has 54 sites, restrooms, and showers, and is open mid-Apr to mid-Oct. You are advised to reserve a campsite; reservations must be made through recreation.gov at least 4 days in advance. Primitive camping is permitted off-season. There is a boat ramp open in-season. Open daily. Admission fee.

Cerro Pedernal. Access is via SR 96, just west of Abiquiu Lake. Georgia O'Keeffe's declaration that God once told her that if she painted her beloved Pedernal (Spanish for "flint") often enough, he'd give it to her, became reality: Her ashes are scattered on the distinctive volcanic landmark. It's a strenuous, 8-mile climb up and back, with an 1,862-foot elevation gain and the need for climbing skills at times. This is only for the fit and prepared. Don't attempt it alone.

Dar Al Islam. (505) 685-4515; daralislam.org. Behind the Abiquiu Inn, off FR 155 on the hill, are 1,600 acres owned by the nonprofit organization Dar Al Islam, which built a Muslim community here in the 1980s. It is now an educational retreat center aimed at fostering peace between the Muslim and non-Muslim world in a contemplative setting. Its large mosque was designed by well-known Egyptian architect Hassan Fathi, and the whole campus is unusual and breathtaking. It is open to visitors on weekdays only; call ahead to make an appointment. There is a hiking trail here to Georgia O'Keeffe's favorite walking area, which she called the "White Place." You will easily recognize these badland cliffs, which can be seen from the painter's studio across the river.

Georgia O'Keeffe Home Tour. (505) 685-4016; okeeffemuseum.org/store/products/abiquiu/abiquiu-home-studio-tour. Reserve well ahead for these popular one-hour guided tours. They are run by the Georgia O'Keeffe Museum in Santa Fe out of the Tour Office in the new Georgia O'Keeffe Welcome Center next to the Abiquiu Inn on US 84, a good place for general information, restrooms, and a few exhibits. Visitors with reservations park, check in, and board a shuttle to reach the nearby home. Group limit is 12, and food and drink, cameras, note taking, and sketching are not permitted. Five tours from early Mar to late Nov, Tues through Fri; first tour at 9:15 a.m., last tour at 3:15 p.m. A special Behind the Scenes tour is offered at 5:30 p.m. Admission fee.

Poshouingue Pueblo. Ancestors of nearby Ohkay Owingeh (San Juan Pueblo) built this pueblo overlooking the Chama River. A steep, half-mile trail leads through the hilltop pueblo ruins, which contain more than 700 rooms surrounding two large plazas and a large kiva. It is managed by the BLM. Look for the parking lot on the left just south of Abiquiu. Interpretive signs include an attractive painting by artist Mary Beath showing how the pueblo would have looked at its zenith. Free.

Pueblo de Abiquiu Library and Cultural Center. (505) 685-4884; abiquiupl.org. Abiquiu Library, across the plaza from the Parish Hall, offers information, cultural events, and walking tours by reservation with local historians for a donation. Open Sun through Thurs 1 to 6 p.m.

where to shop

Bode's Mercantile. 21196 US 84; (505) 685-4422; bodes.com. You can't miss this old-fashioned family-run general store opposite the entrance road to Abiquiu. In business since 1919, it has everything from bandannas and nails to unusual gifts, tasty green chile burgers, homemade pies, and deli foods in the cafe (a good place to get a Wi-Fi signal and check your email). Georgia O'Keeffe used to shop here. You can gas up here for the trip north to

Colorado, and there's an ice cream parlor on the other side of the parking lot. Open Mon through Thurs 6:30 a.m. to 7 p.m., Fri 6:30 a.m. to 8 p.m., and Sat and Sun 7 a.m. to 8 p.m.

Purple Adobe Lavender Farm. US 84; (505) 685-0082; purpleadobelavenderfarm.com. This beautiful 12-acre riverside property is a perfect spot to stop and smell the lavender, buy high-quality skin-care products, and relax among fields of hardy lavender plants with the photogenic mesas forming a backdrop. Dreamed into existence in 2004 as a second career for California escapees Roger and Elizabeth Inman, who have worked hard to make it a success, each season has seen something new here, from new lavender skin-care products made right on the farm and gifts with a lavender theme to a labyrinth and teahouse serving exceptional gluten-free lavender cakes, scones, and gelato. After 15 years, they are hoping to retire for real now but are in no hurry to say good-bye, waiting for the right new owners to take up the reins before retiring to their lovely northern New Mexico home nearby. The farm is open to visitors for tours Apr to Nov and holds a lavender festival in July. The exceptional, high-grade Purple Adobe Lavender products are available in the gift shop here and at nearby Bode's and Abiquiu Inn.

where to eat

Cafe Abiquiu. 21120 US 84; (505) 685-4378, (888) 735-2902; abiquiuinn.com. This restaurant inside the Abiquiu Inn serves inspired and well-priced Southwest and modern American food for breakfast, lunch, and dinner with ingredients that are sourced locally and freshly prepared, including house-smoked trout dip, a nice lamb burger made from local El Rito lamb, and green chile rib eye stew. The adjoining gift store has a great selection of ethnic clothing, regional books, works by local artists, and unique gifts. The inn is part of the Abiquiu Studio Tour in Oct and previews the work of many local artists in a room upstairs. Open daily. $–$$.

where to stay

Abiquiu Inn. 21120 US 84; (505) 685-4378; abiquiuinn.com. This attractive adobe inn, conveniently located next to the Georgia O'Keeffe Welcome Center, has 32 rooms, suites, casitas, and houses for overnight guests that are beautifully decorated with New Mexico touches. Pet-friendly. On-site restaurant and gift store. $$–$$$.

Las Parras de Abiquiu. 21341 US 84, 1.5 miles north of Abiquiu; (505) 685-4200; lasparras.com. Arin and Stan Bader's 55-acre northern New Mexico–style home and working 6-acre vineyard offers an enjoyable glimpse of traditional agriculture in the Chama River valley. Guests stay in a separate casita with 2 spacious, peaceful Southwest rooms, with king-size beds, private baths and patios, and hot tub. Trails lead among vines and gardens to the river. In lieu of breakfast, your hosts bring over a night tray of special treats such as fresh-picked berries and grapes; rooms have coffeemakers, fridges, and microwaves. Arin is a mask artist and Stan makes birdhouses, and they sell their work at the inn. No pets. Closed Nov to Apr. $$.

ghost ranch

Twelve miles northwest of Abiquiu on US 84 is Ghost Ranch. The former dude ranch is set among the badlands and colorful sandstone cliffs of the northeastern edge of the Colorado Plateau, the same red rocks in which the Colorado River and its tributaries have created Utah's canyon country. The main draw here is jaw-dropping scenery, interesting wildlife, outdoor activities, and opportunities for solitude at several spiritual centers.

where to go

Chama River Canyon Wilderness Area. (505) 438-5300 (Santa Fe National Forest HQ); continentaldividetrail.org/project/chama-river-canyon-wilderness-santa-fe-national-forest. This 50,300-acre wilderness is part of Santa Fe National Forest. It includes the Rio Chama, designated a Wild and Scenic River, a popular destination for river running and hiking. The Continental Divide National Scenic Trail passes through here. Access points are Skull Bridge 9.1 miles from US 84 on FR 151, the main graveled route into Chama River Canyon, and Ojitos Canyon on SR 96. Because this is wilderness, the only way you may enter is on foot; no mechanized travel is allowed beyond the forest access roads. Observe "Leave No Trace" wilderness rules. Bring all the food and water and supplies you need, and make sure you have adequate clothing and first-aid kits with you. This is the desert; you will need a gallon of water per person per day, more if you are exerting yourself. Pack out all you pack in, including used toilet paper, and bury human waste in a cat hole 6 inches deep. Fires are not permitted. There is a developed campground along the river a mile before you get to the Christ in the Desert Monastery, where you will find a number of large, attractive, shaded campsites; vault toilets; and water. Dispersed camping is allowed throughout the canyon, including close to the river takeout at Whirlpool. These campsites are very popular during warmer weather, so arrive early to secure a site. During spring and late fall, campsites in the campground may only be used for day-use picnicking, and you will have the campground to yourself much of the time. This is not the place to come in winter, though: It is frigid, and access is poor on the graded forest road.

Echo Canyon Amphitheater. About 3 miles north of Ghost Ranch, on US 84, this enormous amphitheater in the pink sandstone cliffs has been created by wind and water erosion. The weathering and the dark, streaked, desert-varnished rocks have the appearance of blood pouring off the top of the cliffs, and indeed, stories tell that Echo Canyon was once the site of two massacres: a party of white farmers who were set upon by Navajos in 1861, and then, three years later, a group of Navajos who were killed in retribution for the earlier massacre during the Long Walk years. There's a short trail, a picnic area, restrooms, water, and a primitive 9-site campground that makes an excellent overnight stop with views all the way to Abiquiu Lake and Pedernal from this elevated location.

Ghost Ranch Education and Retreat Center. US 84; (505) 685-1000; (877) 804-4678; ghostranch.org. This 21,000-acre former dude ranch was donated to the Presbyterian Church by publisher Arthur Pack and now serves as a popular retreat and workshop center offering arts courses and spiritual retreats. Visitors are welcome to visit for the day and look around, or stay the night (breakfast included; rates vary), if room is available. There are hiking trails into the badlands, where rare dinosaurs were unearthed, and excellent views of Pedernal, the volcanic neck to the west famously painted by Georgia O'Keeffe. The Florence Hawley Ellis Anthropology Museum and Ruth Hall Paleontology Museum offer information on area natural and cultural history, and writers take note: The on-site library is a wonderful place to curl up and read, do research, or work on your computer in a peaceful and lightly used part of the campus. Other activities include camping, hiking, horseback riding, a labyrinth, and special guided tours of Ghost Ranch sites depicted by Georgia O'Keeffe in her paintings. The dining room serves breakfast, lunch, and dinner, available for a set fee to day visitors as well as overnight guests. Check out the weekly menu and price list in the welcome center, where you pay your $5 conservation fee to walk around the campus. There's a good gift shop and a spot to get a cup of coffee and snacks and sit down to watch a film about Ghost Ranch; tours leave from here. Free Wi-Fi in the welcome center and library. The welcome center is open daily 8 a.m. to 7 p.m.; museums are open Mon through Sat 9 a.m. to 5 p.m. and Sun 1 to 5 p.m.; the library is open 24 hours a day.

where to stay

Ghost Ranch Education and Retreat Center. US 84; (505) 685-1000, (877) 804-4678; ghostranch.org. Overnight bed-and-breakfast lodgings at Ghost Ranch include dormitories, no-frills single- and double-occupancy rooms, and a campground that is open year-round for tent and RV camping with showers in the bathhouse. Breakfast is included with the room; other meals are available for separate pricing. No TVs, radios, or phones in rooms. Some hiking is needed to reach most facilities. Wi-Fi is available in the welcome center and library. $$.

Monastery of Christ in the Desert. PO Box 270, Abiquiu; (575) 613-4233; christdesert .org. This lovely Benedictine monastery, 27 miles northwest of Abiquiu, was built in 1962. Guests are welcome to visit for the day or to stay for personal retreats. Single- and double-occupancy guest rooms and suites are in a separate guesthouse and ranch house, which must be reserved ahead of time. Electricity is available in the rooms, but use of electrical devices is discouraged to avoid overloading the system. You are encouraged to help with chores and to attend regular services in the church. Clothing should be modest; no shorts. The on-site gift shop has been expanded to include handmade items from this and other monasteries. The monastery is located 13 miles down FR 151 in Chama River Canyon on a graveled and clay road that is steep, winding, and becomes impassable in snow and rain. Note: This is a silent order; guests are requested to speak softly, if at all, and respect community rules. Bring a flashlight to help navigate the grounds at night and a battery-powered alarm clock to make sure you are on time for meals and services. Two-night minimum; suggested donation includes all refectory meals. $–$$.

tierra amarilla

North of Ghost Ranch on US 84, you enter a *Sound of Music*–like landscape, with Colorado's San Juan Mountains in the distance and lush valleys in between. Tierra Amarilla ("Yellow Earth") is a pastoral landscape, famous for its sheep rearing and wool operations on historic land grants grazed since 1860. It shot to national fame in 1967 when Reies Lopez Tijerina, a charismatic Chicano grassroots activist, led a group of armed Hispanic men in storming the courthouse, triggering a manhunt by the National Guard. The subsequent publicity highlighted a long-standing dispute over land distribution in northern New Mexico, and by the 1970s it had jump-started several social programs, such as the nonprofit Ganados del Valle, aimed at helping poor communities become self-sufficient.

where to shop

Tierra Wools. 91 Main St., Los Ojos; (575) 588-7231; handweavers.com. It's worth a special trip in order to watch freshly sheared wool from native Churro sheep being graded, hand-spun, and colored with natural dyes for weaving into colorful Rio Grande–style blankets and jackets, which are on sale in a beautiful showroom. A weaving school has been set up here, and you can watch the local women who run this cooperative weaving daily. Open Mon through Sat 9 a.m. to 5 p.m. and Sun 11 a.m. to 4 p.m.

chama

Chama is surrounded by the Carson National Forest, a mecca for hiking, camping, fishing, and other outdoor sports. There are numerous pullouts on scenic US 64, which heads east into the Tusas Mountains, south of Chama. El Vado Lake and Heron Lake State Parks contain two of the most popular lakes in New Mexico for recreation. Rustic Chama is best known for the historic 1880 Cumbres & Toltec Scenic Railroad, a remnant of the lines throughout the San Juans that served mining camps and revived in the 1960s.

where to go

Cumbres & Toltec Scenic Railroad. (888) 286-2737; cumbrestoltec.com. A highlight of any trip to the Chama River valley, this scenic 64-mile one-way railway ride between Chama and Antonito is best done in fall, when the aspens are turning, but the trip is lovely anytime. Trains depart every day at 10 a.m., stop for lunch in Osier, and continue to Antonito, where a shuttle bus brings you back to Chama at 5:45 p.m.; you also have the option to take the shuttle to Antonito and come back on the train. Admission fee.

El Vado Lake State Park. (575) 588-7247; emnrd.state.nm.us/SPD/elvadolakestatepark .html. Created by damming the Rio Chama, this lake is 17 miles southwest of Tierra Amarilla and reached via SR 112. In the early 1900s, before the lake was constructed, the town of El Vado was a noisy, bustling railroad-and-lumber center and the largest town in the county. The park has boating, 8 campgrounds with 80 developed sites (19 with hookups), showers, restrooms, and water. It is a good place to spot eagles in winter. Admission fee.

Heron Lake State Park. (575) 588-7470; emnrd.state.nm.us/spd/heronlakestatepark.html. This state park encompasses a large, no-wake lake that is a popular destination for sailing, windsurfing, swimming, and camping. It is 11 miles west of Tierra Amarilla via US 64/84 and SR 95. You'll find a visitor center, 250 developed campsites (54 with electric hookups), primitive beach and boat-in camping, water, showers, and boat ramp. Admission fee.

where to stay

The Lodge at Chama. PO Box 127, Chama; (575) 756-2133; lodgeatchama.com. If you want to go all in with five-star lodging and guided outdoor activities—such as hiking; elk, deer, and bison hunting; clay shooting; and fly-fishing—this elegant hunting lodge located on the historic 36,000-acre Chama Land and Cattle Company Ranch may be just the ticket. It offers luxurious Western rooms in the 27,000-square-foot lodge, stellar gourmet meals, 2 great rooms, and a fitness center. American plan pricing includes all meals, open bar, and activities; expect to push the boat out. $$$$.

Parlor Car Bed & Breakfast. 311 Terrace Ave.; (575) 756-1946, (888) 849-7800; parlorcar .com. Not actually located in a parlor car but within sight (and earshot) of the scenic railroad depot, this pink Tudor-style house is as close to an overnight train experience you can have without actually being on the train. It offers 3 period rooms reminiscent of the golden age of train travel and exudes that stiff, Victorian glamour that will get you in the mood for a train ride. This is a family-run B&B; one of the owners is a veterinarian who will kennel your pooch for you while you are on the train, if you wish. Breakfasts are hearty home-style affairs. $.

day trip 06

northwest

>>>

indian country:
navajo nation, chaco culture national
historical park, bloomfield, aztec, jicarilla
apache nation

This exploration of the New Mexico portion of the Navajo Nation and adjoining Jicarilla Apache Nation is best done as a long weekend trip. Drive north on I-25 to pick up US 550 north from Bernalillo and continue through Cuba and onto the Navajo Nation. The highlight of the trip is a visit to remote Chaco Culture National Historical Park, 21 miles west of US 550 from Nageezi in the San Juan Basin. Chaco Canyon preserves the haunting 11th-century Ancestral Pueblo ruins of the Chaco culture, one of the most influential prehistoric civilizations in Southwest history. Located 144 miles from Albuquerque, it requires an overnight camping trip in the park (no services; fill your tank and bring all water, food, ice, and supplies with you) to see the extensive ruins in the canyon and on the surrounding cliffs. Continuing north on US 550 to its junction with US 64 at Bloomfield on the San Juan River, you can visit the Chacoan "outliers" protected at Salmon Ruins County Park and Aztec Ruins National Monument, distant pueblos linked to Chaco by trade and culture. Jicarilla Apache lands, east of Bloomfield, offer superb hunting, fishing, camping, and other outdoor activities.

navajo nation

The northeastern New Mexico portion of the 29,817-square-mile Navajo Nation is called the Dinetah. It's the original homeland of the Navajo—the Dineh—nomads of the Athabascan culture who came from northwest Canada, perhaps as early as AD 1000, when Ancestral

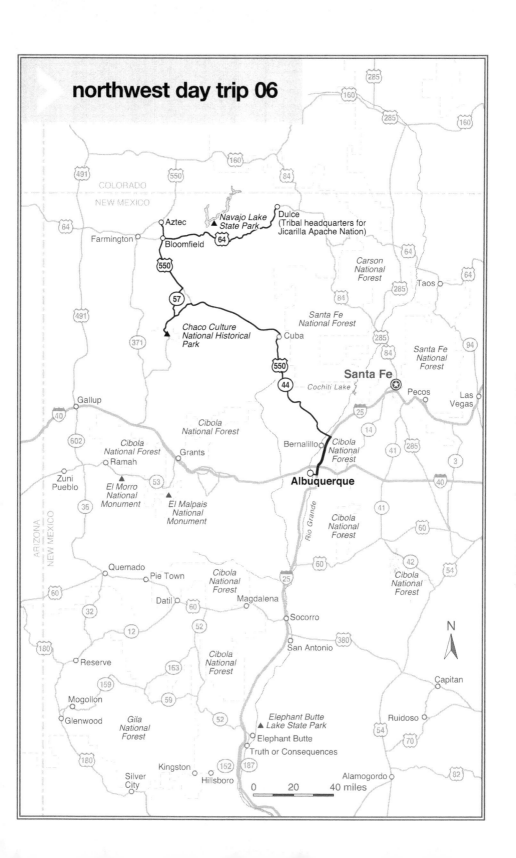

northwest day trip 06

COLORADO
NEW MEXICO

285
160
160
285
160

491
550
84

64

Aztec
Navajo Lake State Park ▲
Dulce
(Tribal headquarters for
Jicarilla Apache Nation)

Farmington

Bloomfield
64

64

Carson National Forest

550

Taos
285

57

64

Chaco Culture National Historical Park ▲

371

Cuba

Santa Fe National Forest

285

84

94

Santa Fe National Forest

Gallup

550

40

44

Cochiti Lake

Santa Fe

Pecos

Las Vegas

602

25

14

Cibola National Forest

Bernalillo

Cibola National Forest

41

285

3

Cibola National Forest

Grants

Albuquerque

40

Ramah

53

Zuni Pueblo

El Morro National Monument ▲

36

El Malpais National Monument ▲

Rio Grande

Cibola National Forest

41

60

Quemado

Pie Town

Cibola National Forest

60

Cibola National Forest

42

54

60

Datil

60

Magdalena

32

12

25

52

180

Socorro

Cibola National Forest

153

San Antonio

380

Reserve

159

Capitan

Mogollon

59

Gila National Forest

52

Glenwood

Elephant Butte Lake State Park ▲

Ruidoso

180

Elephant Butte

54

70

Kingston

152

187

Truth or Consequences

Silver City

Hillsboro

Alamogordo

82

0   20   40 miles

N

Pueblo people were still living in Chaco Canyon. While their Apache relatives remained hunter-gatherers, preferring to live in the mountains, the Navajo successfully adopted farming, weaving, pottery, and other cultural traits from Pueblos, who named them *navaju*, "people of the great cultivated fields."

Navajos fiercely resisted Spanish, Mexican, and finally American colonization that defeated most Pueblos, but they eagerly adopted European innovations: raiding settlements for horses, goats, and sheep; learning silversmithing; and building outdoor ovens. Even the US Army's scorched-earth campaign that ended in the Navajos' 1864–68 incarceration at Fort Sumner in southeastern New Mexico did not defeat them. Since their reservation was created in 1868, the resilient Navajo have grown in numbers and resources, retaining their traditional ways while benefiting from Anglo approaches to education, material goods, political organization, and resource development. Today over 330,000 members strong, half of whom live on the 27,000-square-mile-plus reservation, the Navajo are the largest, wealthiest, and best-educated tribe in the country. Political representation is through a tribal council in Window Rock, Arizona, made up of 88 delegates from 110 chapters, or local councils, across the reservation.

Tribal museums and visitor attractions are mainly located in the tribal headquarters town of Window Rock. The joy of traveling on the reservation is enjoying the sacred landmarks and vistas of the Navajo homeland and sharing warm interactions with Navajo people selling rugs, jewelry, and other handicrafts at roadside booths, fairs, trading posts, and chapter houses.

where to go

Cabezon Peak Wilderness Study Area. BLM, Rio Puerco Field Office; (505) 761-8700; blm.gov/programs/national-conservation-lands/new-mexico/cabezon. Part of the Rio Puerco volcanic region around Mount Taylor and west of US 550, this distinctive volcanic "neck" is a sacred landmark for Navajos. Their origin stories tell that the peak is the head of a giant slain on Mount Taylor and the nearby lava flows, or malpais, are his blood. The 2,000-foot peak is popular with climbers and backpackers. To reach the WSA, turn off US 550 at the sign for San Luis–Cabezon–Torreon, about 20 miles northwest of San Ysidro, near Cuba, and drive west on CR 279 for 12 miles. Open 24 hours year-round. Free.

Torreon. Star Lake Chapter House; (505) 731-2336; torreon.navajochapters.org. The Navajo settlement of Torreon is off US 550, 26 miles southwest of Cuba via SR 197. It typically hosts an interesting annual Eastern Navajo Arts and Crafts Festival in mid-June, which includes rugs, jewelry, folk art, singing, dances, food, drumming, and other activities, such as tours of Chaco Canyon with Navajo guides. It's held in the Star Lake Chapter House, a good place to stop at any time if you get lost. Call for information. Free.

chaco culture national historical park

The important Chaco Project unearthed 3,600 archeological sites in 15-mile-long Chaco Canyon and the 25,000-square-mile San Juan Basin that surrounds it. For most people, though, Chaco's main attractions are its overscaled multistory masonry great houses and great kivas, master-planned by a priestly elite and oriented to cardinal points and astronomical markers, built and repeatedly remodeled using core-and-veneer masonry between AD 850 and 1150. The most impressive of these is Pueblo Bonito, a 3-acre, D-shaped great house begun in AD 1050. It eventually rose five stories in back and had 650 rooms around an enclosed plaza dotted with 3 great kivas and 30 small ones.

After Chaco's 400-mile road system was uncovered by archeologists in the early 1980s, it became obvious that Chaco Canyon was a place of pilgrimage, the Vatican City of the prehistoric world, and it was expanded and upgraded from a small national monument to a national historical park. Current evidence indicates that it was home to a small population of powerful priest-leaders whose role was to observe seasonal planetary movements and call farmers to Chaco to participate in rituals aimed at ensuring good harvests and redistribution of turquoise and trade goods to pueblos throughout the empire and beyond. The Chaco Phenomenon, as it is known, was unique in the prehistoric world—no culture ever matched it for power and national influence. It reached a tipping point in the early 1100s, when a long drought may have created disaffection among villagers, robbing the priests at Chaco of their authority and causing a diaspora of Chacoans throughout the Pueblo world. Chaco's story remains shrouded in mystery, but that's its greatest attraction. Part of the magic here is that the Chaco experience remains pristine—there are no visitor concessions, so you must bring your own food, drink, and ice, and gas up the car before venturing across the reservation to the site. Chaco is scorching and dry in summer and as cold as a meat locker in winter; come prepared with good protection from the elements at any time of the year.

To reach Chaco from Albuquerque, drive US 550 north and look for signs for the national park on the left-hand side at Nageezi, a chapter of the Navajo Nation. A 29-mile dirt road leads into the park, crossing Navajo lands homesteaded by Navajo families with traditional six-sided hogans, shade ramadas, sheep corrals, and sometimes regular houses. Allow plenty of time; it's quite rough. It's about a four-hour drive from Albuquerque, so plan on overnighting in the campground and spending two days here: the first in the main canyon looking at the central ruins; the second visiting backcountry pueblos along the mesas and beyond. Arrive early to get a campsite; no reservations are available.

where to go

Visitor Center. (505) 786-7014; nps.gov/chcu. Stop at the newly rebuilt visitor center to pay the entrance fee and pick up information. The center has ranger talks; occasional guest lectures; interpretive films, including one on Fajada Butte's famous astronomy markers narrated by Robert Redford; a bookstore; a museum; a small planetarium offering stargazing programs out back; restrooms and water faucet; and picnic tables under shade ramadas. Open daily 8 a.m. to 5 p.m. Closed Thanksgiving, Christmas, and New Year's Day. Admission fee.

Canyon Loop Drive. The main ruins sit along linked trails off a 9-mile paved loop west of the visitor center. On the north side is the oldest pueblo—the small unrestored pueblo of Una Vida built in AD 850—and Hungo Pavi, Chetro Ketl, Pueblo Bonito, and Pueblo del Arroyo, all begun in the 1000s and remodeled as the need for additional storage rooms and guest quarters for travelers and traders grew. South of Chaco Wash is the great kiva of Casa Rinconada and several small village sites. Rangers offer guided tours of Pueblo Bonito and other sites between May and Oct.

Backcountry Trails. Longer trails lead to more distant sites in and above the canyon, passing early pit houses and pueblos, remnant fields, stairways, roads, signaling features, water control features, fossilized rocks, rock art sites, and astronomy markers. A trail on the west end of the canyon leads to two 12th-century Mesa Verde–style pueblos—Casa Chiquita and Kin Kletso—which have the type of rough-mortared, inelegant McElmo Phase (AD 1150–1180) stonework typical of later occupation by people from Mesa Verde in the Four Corners region where New Mexico, Arizona, Colorado, and Utah meet. The trail ascends steeply onto the 300-foot-high cliffs to reach the important wayside pueblos of Pueblo Alto and Peñasco Blanco. The Wijiji Trail, across from the Gallo Campground, leads to Wijiji Pueblo, a small pueblo that was built in one phase in AD 1100. It's within sight of Fajada Butte, an important astronomical observation spot for priests. You'll often find painted and ridged potsherds on the ground in a quantity that may indicate ritual breakage. Important: All artifacts in the park are federal property and must not be removed; moreover, once an artifact is moved from its location, it loses its story and is of no value to archeologists anymore. Free permits are required for these backcountry trails; they are open sunrise to sunset.

where to stay

Gallo Campground. (877) 444-6777; recreation.gov. There are 48 individual campsites, 1 ADA-accessible site, and 2 group sites in the small campground. Some are for tent and car campers, some for RVs, some for both; none are protected from the elements. Restrooms and non-potable water available, but no showers or electric hookups. The campground is now on the national reservation system; reserve well ahead, as this is a popular spot. Sites are half price for holders of Interagency Senior and Access Passes. Open year-round, but tent-only sites close for the winter Nov through Feb. $.

bloomfield

Anglo communities like Bloomfield, Farmington, and Aztec above the San Juan River are busy commercial centers driven by oil and gas production, which had been encroaching farther on public lands until a new bill was passed in October 2019 to protect places like Chaco Canyon in the San Juan Basin from drilling. These peripheral towns are not pretty by any means, but they offer the nearest full visitor services to the reservation. To reach Bloomfield, go back to US 550 via SR 57 and continue north, over the San Juan River, to the US 550/64 junction. To reach Farmington (and the Navajo town of Shiprock, beyond) turn left on US 64; to reach the town of Aztec, continue north on US 550.

where to go

Salmon Ruins County Park. 6131 US 64; (575) 632-2013; salmonruins.com. This 217-room Chaco outlier started construction in AD 1064 and was primarily built between AD 1088 and 1092. It's often overlooked as people whizz along US 64 between Chaco, Aztec, and Mesa Verde, but I think it is really worth your time and hope you stop and take a look. Originally, this outlier pueblo specialized in growing a hardy form of dent corn, which it traded with Chaco Canyon using roads that went through Kurtz Canyon and the San Juan River via Aztec Pueblo to the north and Twin Angels Pueblo to the east. It was abandoned in AD 1138, possibly due to flooding danger in the San Juan River floodplain, and inhabitants moved to nearby Aztec Pueblo. A second occupation began in AD 1160 by people from various culture groups, including potters from Mesa Verde to the northwest, who made their distinctive black-on-white pottery using local clays. Archeologists have recently named this period the San Juan Occupation. A trail from the kiva-shaped visitor center descends to the ruins and links with another that takes you through the Salmon family homestead, where you can see a 19th-century adobe home, a Navajo hogan, a Ute brush wickiup, and a Jicarilla Apache tepee. At the park museum, ask about daylong guided tours of remote Navajo "pueblitos" like Three Corn Ruin in nearby Gobernador and Largo Canyons, which sheltered Navajo and Pueblo people during the Pueblo Revolt in the 17th century and again during Comanche raids in the 1700s. This park has terrific archeological programs for kids and also provides a fun and educational touch-screen computer virtual tour of Chacoan outliers in the area. A holiday crafts fair takes place here in early Dec. Open year-round Mon through Fri 8 a.m. to 5 p.m. and weekends 9 a.m. to 5 p.m. (Sun noon to 5 p.m. Nov through Apr). Admission fee; children under 5 free.

aztec

The town of Aztec is located on US 550 and lies south of Durango, Colorado, on the pretty Animas River. It grew up around the ruins of Aztec Pueblo, a large Chacoan great house pueblo that was built between AD 1109 and the 1120s. The largest pueblo in the Animas

River valley, this outlier may have been intended as a successor to Chaco Canyon, after drought and failing harvests possibly led the priest-leaders to relocate their power center to this more fertile, well-watered area in the 1100s. Not for long, though: All the pueblos in the Four Corners were empty by AD 1300, following the Great Drought, and their occupants relocated to the Rio Grande and Rio Puerco regions and the Little Colorado River in Arizona, where their descendants live today.

where to go

Aztec Ruins National Monument. 84 CR 2900 (Ruins Road); (575) 334-6174; nps.gov/ azru. Of the three Chacoan great houses serving 100 nearby pueblos at Aztec, only the 400-room, three-story West Ruin is open to the public. It was excavated by archeologist Errol Morris between 1916 and 1923 and is remarkable for the fascinating contrast of its elegant, tightly banded Chacoan masonry with later, more rustic rough-mortared stonework, particularly evident on unusual triwalled kivas added by later occupants from Mesa Verde. Aztec has the only reconstructed great kiva in the National Park System, an atmospheric 41-foot-high cathedral-like ceremonial room with massive supports holding up the roof. The visitor center is in an attractive historic building and has a gift shop and small museum displaying pottery, yucca sandals, and other artifacts. Information, ranger talks, cultural demonstrations, scholarly lectures in summer, and occasional weekend tours of the unexcavated East Ruin. Open daily 8 a.m. to 6 p.m. in summer, until 5 p.m. the rest of the year. Admission fee.

jicarilla apache nation

The 3,400-member Jicarilla Apache tribe at one time roamed freely throughout the mountains and canyons of northeastern New Mexico. They were forced onto this 850,000-acre reservation just south of the Colorado border in 1887, following conflicts with settlers, and remain here today, their homes in and around Dulce, the sleepy tribal capital. Jicarilla lands are wild and beautiful high-desert steppes dotted with lakes at the foot of the southern Rockies that are mainly used for residences, grazing, fishing, camping, boating, birding, and hiking. Horse Lake Mesa Game Park has the largest single elk enclosure in the country, and big-game hunting is popular here. The Little Beaver Roundup Powwow takes place in July and features parades, rodeo, dancing, concerts, a softball tournament, even a Spam-carving competition. September's Go-Jii-Yah Feast is a campout at Stone Lake, with feasting, dancing, crafts, and a relay race between the Llaneros (plains people) and Olleros (mountain people), representing the social division among the Jicarilla. The two teams also represent the sun and moon in a mythical race to escape the underworld. Jicarillas specialize in beadwork, basketry, micaceous pottery, paintings, buckskin clothing, and ribbon shirts. Artist and musician Darren Vigil Gray is from Jicarilla and produces paintings capturing the raw beauty of this land that are in the collections of musicians Paul McCartney and Steve

Miller. To reach the Jicarilla Apache Nation, drive east on US 64 from US 550; Dulce, the tribal headquarters, is right on the highway.

where to go

Dulce. US 64; (575) 759-3242; newmexico.org/places-to-visit/native-culture/jicarilla -apache-nation. Make a stop at this New Mexico town, the headquarters of the Jicarilla Apache Nation, to visit government offices, pick up permits, and get information on outdoor activities. There's not a lot to do in town. Tribal office is open Mon through Fri 8 a.m. to 5 p.m.

Jicarilla Game and Fish. (575) 759-3255; jicarillahunt.com. Contact the tribe's game and fish department for information and permits for hunting mule deer, elk, mountain lion, black bear, and turkey. Trout fishing on seven fishing lakes, wildlife watching, and lakeside camping are also available. Open Mon through Fri 8 a.m. to 5 p.m.

where to stay

Wildhorse Casino and Hotel. 13603 US 64; (575) 759-3663, (855) 516-1090; reserva tions.com/Hotel/best-western-jicarilla-inn-casino-dulce-nm. This casino-hotel has 42 well-equipped rooms and suites, an on-site restaurant, lounge, fitness center, and high-speed Internet access. Pet-friendly. Note: Nonsmoking rooms and suites are available, but try to book a room as far away from the casino as possible; the casino allows smoking, and the smoke tends to carry along the corridors. $.

worth more time

Navajo Lake State Park. (575) 632-2278; emnrd.state.nm.us/SPD/navajolakestatepark .html. Navajo Lake above Navajo Dam on the San Juan River spans the New Mexico–Colorado border. At 15,590 acres, it is the second-largest lake in the state and one of the top places for fishing, with abundant native brown trout, kokanee salmon, black bass, bluegill, and crappie. Pine River and Sims Mesa are the most developed areas of the lake. Each has a visitor center with interpretive exhibits, developed campsites, and a full-service marina. There are 246 campsites spread across several campgrounds; the most popular is Cottonwood Canyon Campground, which has rare shaded spots among the red rocks. Admission fee.

regional information

north

Albuquerque Convention & Visitors Bureau
20 First Plaza, Ste. 601
Albuquerque, NM 87125-6866
(800) 284-2282
visitalbuquerque.org

Los Alamos Meeting and Visitor Bureau
475 20th St., Ste. A (Central Park Square)
Los Alamos, NM 87544
(505) 662-8105, (800) 444-0707
visitlosalamos.org

Tourism Santa Fe
201 W. Marcy St.
Santa Fe, NM 87501
(505) 955-6200, (800) 777-2489
santafe.org

northeast

Angel Fire Chamber of Commerce
3407 Mountain View Blvd.
Angel Fire, NM 87710
(575) 377-6353, (800) 446-8117
angelfirechamber.org

Cimarron Chamber of Commerce
104 N. Lincoln Ave.
Cimarron, NM 88415
(575) 376-2417
cimarronnm.com

Las Vegas/San Miguel Chamber of
Commerce
500 Railroad Ave.
Las Vegas, NM 87701
(575) 425-8631
lasvegasnewmexico.com

Raton Chamber of Commerce
100 Clayton Rd.
Raton, NM 87740
(575) 445-3689
raton.info

Red River Visitor Center
100 W. River St.
Red River, NM 87558
(575) 754-3030
redriver.org

Taos Visitor Center
1139 Paseo del Pueblo Sur
Taos, NM 87571
(800) 732-8267
taos.org

Turquoise Trail Association
PO Box 303
Sandia Park, NM 87047
(505) 281-5233
turquoisetrail.org

Village of Taos Ski Valley Chamber of
Commerce
PO Box 91
Taos Ski Valley, NM 87525
(575) 776-1413, (800) 517-9816
taosskivalley.com

east

Belen Chamber of Commerce/Visitor Center
712 Dalies Ave.
Belen, NM 87002
(505) 864-8091
belenchamber.com

Clovis/Curry County Chamber of Commerce
105 E. Grand Ave.
Clovis, NM 88101
(505) 763-3435
clovisnm.org

Fort Sumner/De Baca County Chamber of
Commerce
3501 Billy the Kid Dr.
Fort Sumner, NM 88119
(575) 355-7705
fortsumnerchamber.net

East Mountain Regional Chamber
(Tijeras, Cedar Crest, Sandia Park, Moriarty)
PO Box 1945
Edgewood, NM 87015
(575) 281-1999
eastmountainchamber.com

New Mexico Route 66 Association
1415 Central Ave. NE
Albuquerque, NM 87106
(505) 385-1410
rt66nm.org

Portales/Roosevelt County Chamber
100 S. Avenue A
Portales, NM 88130
(800) 635-8036
portales.com

Santa Rosa Visitor Information Center
1085 Blue Hole Rd.
Santa Rosa, NM 88435
(575) 472-3763
visitsantarosanm.com

southeast

Alamogordo Chamber of Commerce
1301 N. White Sands Blvd.
Alamogordo, NM 88310
(575) 437-6120
alamogordo.com

Capitan Chamber of Commerce
114 Lincoln Ave.
Capitan, NM 88316
(575) 354-2247
villageofcapitan.org

Carlsbad Chamber of Commerce
302 S. Canal
Carlsbad, NM 88220
(575) 887-6516
visitcarlsbadchamber.com

Cloudcroft Chamber of Commerce
1001 James Canyon Hwy.
Cloudcroft, NM 88415
(575) 682-2733
coolcloudcroft.com

Las Cruces Convention & Visitors Bureau
336 S. Main St.
Las Cruces, NM 88001
(575) 541-2444
lascrucescvb.org

Mountainair Chamber of Commerce
PO Box 258
Mountainair, NM 87036-0595
(505) 847-3580
discovermountainairnm.com

Roswell Visitors Center
426 N. Main St.
Roswell, NM 88201
(575) 623-3442
seeroswell.com

Ruidoso Valley Chamber of Commerce
720 Sudderth Dr.
Ruidoso, NM 88345
(575) 257-7395
ruidosonow.com

south

Socorro Heritage and Visitors Center
217 Fisher Ave.
Socorro, NM 87801
(575) 835-8927
socorronm.org

Truth or Consequences Chamber of
Commerce
207 S. Foch St.
Truth or Consequences, NM 87901
(575) 894-3536
torcchamber.org

southwest

Magdalena Chamber of Commerce
902 W. First St.
Magdalena, NM 87825
(866) 854-3560
magdalena-nm.com

Silver City/Grant County Chamber of
Commerce
3031 US 180
Silver City, NM 88061
(800) 548-9378
silvercity.org

west

Gallup/McKinley County Chamber of
Commerce
106 W. US 66
Gallup, NM 87301
(505) 772-2228, (800) 380-4989
thegallupchamber.com

Grants/Cibola County Chamber of
Commerce
100 Iron Ave.
PO Box 297
Grants, NM 87020
(505) 287-4802
grants.org

Northwest New Mexico Visitor Center
I-40, exit 85
Grants, NM 87020
(505) 876-2783
nps.gov/archive/elma/mac.htm

Sky City Cultural Center and Haak'u
Museum
Haak'u Road
Acoma Pueblo, NM 87034
(505) 552-7861
acomaskycity.org

northwest

Chama Valley Chamber of Commerce
2372 S. State, NM 17
Chama, NM 87520
(575) 756-2306
chamavalley.com

Corrales MainStreet
4324 Corrales Rd.
Corrales, NM 87048
(505) 350-3955
visitcorrales.com

Cuba Area Chamber of Commerce
41 Martinez Dr.
Cuba, NM 87013
(575) 289-3514
cubanewmexico.com

Española Valley Chamber of Commerce
101 Calle de las Españolas, #F
Española, NM 87532
(505) 753-2831
espanolanmchamber.com

Greater Sandoval County Chamber of
Commerce
282 Camino del Pueblo
Bernalillo, NM 87004
(505) 404-8492
sandovalchamber.sks.com

Jicarilla Apache Nation
PO Box 507
Dulce, NM
(575) 759-3242

Navajo Tourism Dept.
PO Box 663
Window Rock, AZ 86515
(928) 810-8501
discovernavajo.com

Rio Rancho Convention and Visitors Bureau
3001 Civic Center Circle NE
Rio Rancho, NM 87114
(505) 891-7258
visitriorancho.org

general information

Bureau of Land Management
New Mexico Office
301 Dinosaur Trail
Santa Fe, NM 87508
(505) 954-2000
blm.gov/new-mexico

Indian Pueblo Cultural Center
2401 12th St. NW
Albuquerque, NM 87104
(505) 843-7270
indianpueblo.org
(Information on all New Mexico's pueblos)

National Park Service
Southwest Regional Office (Region III HQ
Building)
1100 Old Santa Fe Trail
Santa Fe, NM 87505
(505) 988-6888
nps.gov

National Park Service Intermountain Region
12795 W. Alameda Pkwy.
Lakewood, CO 80228
(303) 969-2500
nps.gov/orgs/1072/index.htm

New Mexico Department of Game and Fish
1 Wildlife Way
Santa Fe, NM 87505
(505) 476-8000, (888) 248-6866
wildlife.state.nm.us

New Mexico Energy, Minerals, and Natural
Resources Dept. (State Parks)
1220 S. St. Francis Dr.
Santa Fe, NM 87505
(888) 667-2757
emnrd.state.nm.us/SPD

New Mexico Historic Sites
Administrative Office
725 Camino Lejo
Santa Fe, NM 87504
(505) 476-1130
nmmonuments.org

New Mexico Public Lands Information
Center
301 Dinosaur Trail
Santa Fe, NM 87508
(505) 954-2002
publiclands.org

New Mexico Tourism Department
491 Old Santa Fe Trail
Santa Fe, NM 87501
(505) 827-7400
newmexico.org

US Fish & Wildlife Service
Southwest Region
500 Gold Ave. SW
Albuquerque, NM 87102
(505) 248-6911
fws.gov/southwest

US Forest Service
Southwestern Region (Region 3)
333 Broadway Blvd. SE
Albuquerque, NM 87102
(505) 842-3292
fs.usda.gov/r3

festivals and celebrations

NOTE: Contact numbers can change from year to year. Your best bet is to call tourism information numbers for the cities or counties listed in Regional Information. Dates are always subject to change.

january

All Kings Day. This is a celebration in honor of new tribal officials on Jan 6 (Epiphany) and includes most northern pueblos. indianpueblo.org

Picurís Pueblo Feast Day. Celebrations on Jan 25 include various dances. (575) 587-2519; picurispueblo.org

San Ildefonso Pueblo Feast Day. Celebrations on Jan 22 and 23 include various dances. (505) 455-3549; sanipueblo.org

Transfer of the Canes. This is the New Year's Day inauguration of new tribal officials. Various dances. Most pueblos.

Winter Wine Festival. Sister to the Santa Fe Wine and Chile Fiesta, this festival of the grape takes place in Taos Ski Valley, Jan 30 to Feb 2. (505) 577-9042; taoswinterwinefest.com

february

Crownpoint Navajo Rug Auction. Buy rugs directly from Navajo weavers at the monthly auction in the elementary school in Crownpoint, near Gallup. (505) 362-8502; crownpoint rugauction.com

Mardi Gras in the Mountains. Red River has a lively Lent celebration echoing New Orleans Mardi Gras. (575) 754-2366; redriver.org

Mount Taylor Winter Quadrathlon. Get your heart pumping on Valentine's Day by biking, running, skiing, and snowshoeing from Grant to the top of Mount Taylor and back, 22 miles round-trip. (505) 287-4802; mttaylorquad.org

Ohkay Owingeh (San Juan Pueblo). The Deer Dance is performed in late Feb.

Souper Bowl Sunday. Attendees at this fund-raiser, timed to coincide with the real Super Bowl, sample special soups created by 24 top Santa Fe restaurants and vote on their favorite. Benefits the Food Depot. (505) 471-1633; thefooddepot.org/souperbowl

march

Ernie Blake Birthday Celebration and Fireworks. Taos Ski Valley honors its founder with fireworks and a torchlight parade on the occasion of his birthday every year. (866) 968-7386; taosskivalley.com

Jeff Gladfelter Memorial Bump Run. The area's best mogul skiers and snowboarders compete for prizes in this event at Santa Fe Ski Basin named for a local photographer. (505) 982-4429; skisantafe.com

april

Chimayó Pilgrimage. Thousands of pilgrims walk to the Santuario de Chimayó during Holy Week, arriving in Chimayó on Good Friday.

Easter Dances. Most pueblos hold dances over Easter weekend.

may

Corrales Art Studio Tour. More than 50 artists open their studios for this tour. (505) 899-3430; corralessocietyofartists.org

Jemez Red Rocks Arts and Crafts Show. Jemez Pueblo holds its big art show among the red rocks at Walatowa Visitor Center near Jemez Springs. (575) 834-7235; jemezarts andcrafts.com/jemezredrocksshow.php

San Felipe Feast Day. Festivities at San Felipe Pueblo include the Corn Dance and other dances. (505) 867-3381

Santa Cruz Feast Day. Festivities at Taos Pueblo include dances and the blessing of the fields and corn. (575) 758-1028; taospueblo.com

Santa Fe Century Bicycle Ride. More than 2,600 bicyclists take part on 25-, 50-, and 75-mile loops along the Turquoise Trail. (505) 600-1840; santafecentury.com

Santa Maria Feast Day. Dances at Acoma Pueblo. (800) 747-0181; skycity.org or puebloofacoma.org

Silver City Blues Festival. This free event in Silver City put on by the Mimbres Region Arts Council features top blues entertainers playing in Gough Park. (575) 538-2505; silvercity bluesfestival.org

june

Annual Plaza Arts and Crafts Festival. Food, music, and art exhibits on the Santa Fe Plaza benefit Challenge New Mexico's therapeutic recreation programs for the disabled. (505) 470-9088; challengenewmexico.com/arts-and-crafts-festival

ARTsmart Edible Feast Tour. An inspired pairing of fine art and gourmet food over two nights at Santa Fe's art galleries benefiting local arts programs. (505) 992-2787; artsmartnm .org/artsmarts-edible-art-tour

Blessing of the Fields. The Corn Dance is performed at Tesuque Pueblo the first Sat in June. (505) 983-2667; tesuquecasino.com

Buckaroo Ball. Now held at La Mesita Ranch Estate, Santa Fe's biggest fund-raiser has big-name musical acts and a live auction. Proceeds benefit northern New Mexico kids; tickets through the Lensic Box Office. (505) 988-1234; lensic.org

Clovis Draggin' Main Music Festival. A three-day music festival celebrates Buddy Holly, Roy Orbison, and other greats who recorded at the Norman Petty Recording Studios, as well as drag racing. (575) 763-3435; clovisnm.org

Eastern Navajo Arts and Crafts Festival. The small Navajo settlement of Torreon hosts this annual festival in the chapter house in mid-June. (505) 731-2422; facebook.com/ Eastern-Navajo-Arts-Crafts-Festival-190189714381328

Ohkay Owingeh (San Juan Pueblo) Feast Day. The Buffalo, Corn, and Comanche Dances are performed on June 24. (505) 842-4400; ohkay.org

Old Fort Days. Held in Fort Sumner the second week in June, this fun annual rodeo also features novel Western activities such as goat roping, the Great American Cow Plop, and the Billy the Kid Tombstone Race. (575) 355-7705; fortsumnerchamber.net

Rodeo de Santa Fe. Bareback and saddle bronc riding, steer wrestling, barrel racing, and bull riding bring thousands to the Rodeo Grounds the last four days in June. (505) 471-4300; rodeodesantafe.org

San Antonio Feast Day. The Comanche Dance is performed at Santa Clara Pueblo and San Ildefonso Pueblo on June 13. Santa Clara Pueblo: (505) 753-7326; San Ildefonso Pueblo: (505) 455-3549, sanipueblo.org

Taos Solar Music Festival. Non-electrified acoustic music by big-name acts takes place in Kit Carson Park in downtown Taos. (575) 758-9191; solarmusicfest.com

july

Bach Festival. Santa Fe Pro Musica is joined by the Smithsonian Chamber Players for several Bach concerts in beautiful Loretto Chapel. (505) 982-1890; santafechambermusic .com/series-spotlight-bach-plus

Eight Northern Pueblos Arts and Crafts Show. Ohkay Owingeh (San Juan Pueblo) displays artwork by artisans from the Eight Northern Pueblos every Sat from July to Oct. (505) 852-4400; ohkay.com

International Folk Art Market. Scores of folk artists from around the world show their work at Milner Plaza on Museum Hill in Santa Fe at one of Santa Fe's newest and most popular summer festivals. Music, food, and home tours. (505) 476-1203; folkartmarket.org

Jicarilla Apache Little Beaver Roundup and Rodeo. This annual celebration in Dulce is a good reason to visit the beautiful Apache lands in northeastern New Mexico. It features parades, rodeo, dancing, concerts, a softball tournament, and even a Spam-carving competition. (575) 759-4375/4378; newmexicorodeoassociation.org

Mescalero Apache Fourth of July Rodeo. Apache cowboys show off their bull riding, roping, and other skills at this popular rodeo at Mescalero on the Mescalero Apache Reservation in the Sacramento Mountains. Celebrations include a powwow; dances featuring *gaan*, or mountain spirit dancers; and the three-day puberty ritual for young girls. (575) 464-4494; innofthemountaingods.com/the-top-mescalero-ruidoso-nm-events-in-july

New Mexico Pork and Brew State Barbecue Championship. The big cook-off takes place in the new Civic Center in Rio Rancho. (505) 891-7258; rioranchonm.org

New Mexico Wine Festival. Held at El Rancho de las Golondrinas, this festival allows visitors to taste samples from 20 New Mexico wineries and enjoy food and music. (505) 471-2261; golondrinas.org/event/wine-festival-2

San Buenaventura Feast Day. Cochiti Pueblo holds a Corn Dance on its feast day on July 14. (505) 465-2244; pueblodecochiti.org

Santa Fe Chamber Music Festival. Pinchas Zukerman, R. Carlos Nakai, and other famous musicians play concerts in the St. Francis Auditorium at the New Mexico Museum of Art and the Lensic Performing Arts Center. Lunchtime rehearsal concerts in St. Francis Auditorium are free. (505) 983-2075; santafechambermusic.com

Santa Fe Opera. The performance season begins at the Santa Fe Opera and continues through Aug. Backstage tours. Free community concerts are offered in the Cathedral Basilica of St. Francis. (800) 280-4564; santafeopera.org

Taos Pueblo Annual Pow Wow. Dances, food, and music are offered during the pueblo's annual powwow at the Taos Pueblo Pow Wow Grounds. (888) 285-6244; taospueblo.org

Traditional Spanish Market. Two hundred artists display *santos*, tinwork, silver filigree jewelry, wood carving, straw inlay, *colcha* embroidery, and weaving at this juried show organized by the Spanish Colonial Arts Society on the Santa Fe Plaza the last weekend in July. Contemporary Spanish Market runs nearby. (505) 982-2226; spanialcolonial.org

august

Gallup Inter-Tribal Indian Ceremonial. Red Rock Park, just east of Gallup, hosts this huge Indian powwow, which features competitive and social dances, arts and crafts, a rodeo, music, and food. (505) 863-3896; gallupceremonial.com

Great American Duck Race. This annual hometown event is one of the best attended in New Mexico and features, yes, duck racing in mesh lanes, a cookout, arts and crafts, and entertainment at McKinley Duck Downs, Courthouse Park, Deming. (575) 546-2674; demingduckrace.com

San Lorenzo Feast Day. Dances at Acoma and Cochiti Pueblos take place on the feast day of San Lorenzo on Aug 10. Acoma: (800) 747-0181; Cochiti: (505) 465-2244

Santa Fe Indian Market. The largest exhibition of American Indian arts and crafts in the world takes over the Santa Fe Plaza for this juried show every year. About 1,000 artists show here, and hundreds of thousands of international visitors attend. Concurrent Native cultural events, such as independent movies, concerts, and fashion shows, take place around town. (505) 983-5220; swaia.org

Santo Domingo Feast Day. Kewa (Santo Domingo) Pueblo holds its big Corn Dance at the beginning of Aug. (505) 465-2214; santodomingotribe.org

Sunflower Festival. Art shows, entertainment, chili cook-off, sunflower hat contest, and Poets' and Writers' Picnic take place in Mountainair at this annual festival put on by the Manzano Mountain Art Council. (505) 847-0109; manzanomountainartcouncil.org/sunflowerfestival.html

Zuni Cultural Arts Expo. This annual fair includes Zuni's famous channel inlay turquoise-and-silver jewelry and carved fetishes, among other arts and crafts. (575) 782-7238; zuni-tourism.com

september

Burning of Zozobra. This unique community event in Fort Marcy Park has its roots in pagan community rituals and has been staged the Friday before Fiesta for over 95 years. It was created in 1924 by artist Will Shuster, one of the famed Cinco Pintores, and involves the burning of a strangely waving, giant marionette, Zozobra, or Old Man Gloom, as a form of cathartic letting go of troubles. Thousands attend. (855) 969-6272; burnzozobra.com

Fiesta de Santa Fe. The big party marking de Vargas's 1692 reconquest (and nowadays, Native American cultural perspectives) is a weeklong Labor Day celebration featuring parades, dances, parties, and a fashion show. Highlights are the popular Desfile de los Niños, or Children's Pet Parade, on Saturday morning; Sunday's Historical/Hysterical parade; the Fiesta Mass at the cathedral; and the candlelight procession from the cathedral to the Cross of the Martysrs. (505) 470-6325; santafefiesta.org

Go-Jii-Yah Feast. This Jicarilla Apache harvest celebration in Dulce is a campout at Stone Lake, with feasting, dancing, a powwow, crafts, and a foot relay race between the Llaneros (plains people) and Olleros (mountain people), representing the social division within the Jicarilla tribe. The two teams also represent the sun and moon in a mythical race to escape the underworld. (575) 759-3225

High Road Art Tour. Travel the High Road to Taos the last two weekends in Sept and visit artist studios in Chimayó, Cordova, Las Trampas, Truchas, and Ojo Sarco. (888) 866-3643; highroadnewmexico.com

Northern Navajo Nation Fair. Held in the northern New Mexico reservation town of Shiprock at the fairgrounds, this tribal fair includes dances, a beauty pageant, food, and arts and crafts. (505) 368-4305; farmingtonnm.org

Pie Festival. Held in Pie Town, in southwestern New Mexico, this annual weekend festival is the highlight of the year for Pie Town bakers and those who love pie. There are pie-eating contests, pie judging, a pie fun run, dancing, and fun. (888) 743-8696; piefestival.org

october

Abiquiu Artists Studio Tour. More than 50 artists take part in this popular art tour in Georgia O'Keeffe Country over three days in mid-Oct. (505) 500-4692; abiquiustudiotour.org

Albuquerque International Balloon Fiesta. The nine-day balloon extravaganza features more than 600 balloons, mass ascensions, food, and live music at Balloon Fiesta Park. (505) 821-1000; balloonfiesta.com

Cerrillos, Madrid, and San Marcos Studio Tours. These communities have first weekend in Oct art studio tours. (505) 438-7003; madridcerrillosstudiotour.com

Galisteo Studio Tour. Arts, crafts, and Native cooking are featured on this weekend tour, which takes place in mid-Oct. galisteostudiotour.org

november

Dixon Studio Tour. More than 40 artists and 6 businesses participate in this delightful art tour in the Rio Grande Gorge. (575) 579-4574; dixonarts.org

Fall Fiber Fiesta. This art show organized by the Española Fiber Arts Center includes an artist reception and silent auction at the Scottish Rite Temple in Santa Fe. (505) 747-3577; evfac.org

Festival of the Cranes. Guided bus tours and more than 100 special events celebrate the return of thousands of sandhill cranes, snow geese, and other migratory waterfowl to Bosque del Apache National Wildlife Refuge. (575) 835-1828; friendsofbosquedelapache .org

december

Aid and Comfort Gala. The main fund-raiser for Southwest Care Center, which coordinates Santa Fe's AIDS services, this dress-up ball is held at the Eldorado Hotel and Spa on the Sat after Thanksgiving. (505) 989-8132; southwestcare.org

Christmas at the Palace. This popular family event with music, stories, puppet shows, dance, and Santa Claus is held at the Palace of the Governors the second week in Dec. Cider and *bizcochitos* (little anise cookies) are served. (505) 476-5200; nmhistorymuseum .org

Christmas Eve Canyon Road Farolito Walk. This Santa Fe tradition attracts thousands of locals and visitors to Canyon Road to enjoy *farolitos*, *luminarias*, carol singing, and seasonal cheer. farolitowalk.com

Christmas in Madrid. Christmas in Madrid means lots of fairy lights and festivities, including late-night shopping in unique boutiques and a community open house. (505) 471-1054; visitmadridnm.com

Winter Spanish Market. The sister event to July's Traditional Spanish Market is held at the National Hispanic Cultural Center in Albuquerque at holiday time. (505) 922-2226; spanish colonial.org

index